MAJOR DEVELOPMENT IN ISLAMIC WORLD

MAJOR DEVELOPMENT IN ISLAMIC WORLD

Masood Ali

CYBER TECH PUBLICATIONS
4264/3, Ansari Road, Daryaganj, New Delhi-110002 (India)
Ph.: 011-23244078. Fax: 011-23280028
E-Mail: cyberpublicationsdelhi@yahoo.com

MAJOR DEVELOPMENT IN ISLAMIC WORLD

Masood Ali

First Edition 2009

Published by :

G.S. Rawat for **Cyber Tech Publications**
4264/3, Ansari Road, Daryaganj, New Delhi-110002 (India)
Ph.: 011-23244078. Fax: 011-23280028
E-Mail: cyberpublicationsdelhi@yahoo.com

Printed at :

Preface

Every revealed religion is the religion and a religion, the religion in as much as it contains within itself the Truth and means of attaining the Truth, a religion since it emphasizes a particular aspect of the Truth in conformity with the spiritual and psychological needs of the humanity for whom it is destined and to whom it is addressed. Religion itself is derived from the word religion whose root meaning is to bind. It is that which binds man to the truth. As such every religion possesses ultimately two essential elements which are its basis and foundation: a doctrine which distinguishes between the Absolute and the relative, between the absolutely Real and the relatively real, between that Which has absolute value and that whose value is relative; and a method of concentrating upon the Real, of attaching oneself to the Absolute and living according to the Will of Heaven in accordance with the purpose and meaning of human existence.

These two elements, the doctrine and the method, the means of distinguishing between what is Real and what appears to be real, and attaching oneself to the Real, exist in every orthodox and integral religion and are in fact the essence of every religion. No religion, whether it be Islam or Christianity, Hinduism or Buddhism, can be without a doctrine as to what is Absolute and what is relative. Only the doctrinal language differs from one tradition to another. Nor can any religion be without a method of concentrating on the Real and living according to it although the means again differ in different traditional climates.

—*Author*

CONTENTS

1

INTRODUCTION

Islam is a monotheistic Abrahamic religion originating with the teachings of Muhammad, a 7th century Arab religious and political figure. The word *Islam* means "submission", or the total surrender of oneself to God (Arabic: 'DDG, Allh). An adherent of Islam is known as a Muslim, meaning "one who submits (to God)". There are between 1.1 billion and 1.8 billion Muslims, making Islam the second-largest religion in the world, after Christianity.

Muslims believe that God revealed the Qur'an to Muhammad, God's final prophet, and regard the Qur'an and the Sunnah (words and deeds of Muhammad) as the fundamental sources of Islam. They do not regard Muhammad as the founder of a new religion, but as the restorer of the original monotheistic faith of Abraham, Moses, Jesus, and other prophets. Islamic tradition holds that Jews and Christians distorted the revelations God gave to these prophets by either altering the text, introducing a false interpretation, or both.

Islam includes many religious practices. Adherents are generally required to observe the Five Pillars of Islam, which are five duties that unite Muslims into a community. In addition to the Five Pillars, Islamic law (*sharia*) has developed a tradition of rulings that touch on virtually all aspects of life and society. This tradition encompasses everything from practical matters like dietary laws and banking to warfare.

Almost all Muslims belong to one of two major denominations, the Sunni and Shi'a. The schism developed in the late 7th century following disagreements over the religious and political leadership of the Muslim community. Roughly 85 percent of Muslims are Sunni and 15 percent are Shi'a. Islam is the predominant religion throughout the Middle East, as well as in parts of Africa and Asia. Large communities are also found in China, the Balkan Peninsula in Eastern Europe and Russia. There are also large Muslim immigrant communities in other parts of the world such as Western Europe. About 20 percent of Muslims live in Arab countries.

ETYMOLOGY AND MEANING

The word *Islm,* from the triliteral root *s-l-m,* is derived from the Arabic verb *Aslama,* which means "to accept, surrender or submit." Thus, Islam means acceptance of and submission to God, and believers must demonstrate this by worshiping him, following his commands, and avoiding polytheism. The word is given a number of meanings in the Qur'an. In some verses *(ayat),* the quality of Islam as an internal conviction is stressed: "Whomsoever God desires to guide, He expands his breast to Islam." Other verses connect *islm* and *d+n* (usually translated as "religion"): "Today, I have perfected your religion (*d+n*) for you; I have completed My blessing upon you; I have approved Islam for your religion." Still others describe Islam as an action of returning to God—more than just a verbal affirmation of faith.

ARTICLES OF FAITH

According to the Qur'an all Muslims have to believe in God, his revelations, his angels, his messengers, and in the "Day of Judgment". Also, there are other beliefs that differ between particular sects. The Sunni concept of predestination is called divine decree, while the Shi'a version is called divine justice. Unique to the Shi'a is the doctrine of *Imamah,* or the political and spiritual leadership of the Imams.

Muslims believe that God revealed his final message to humanity through the Islamic prophet Muhammad via the angel Gabriel. For them, Muhammad was God's final prophet and the Qur'an is the revelations he received over more than two decades. In Islam, prophets are men selected by God to be his messengers. Muslims believe that prophets are human and not divine, though some are able to perform miracles to prove their claim. Islamic prophets are considered to be the closest to perfection of all humans, and are uniquely the recipients of divine revelation—either directly from God or through angels. The Qur'an mentions the names of numerous figures considered prophets in Islam, including Adam, Noah, Abraham, Moses and Jesus, among others. Islamic theology says that all of God's messengers since Adam preached the message of Islam—submission to the will of the one God. Islam is described in the Qur'an as "the primordial nature upon which God created mankind", and the Qur'an states that the proper name *Muslim* was given by Abraham.

As a historical phenomenon, Islam originated in Arabia in the early 7th century. Islamic texts depict Judaism and Christianity as prophetic successor traditions to the teachings of Abraham. The Qur'an calls Jews and Christians "People of the Book" (*ahl al-kitb*), and distinguishes them from polytheists. Muslims believe that parts of the previously revealed scriptures, the *Tawrat* (Torah) and the *Injil* (Gospels), had become distorted—either in interpretation, in text, or both.God

Islam's fundamental theological concept is *tawh+d*—the belief that there is only one God. The Arabic term for God is *Allh*; most scholars believe it was derived from a contraction of the words *al-*(the) and *¾ilh* (deity, masculine form), meaning "the God" (*al-ilh*), but others trace its origin to the Aramaic *Alh*. The first of the Five Pillars of Islam, *tawh+d* is expressed in the *shahadah* (testification), which declares that there is no god but God, and that Muhammad is God's messenger. In traditional Islamic theology, God is beyond all comprehension; Muslims are not expected to visualize God but to worship and adore him as a protector. Although Muslims believe that Jesus was a prophet, they reject the Christian doctrine of the Trinity, comparing it to polytheism. In Islamic theology, Jesus was just a man and not the son of God; God is described in a chapter (*sura*) of the Qur'an as "...God, the One and Only; God, the Eternal, Absolute; He begetteth not, nor is He begotten; And there is none like unto Him."Qur'an

Muslims consider the Qur'an to be the literal word of God; it is the central religious text of Islam. Muslims believe that the verses of the Qur'an were revealed to Muhammad by God through the angel Gabriel on many occasions between 610 and his death on July 6, 632. The Qur'an was written down by Muhammad's companions (*sahabah*) while he was alive, although the prime method of transmission was orally. It was compiled in the time of Abu Bakr, the first caliph, and was standardized in the time of Uthman, the third caliph. The Qur'an in its actual form is generally considered by academic scholars to record the words spoken by Muhammad because the search for variants in Western academia has not yielded any differences of great significance and that historically controversy over the content of the Qur'an has never become a main point.

The Qur'an is divided into 114 suras, or chapters, which combined, contain 6,236 *yt*, or verses. The chronologically earlier suras, revealed at Mecca, are primarily concerned with ethical and spiritual topics. The later Medinan suras mostly discuss social and moral issues relevant to the Muslim community. The Qur'an is more concerned with moral guidance than legal instruction, and is considered the "sourcebook of Islamic principles and values". Muslim jurists consult the *hadith*, or the written record of Muhammad's life, to both supplement the Qur'an and assist with its interpretation. The science of Qur'anic commentary and exegesis is known as *tafsir*.

The word *Qur'an* means "recitation". When Muslims speak in the abstract about "the Qur'an", they usually mean the scripture as recited in Arabic rather than the printed work or any translation of it. To Muslims, the Qur'an is perfect only as revealed in the original Arabic; translations are necessarily deficient because of language differences, the fallibility of translators, and the impossibility of preserving the original's inspired style. Translations are therefore regarded only as commentaries on the Qur'an, or "interpretations of its meaning", not as the Qur'an itself.Angels

Belief in angels is crucial to the faith of Islam. The Arabic word for Angels (*malak*) means "messenger", like its counterparts in Hebrew (*malakh*) and Greek (*angelos*). According to the Qur'an, angels do not possess free will, and worship God in perfect obedience. Angels' duties include communicating revelations from God, glorifying God, recording every person's actions, and taking a person's soul at the time of death. They are also thought to intercede on man's behalf. The Qur'an describes angels as "messengers with wings—two, or three, or four (pairs): He [God] adds to Creation as He pleases..."Muhammad

Muhammad (c. 570 – July 6, 632) was an Arab religious, political, and military leader who founded the religion of Islam as a historical phenomenon. Muslims view him not as the creator of a new religion, but as the restorer of the original, uncorrupted monotheistic faith of Adam, Abraham and others. In Muslim tradition, Muhammad is viewed as the last and the greatest in a series of prophets—as the man closest to perfection, the possessor of all virtues. For the last 23 years of his life, beginning at age 40, Muhammad reported receiving revelations from God. The content of these revelations, known as the Qur'an, was memorized and recorded by his companions.

During this time, Muhammad preached to the people of Mecca, imploring them to abandon polytheism. Although some converted to Islam, Muhammad and his followers were persecuted by the leading Meccan authorities. After 13 years of preaching, Muhammad and the Muslims performed the *Hijra* ("emigration") to the city of Medina (formerly known as *Yathrib*) in 622. There, with the Medinan converts (*Ansar*) and the Meccan migrants (*Muhajirun*), Muhammad established his political and religious authority. Within years, two battles had been fought against Meccan forces: the Battle of Badr in 624, which was a Muslim victory, and the Battle of Uhud in 625, which ended inconclusively. Conflict with Medinan Jewish clans who opposed the Muslims led to their exile, enslavement or death, and the Jewish enclave of Khaybar was subdued. At the same time, Meccan trade routes were cut off as Muhammad brought surrounding desert tribes under his control. By 629 Muhammad was victorious in the nearly bloodless Conquest of Mecca, and by the time of his death in 632 he ruled over the Arabian peninsula.

In Islam, the "normative" example of Muhammad's life is called the *Sunnah* (literally "trodden path"). This example is preserved in traditions known as hadith ("reports"), which recount his words, his actions, and his personal characteristics. The classical Muslim jurist ash-Shafi'i (d. 820) emphasized the importance of the Sunnah in Islamic law, and Muslims are encouraged to emulate

Muhammad's actions in their daily lives. The Sunnah is seen as crucial to guiding interpretation of the Qur'an.Resurrection and judgment

Belief in the "Day of Resurrection", *yawm al-Qiymah* (also known as *yawm ad-d+n*, "Day of Judgment" and *as-s`a*, "the Last Hour") is also crucial for Muslims. They believe that the time of *Qiymah* is preordained by God but unknown to man. The trials and tribulations preceding and during the *Qiymah* are described in the Qur'an and the hadith, and also in the commentaries of Islamic scholars. The Qur'an emphasizes bodily resurrection, a break from the pre-Islamic Arabian understanding of death. It states that resurrection will be followed by the gathering of mankind, culminating in their judgment by God.

The Qur'an lists several sins that can condemn a person to hell, such as disbelief, usury and dishonesty. Muslims view paradise (*jannah*) as a place of joy and bliss, with Qur'anic references describing its features and the physical pleasures to come. There are also references to a greater joy—acceptance by God (*ridwn*). Mystical traditions in Islam place these heavenly delights in the context of an ecstatic awareness of God.Predestination

In accordance with the Islamic belief in predestination, or divine preordainment (*al-qad wa'l-qadar*), God has full knowledge and control over all that occurs. This is explained in Qur'anic verses such as "Say: 'Nothing will happen to us except what Allah has decreed for us: He is our protector'..." For Muslims, everything in the world that occurs, good or evil, has been preordained and nothing can happen unless permitted by God. In Islamic theology, divine preordainment does not suggest an absence of God's indignation against evil, because any evils that do occur are thought to result in future benefits men may not be able to see. According to Muslim theologians, although events are pre-ordained, man possesses free will in that he has the faculty to choose between right and wrong, and is thus responsible for his actions. According to Islamic tradition, all that has been decreed by God is written in *al-Lawh al-Mahfkz*, the "Preserved Tablet".

The Shi'a understanding of predestination is called "divine justice" (*Adalah*). This doctrine, originally developed by the Mu'tazila, stresses the importance of man's responsibility for his own actions. In contrast, the Sunni deemphasize the role of individual free will in the context of God's creation and foreknowledge of all things.

DUTIES AND PRACTICES

Five Pillars

The Five Pillars of Islam (Arabic: '1C'F 'D/JF) are five practices essential to Sunni Islam. Shi'a Muslims subscribe to eight ritual practices which substantially overlap with the Five Pillars. They are:

The ***shahadah***, which is the basic creed or tenet of Islam: *"'aðhadu 'al-lâ ilâha illâ-llâhu wa 'aðhadu 'anna mu'ammadan rasûlu-llâh"*, or "I testify that there is none worthy of worship except God and I testify that Muhammad is the Messenger of God." This testament is a foundation for all other beliefs and practices in Islam (although technically the Shi'a do not consider the *shahadah* to be a separate pillar, just a belief). Muslims must repeat the *shahadah* in prayer, and non-Muslims wishing to convert to Islam are required to recite the creed.

Salah, or ritual prayer, which must be performed five times a day. (However, the Shi'a are permitted to run together the noon with the afternoon prayers, and the evening with the night prayers). Each salah is done facing towards the Kaaba in Mecca. Salah is intended to focus the mind on God, and is seen as a personal communication with him that expresses gratitude and worship. Salah is compulsory but flexibility in the specifics is allowed depending on circumstances. In many Muslim countries, reminders called Adhan (call to prayer) are broadcast publicly from local mosques at the appropriate times. The prayers are recited in the Arabic language, and consist of verses from the Qur'an.

Zakat, or alms-giving. This is the practice of giving based on accumulated wealth, and is obligatory for all Muslims who can afford it. A fixed portion is spent to help the poor or needy, and also to assist the spread of Islam. The zakat is considered a religious obligation (as opposed to voluntary charity) that the well-off owe to the needy because their wealth is seen as a "trust from God's bounty". The Qur'an and the hadith also suggest a Muslim give even more as an act of voluntary alms-giving (*sadaqah*). Many Shi'ites are expected to pay an additional amount in the form of a *khums* tax, which they consider to be a separate ritual practice.

Sawm, or fasting during the month of Ramadan. Muslims must not eat or drink (among other things) from dawn to dusk during this month, and must be mindful of other sins. The fast is to encourage a feeling of nearness to God, and during it Muslims should express their gratitude for and dependence on him, atone for their past sins, and think of the needy. *Sawm* is not obligatory for several groups for whom it would constitute an undue burden. For others, flexibility is allowed depending on circumstances, but missed fasts usually must be made up quickly.

The ***Hajj***, which is the pilgrimage during the Islamic month of *Dhu al-Hijjah* in the city of Mecca. Every able-bodied Muslim who can afford it must make the pilgrimage to Mecca at least once in his or her lifetime. When the pilgrim is about ten kilometers from Mecca, he must dress in *Ihram* clothing, which consists of two white seamless sheets. Rituals of the Hajj include walking seven times around the Kaaba, touching the Black Stone, running seven times between Mount Safa and Mount Marwah, and symbolically stoning the Devil in Mina. The pilgrim, or the *hajji*, is honored in his or her community, although Islamic teachers say that the Hajj should be an expression of devotion to God instead of a means to gain social standing.

In addition to the *khums* tax, Shi'a Muslims consider three additional practices essential to the religion of Islam. The first is jihad, which is also important to the Sunni, but not considered a pillar. The second is *Amr-Bil-Ma'rkf*, the "Enjoining to Do Good", which calls for every Muslim to live a virtuous life and to encourage others to do the same. The third is *Nahi-Anil-Munkar*, the "Exhortation to Desist from Evil", which tells Muslims to refrain from vice and from evil actions and to also encourage others to do the same.Law

The *Sharia* (literally: "the path leading to the watering place") is Islamic law formed by traditional Islamic scholarship. In Islam, Sharia is the expression of the divine will, and "constitutes a system of duties that are incumbent upon a Muslim by virtue of his religious belief".

Islamic law covers all aspects of life, from matters of state, like governance and foreign relations, to issues of daily living. The Qur'an defines *hudud* as the punishments for five specific crimes: unlawful intercourse, false accusation of unlawful intercourse, consumption of alcohol, theft, and highway robbery. The Qur'an and Sunnah also contain laws of inheritance, marriage, and restitution for injuries and murder, as well as rules for fasting, charity, and prayer. However, these prescriptions and prohibitions may be broad, so their application in practice varies. Islamic scholars (known as *ulema*) have elaborated systems of law on the basis of these rules and their interpretations.

Fiqh, or "jurisprudence", is defined as the knowledge of the practical rules of the religion. The method Islamic jurists use to derive rulings is known as *usul al-fiqh* ("legal theory", or "principles of jurisprudence"). According to Islamic legal theory, law has four fundamental roots, which are given precedence in this order: the Qur'an, the Sunnah (actions and sayings of Muhammad), the consensus of the Muslim jurists (*ijma*), and analogical reasoning (*qiyas*). For early Islamic jurists, theory was less important than pragmatic application of the law. In the 9th century, the jurist ash-Shafi'i provided a theoretical basis for Islamic law by codifying the principles of jurisprudence (including the four fundamental roots) in his book *ar-Rislah*.Religion and state

Islamic law does not distinguish between "matters of church" and "matters of state"; the ulema function as both jurists and theologians. In practice, Islamic rulers frequently bypassed the Sharia courts with a parallel system of so-called "Grievance courts" over which they had sole control. As the Muslim world came into contact with Western secular ideals, Muslim societies responded in different ways. Turkey has been governed as a secular state ever since the reforms of Mustafa Kemal Atatürk. In contrast, the 1979 Iranian Revolution replaced a mostly secular regime with an Islamic republic led by the Ayatollah Ruholla Khomeini.Etiquette and diet

Many practices fall in the category of *adab*, or Islamic etiquette. This includes greeting others with "*as-salamu `alaykum*" ("peace be unto you"), saying *bismillah* ("in the name of God") before meals, and using only the right hand for eating and drinking.

Islamic hygienic practices mainly fall into the category of personal cleanliness and health, such as the circumcision of male offspring. Islamic burial rituals include saying the *Salat al-Janazah* ("funeral prayer") over the bathed and enshrouded dead body, and burying it in a grave. Muslims, like Jews, are restricted in their diet, and prohibited foods include pig products, blood, carrion, and alcohol. All meat must come from a herbivorous animal slaughtered in the name of God by a Muslim, Jew, or Christian, with the exception of game that one has hunted or fished for oneself. Food permissible for Muslims is known as halal food.Jihad

Jihad means "to strive or struggle," and is considered the "sixth pillar of Islam" by a minority of Muslim authorities. Jihad, in its broadest sense, is classically defined as "exerting one's utmost power, efforts, endeavors, or ability in contending with an object of disapprobation." Depending on the object being a visible enemy, the devil, and aspects of one's own self, different categories of Jihad are defined. Jihad when used without any qualifier is understood in its military aspect. Jihad also refers to one's striving to attain religious and moral perfection. Some Muslim authorities, especially among the Shi'a and Sufis, distinguish between the "greater jihad", which pertains to spiritual self-perfection, and the "lesser jihad", defined as warfare.

Within Islamic jurisprudence, jihad is usually taken to mean military exertion against non-Muslim combatants in the defense or expansion of the Islamic state, the ultimate purpose of which is to establish the universal domination of Islam. Jihad, the only form of warfare permissible in Islamic law, may be declared against states which refuse to convert to Islam or submit to the authority of Islam. Treaties (*'ahd*) may be established, subject to payment of the *kharaj*, although jurists differ over its permitted longevity. Most Muslims today interpret Jihad as only a defensive form of warfare: the external Jihad includes a struggle to make the Islamic societies conform to the Islamic norms of justice.

Under most circumstances and for most Muslims, jihad is a collective duty (*fard kifaya*): its performance by some individuals exempts the others. Only for those vested with authority, especially the sovereign (imam), does jihad become an individual duty. For the rest of the populace, this happens only in the case of a general mobilization. For most Shias, offensive jihad can only be declared by a divinely appointed leader of the Muslim community, and as such is suspended since Muhammad al-Mahdi's occultation in 868 AD. History

Islam's historical development resulted in major political, economic, and military effects inside and outside the Islamic world. Within a century of Muhammad's first recitations of the Qur'an, an Islamic empire stretched from the Atlantic Ocean in the west to Central Asia in the east. This new polity soon broke into civil war, and successor states fought each other and outside forces. However, Islam continued to spread into regions like Africa, the Indian subcontinent, and Southeast Asia. The Islamic civilization was one of the most advanced in the world during the Middle Ages, but was surpassed by Europe with the economic and military growth of the West. During the 18th and 19th centuries, Islamic dynasties such as the Ottomans and Mughals fell under the sway of European imperial powers. In the 20th century new religious and political movements and newfound wealth in the Islamic world led to both rebirth and conflict.

RISE OF THE CALIPHATE (632–750)

Muhammad began preaching Islam at Mecca before migrating to Medina, from where he united the tribes of Arabia into a singular Arab Muslim religious polity. With Muhammad's death in 632, disagreement broke out over who would succeed him as leader of the Muslim community. Umar ibn al-Khattab, a prominent companion of Muhammad, nominated Abu Bakr, who was Muhammad's intimate friend and collaborator. Others added their support and Abu Bakr was made the first caliph. This choice was disputed by some of Muhammad's companions, who held that Ali ibn Abi Talib, his cousin and son-in-law, had been designated his successor. Abu Bakr's immediate task was to avenge a recent defeat by Byzantine (or Eastern Roman Empire) forces, although he first had to put down a rebellion by Arab tribes in an episode known as the Ridda wars, or "Wars of Apostasy".

His death in 634 resulted in the succession of Umar as the caliph, followed by Uthman ibn al-Affan and Ali ibn Abi Talib. These four are known as *al-khulaf ar-rshidkn* ("Rightly Guided

Caliphs"). Under them, the territory under Muslim rule expanded deeply into Persian and Byzantine territories.

When Umar was assassinated in 644, the election of Uthman as successor was met with increasing opposition. In 656, Uthman was also killed, and Ali assumed the position of caliph. After fighting off opposition in the first civil war (the "First Fitna"), Ali was assassinated by Kharijites in 661. Following this, Mu'awiyah, who was governor of Levant, seized power and began the Umayyad dynasty.

These disputes over religious and political leadership would give rise to schism in the Muslim community. The majority accepted the legitimacy of the three rulers prior to Ali, and became known as Sunnis. A minority disagreed, and believed that Ali was the only rightful successor; they became known as the Shi'a. After Mu'awiyah's death in 680, conflict over succession broke out again in a civil war known as the "Second Fitna". Afterward, the Umayyad dynasty prevailed for seventy years, and was able to conquer the Maghrib and Al-Andalus (the Iberian Peninsula, former Visigothic Hispania) and the Narbonnese Gaul} in the west as well as expand Muslim territory into Sindh and the fringes of Central Asia.. While the Muslim-Arab elite engaged in conquest, some devout Muslims began to question the piety of indulgence in a worldly life, emphasizing rather poverty, humility and avoidance of sin based on renunciation of bodily desires. Devout Muslim ascetic exemplars such as Hasan al-Basri would inspire a movement that would evolve into Sufism.

For the Umayyad aristocracy, Islam was viewed as a religion for Arabs only; the economy of the Umayyad empire was based on the assumption that a majority of non-Muslims (Dhimmis) would pay taxes to the minority of Muslim Arabs. A non-Arab who wanted to convert to Islam was supposed to first become a client of an Arab tribe. Even after conversion, these new Muslims (*mawali*) did not achieve social and economic equality with the Arabs. The descendants of Muhammad's uncle Abbas ibn Abd al-Muttalib rallied discontented *mawali*, poor Arabs, and some Shi'a against the Umayyads and overthrew them with the help of their propagandist and general Abu Muslim, inaugurating the Abbasid dynasty in 750. Under the Abbasids, Islamic civilization flourished in the "Islamic Golden Age", with its capital at the cosmopolitan city of Baghdad.Golden Age (750–1258)

By the late 9th century, the Abbasid caliphate began to fracture as various regions gained increasing levels of autonomy. Across North Africa, Persia, and Central Asia emirates formed as provinces broke away.

The monolithic Arab empire gave way to a more religiously homogenized Muslim world where the Shia Fatimids contested even the religious authority of the caliphate. By 1055 the Seljuq Turks had eliminated the Abbasids as a military power, nevertheless they continued to respect the caliph's titular authority. During this time expansion of the Muslim world continued, by both conquest and peaceful proselytism even as both Islam and Muslim trade networks were extending into sub-Saharan West Africa, Central Asia, Volga Bulgaria and the Malay archipelago.

The Golden Age saw new legal, philosophical, and religious developments. The major hadith collections were compiled and the four modern Sunni Madh'habs were established. Islamic law was advanced greatly by the efforts of the early 9th century jurist al-Shafi'i; he codified a method to establish the reliability of hadith, a topic which had been a locus of dispute among Islamic scholars. Philosophers Ibn Sina (Avicenna) and Al-Farabi sought to incorporate Greek principles into Islamic theology, while others like the 11th century theologian Abu Hamid al-Ghazzali argued against them and ultimately prevailed. Finally, Sufism and Shi'ism both underwent major changes in the 9th century. Sufism became a full-fledged movement that had moved towards mysticism and away from its ascetic roots, while Shi'ism split due to disagreements over the succession of Imams.

The spread of the Islamic dominion induced hostility among medieval ecclesiastical Christian authors who saw Islam as an adversary in the light of the large numbers of new Muslim converts. This opposition resulted in polemical treatises which depicted Islam as the religion of the antichrist and of Muslims as libidinous and subhuman. In the medieval period, a few Arab philosophers like the poet Al-Ma'arri adopted a critical approach to Islam, and the Jewish philosopher Maimonides contrasted Islamic views of morality to Jewish views that he himself elaborated.

Starting in the 9th century, Muslim conquests in the West began to be reversed. The Reconquista was launched against Muslim principalities in Iberia, and Muslim Italian possessions were lost to the Normans. From the 11th century onwards alliances of European Christian kingdoms mobilized to launch a series of wars known as the Crusades, bringing the Muslim world into conflict with Christendom.

Initially successful in their goal of taking the Holy land, and establishing the Crusader states, Crusader gains in the Holy Land were later reversed by subsequent Muslim generals such as Saladin; who recaptured Jerusalem during the Second Crusade. In the east the Mongol Empire put an end to the Abbassid dynasty at the Battle of Baghdad in 1258, as they overran in Muslim lands in a series of invasions. Meanwhile in Egypt, the slave-soldier Mamluks took control in an uprising in 1250 and in alliance with the Golden Horde were able halt the Mongol armies at the Battle of Ain Jalut. Mongol rule extended across the breadth of almost all Muslim lands in Asia and Islam was temporarily replaced by Buddhism as the official religion of the land. Over the next century the Mongol Khanates converted to Islam and this religious and cultural absorption ushered in a new age of Mongol-Islamic synthesis that shaped the further spread of Islam in central Asia and the Indian subcontinent.

OTTOMANS AND ISLAMIC EMPIRES IN INDIA (1258–1918)

The Seljuk Turks conquered Abbassid lands and adopted Islam and become the *de facto* rulers of the caliphate. They captured Anatolia by defeating the Byzantines at the Battle of Manzikert, thereby precipitating the call for Crusades. They however fell apart rapidly in the second half of the 12th century giving rise to various semi-autonomous Turkic dynasties. In the 13th and 14th centuries the Ottoman empire (named after Osman I) emerged from among these *"Ghazi emirates"* and established itself after a string of conquests that included the Balkans, parts of Greece, and western Anatolia. In 1453 under Mehmed II the Ottomans laid siege to Constantinople, the capital of Byzantium. The Byzantine fortress succumbed shortly thereafter, having been battered by superior Ottoman cannonry.

Beginning in the 13th century, Sufism underwent a transformation, largely as a result of the efforts of al-Ghazzali to legitimize and reorganize the movement. He developed the model of the Sufi order—a community of spiritual teachers and students. Also of importance to Sufism was the creation of the Masnavi, a collection of mystical poetry by the 13th century Persian poet Rumi. The Masnavi had a profound influence on the development of Sufi religious thought; to many Sufis it is second in importance only to the Qur'an.

In the early 16th century, the Shi'ite Safavid dynasty assumed control in Persia and established Shi'a Islam as an official religion there, and despite periodic setbacks, the Safavids remained powerful for two centuries. Meanwhile, Mamluk Egypt fell to the Ottomans in 1517, who then launched a European campaign which reached as far as the gates of Vienna in 1529.

After the invasion of Persia, and sack of Baghdad by the Mongols in 1258, Delhi became the most important cultural centre of the Muslim east. Many Islamic dynasties ruled parts of the Indian subcontinent starting from the 12th century. The prominent ones include the Delhi Sultanate (1206–1526) and the Mughal empire (1526–1857). These empires helped in the spread of Islam in South Asia. but by the mid-18th century the British empire had ended the Mughal dynasty. In the 18th century the Wahhabi movement took hold in Saudi Arabia. Founded by the preacher Ibn Abd al-Wahhab, Wahhabism is a fundamentalist ideology that condemns practices like Sufism and the veneration of saints as un-Islamic.

By the 17th and 18th centuries, despite attempts at modernization, the Ottoman empire had begun to feel threatened by European economic and military advantages. In the 19th century, the rise of nationalism resulted in Greece declaring and winning independence in 1829, with several Balkan states following suit after the Ottomans suffered defeat in the Russo-Turkish War of 1877–1878. The Ottoman era came to a close at the end of World War I.

In the 19th century, the Salafi, Deobandi and Barelwi movements were initiated.

MODERN TIMES (1918–PRESENT)

After World War I losses, the remnants of the empire were parceled out as European protectorates or spheres of influence. Since then most Muslim societies have become independent nations, and new issues such as oil wealth and relations with the State of Israel have assumed prominence.

The 20th century saw the creation of many new Islamic "revivalist" movements. Groups such as the Muslim Brotherhood in Egypt and Jamaat-e-Islami in Pakistan advocate a totalistic and theocratic alternative to secular political ideologies. Sometimes called Islamist, they see Western cultural values as a threat, and promote Islam as a comprehensive solution to every public and private question of importance. In countries like Iran and Afghanistan (under the Taliban), revolutionary movements replaced secular regimes with Islamist states, while transnational groups like Osama bin Laden's al-Qaeda engage in terrorism to further their goals. In contrast, Liberal Islam is a movement that attempts to reconcile religious tradition with modern norms of secular governance and human rights. Its supporters say that there are multiple ways to read Islam's sacred texts, and stress the need to leave room for "independent thought on religious matters".

In modern times Islam has come under criticism from idealogues such as Ibn Warraq who criticize Islamic law and question the morality of the Qur'an; for example, they say that its contents justify mistreatment of women and encourage antisemitic remarks by Muslim theologians; such claims are disputed by Muslim scholars. Montgomery Watt, Norman Daniel, and Edward Said dismiss many of the criticisms as the product of old myths and medieval European polemics. The rise of Islamophobia, according to Carl Ernst, had contributed to the negative views about Islam and Muslims in the West.Community

Demographics

Commonly cited estimates of the Muslim population in 2007 range from 1.1 billion to 1.8 billion. Approximately 85% are Sunni and 15% are Shi'a, with a small minority belonging to other sects. Some 30–40 countries are Muslim-majority, and Arabs account for around 20% of all Muslims worldwide. South Asia and Southeast Asia contain the most populous Muslim countries, with Indonesia, India, Pakistan, and Bangladesh having more than 100 million adherents each. According to U.S. government figures, in 2006 there were 20 million Muslims in China. In the Middle East, the non-Arab countries of Turkey and Iran are the largest Muslim-majority countries; in Africa, Egypt and Nigeria have the most populous Muslim communities. Islam is the second largest religion after Christianity in many European countries.Mosques

A mosque is a place of worship for Muslims, who often refer to it by its Arabic name, *masjid*. The word *mosque* in English refers to all types of buildings dedicated to Islamic worship, although there is a distinction in Arabic between the smaller, privately owned mosque and the larger, "collective" mosque (*masjid jmi`*). Although the primary purpose of the mosque is to serve as a place of prayer, it is also important to the Muslim community as a place to meet and study. Modern mosques have evolved greatly from the early designs of the 7th century, and contain a variety of architectural elements such as minarets.Family life

The basic unit of Islamic society is the family, and Islam defines the obligations and legal rights of family members. The father is seen as financially responsible for his family, and is obliged to cater for their well-being. The division of inheritance is specified in the Qur'an, which states that most of it is to pass to the immediate family, while a portion is set aside for the payment of debts and the making of bequests. The woman's share of inheritance is generally half of that of a man with the same rights of succession. Marriage in Islam is a civil contract which consists of an offer and acceptance between two qualified parties in the presence of two witnesses. The groom is required to pay a dowry (*mahr*) to the bride, as stipulated in the contract.

A man may marry up to four wives if he believes he can treat them equally, while a woman may marry one man only. In most Muslim countries, the process of divorce in Islam is known as *talaq*, which the husband initiates by pronouncing the word "divorce". Scholars disagree whether Islamic holy texts justify traditional Islamic practices such as veiling and seclusion (purdah). Starting in the 20th century, Muslim social reformers argued against these and other practices such as polygamy, with varying success. At the same time, many Muslim women have attempted to reconcile tradition with modernity by combining an active life with outward modesty. Certain Islamist groups like the Taliban have sought to continue traditional law as applied to women.

The formal beginning of the Muslim era was chosen to be the Hijra in 622 CE, which was an important turning point in Muhammad's fortunes. The assignment of this year as the year 1 AH (*Anno Hegirae*) in the Islamic calendar was reportedly made by Caliph Umar. It is a lunar calendar, with nineteen ordinary years of 354 days and eleven leap years of 355 days in a thirty-year cycle. Islamic dates cannot be converted to CE/AD dates simply by adding 622 years: allowance must also be made for the fact that each Hijri century corresponds to only 97 years in the Christian calendar. The year 1428 AH coincides almost completely with 2007 CE. Islamic holy days fall on fixed dates of the lunar calendar, which means that they occur in different seasons in different years in the Gregorian calendar. The most important Islamic festivals are *Eid al-Fitr* (Arabic: 9J/ 'DA71) on the 1st of *Shawwal*, marking the end of the fasting month *Ramadan*, and *Eid al-Adha* (Arabic: 9J/ 'D#6-I) on the 10th of *Dhu al-Hijjah*, coinciding with the pilgrimage to Mecca.Other religions

According to Islamic doctrine, Islam was the primordial religion of mankind, professed by Adam. At some point, a religious split occurred, and God began sending prophets to bring his revelations to the people. In this view, Abraham, Moses, Hebrew prophets, and Jesus were all prophets of Islam, but their message and the texts of the Torah and the Gospels were corrupted by Jews and Christians. Similarly, children of non-Muslim families are born Muslims, but are converted to another faith by their parents. The idea of Islamic supremacy is encapsulated in the formula "Islam is exalted and nothing is exalted above it." Pursuant to this principle, Muslim women may not marry non-Muslim men, defamation of Islam is prohibited, and the testimony of a non-Muslim is inadmissible against a Muslim.

Islamic law divides non-Muslims into several categories, depending on their relation with the Islamic state. Christians and Jews who live under Islamic rule are known as *dhimmis* ("protected peoples"). According to this pact, the personal safety and security of property of the dhimmis were guaranteed in return for paying tribute (*jizya*) to the Islamic state and acknowledging Muslim supremacy. Historically, dhimmis enjoyed a measure of communal autonomy under their own religious leaders, but were subject to legal, social and religious restrictions meant to highlight their inferiority. The status was extended to Zoroastrians and sometimes to polytheists (such as Hindus), but not to atheists or agnostics. Those who live in non-Muslim lands (*dar al-harb*) are known as *harbis,* and upon entering into an alliance with the Muslim state become known as *ahl al-ahd*. Those who receive a guarantee of safety while residing temporarily in Muslim lands are known as *ahl al-amn*. Their legal position is similar to that of the dhimmi except that they are not required to pay the jizya. The people of armistice (*ahl al-hudna*) are those who live outside of Muslim territory and agree to refrain from attacking the Muslims. Apostasy is prohibited, and is punishable by death.Denominations

Islam consists of a number of religious denominations that are essentially similar in belief but which have significant theological and legal differences. The primary division is between the Sunni and the Shi'a, with Sufism generally considered to be a mystical inflection of Islam rather than a distinct school. According to most sources, approximately 85% of the world's Muslims are Sunni and approximately 15% are Shi'a, with a small minority who are members of other Islamic sects.Sunni

Sunni Muslims are the largest group in Islam. In Arabic, *as-Sunnah* literally means "principle" or "path". The Sunnah (the example of Muhammad's life) as recorded in the Qur'an and the hadith is the main pillar of Sunni doctrine. Sunnis believe that the first four caliphs were the rightful successors to Muhammad; since God did not specify any particular leaders to succeed him, those leaders had to be elected. Sunnis recognize four major legal traditions, or madhhabs: Hanafi, Maliki, Shafi'i and Hanbali. All four accept the validity of the others and a Muslim might choose any one that he or she finds agreeable, but other Islamic sects are believed to have departed from the majority by introducing innovations (*bidah*). There are also several orthodox theological or philosophical traditions within Sunnism. For example, the recent

Salafi movement sees itself as restorationist and claims to derive its teachings from the original sources of Islam.Shi'a

The Shi'a, who constitute the second-largest branch of Islam, believe in the political and religious leadership of infallible Imams from the progeny of Ali ibn Abi Talib. They believe that he, as the cousin and son-in-law of Muhammad, was his rightful successor, and they call him the first *Imam* (leader), rejecting the legitimacy of the previous Muslim caliphs. To them, an Imam rules by right of divine appointment and holds "absolute spiritual authority" among Muslims, having final say in matters of doctrine and revelation. Although the Shi'a share many core practices with the Sunni, the two branches disagree over the proper importance and validity of specific collections of hadith. The Shi'a follow a legal tradition called Ja'fari jurisprudence. Shi'a Islam has several branches, the largest of which is the Twelvers (*ion¿ašariyya*), while the others are the Ismaili, the Seveners, and the Zaidiyyah.Sufism

Not strictly a denomination, Sufism is a mystical-ascetic form of Islam. By focusing on the more spiritual aspects of religion, Sufis strive to obtain direct experience of God by making use of "intuitive and emotional faculties" that one must be trained to use. Sufism and Islamic law are usually considered to be complementary, although Sufism has been criticized by some Muslims for being an unjustified religious innovation. Most Sufi orders, or *tariqas*, can be classified as either Sunni or Shi'a.Others

The Kharijites are a sect that dates back to the early days of Islam. The only surviving branch of the Kharijites is Ibadism. Unlike most Kharijite groups, Ibadism does not regard sinful Muslims as unbelievers. The Imamate is an important topic in Ibadi legal literature, which stipulates that the leader should be chosen solely on the basis of his knowledge and piety, and is to be deposed if he acts unjustly. Most Ibadi Muslims live in Oman.

The Alevi, Yazidi, Druze, Ahmadiyya, Bábí, Bahá'í, Berghouata and Ha-Mim movements either emerged out of Islam or came to share certain beliefs with Islam. Some consider themselves separate while others still sects of Islam though controversial in certain beliefs with mainstream Muslims. Sikhism, founded by Guru Nanak in late fifteenth century Punjab, incorporates aspects of both Islam and Hinduism.

2

ISLAM AND THE CLASH OF CIVILIZATIONS

Islam is a seventh century religion. For a moment, think about that statement. I doubt anyone would consider Christianity a first century religion. You might acknowledge that it began in the first century, but you wouldn't probably describe it as a religion of the first century because the timeless principles of the gospel have adapted to the times in which they are communicated.

In many ways, Islam has remained stuck in the century in which it developed. One of the great questions of the twenty-first century is whether it will adapt to the modern era. Certainly many Muslims have done so, but radical Muslims have not.

Perhaps the leading scholar on Islam in this country is the emeritus professor from Princeton University, Bernard Lewis. This is what he had to say about Islam and the modern world:

> *Islam has brought comfort and peace of mind to countless millions of men and women. It has given dignity and meaning to drab and impoverished lives. It has taught people of different races to live in brotherhood and people of different creeds to live side by side in reasonable tolerance. It inspired a great civilization in which others besides Muslims lived creative and useful lives and which, by its achievement, enriched the whole world. But Islam, like other religions, has also known periods when it inspired in some of its followers a mood of hatred and violence. It is our misfortune that part, though by no means all or even most, of the Muslim world is now going through such a period, and that much, though again not all, of that hatred is directed against us.*

This certainly does not mean that all Muslims want to engage in jihad warfare against America and the West. But it does mean that there is a growing clash of civilizations. Bernard Lewis continues:

> *In the classical Islamic view, to which many Muslims are beginning to return, the world and all mankind are divided into two: the House of Islam, where the Muslim law and faith prevail, and the rest, known as the House of Unbelief or the House of War, which it is the duty of Muslims ultimately to bring to Islam.*
>
> *It should by now be clear that we are facing a mood and a movement far transcending the level of issues and policies and the governments that pursue them. This is no less than a clash of civilizations—the perhaps irrational but surely historic reaction of an ancient rival against our Judeo-Christian heritage, our secular present, and the worldwide expansion of both. It is crucially important that we on our side should not be provoked into an equally historic but also equally irrational reaction against the rival.*

This is the challenge for the twenty-first century. Will Islam adapt to the modern world, or will there continue to be a clash of civilizations?

Muslim Intelligentsia

Not everyone accepts the clash of civilizations analysis. William Tucker, writing in the *American Spectator,* believes that the actual conflict results from what he calls the Muslim Intelligentsia.

> *He says "that we are not facing a clash of civilizations so much as a conflict with an educated segment of a civilization that produces some very weird, sexually disoriented men. Poverty has nothing to do with it. It is stunning to meet the al Qaeda roster—one highly accomplished scholar after another with advanced degrees in chemistry, biology, medicine, engineering, a large percentage of them educated in the United States."*

This analysis is contrary to the many statements that have been made in the past that poverty breeds terrorism. While it is certainly true that many recruits for jihad come from impoverished situations, it is also true that the leadership comes from those who are well-educated and highly accomplished. William Tucker believes that those who wish to engage in jihad warfare against the U.S. and the West bear a striking resemblance to the student revolutionaries during the 1960s on American universities. He calls them "overprivileged children" who he believes need to prove themselves (and their manhood) in the world. He also believes that "this is confounded by a polygamous society where fathers are often distant from their sons and where men and women barely encounter each other as young adults."

> *Tucker says that our current conflict with Islam is not a war against a whole civilization. He point out that the jihad warriors are despised as much in their own countries as they are in the West. "Egyptians are sick to death of the Muslim Brotherhood and its casual slaughter. The war between Fundamentalists and secular authorities in Algeria cost 100,000 lives."*

He concludes that we are effectively at war with a Muslim intelligentsia. These are essentially "the same people who brought us the horrors of the French Revolution and 20th century Communism. With their obsession for moral purity and their rational hatred that goes beyond all irrationality, these warrior-intellectuals are wreaking the same havoc in the Middle East as they did in Jacobin France and Mao Tse-tung's China." Certainly we are facing a clash of civilizations between Islam and the West. But it is helpful to understand Tucker's analysis. In any war it is important to know who you are fighting and what their motives might be. This understanding is one more important piece of the puzzle in the war on terrorism.

EXTENT OF THE RADICAL MUSLIM THREAT

What is the extent of the threat from radical Muslims? This is hard to guess, but there are some commentators who have tried to provide a reasonable estimate. Dennis Prager provides an overview of the extent of the threat:

> *Anyone else sees the contemporary reality—the genocidal Islamic regime in Sudan; the widespread Muslim theological and emotional support for the killing of a Muslim who converts to another religion; the absence of freedom in Muslim-majority*

countries; the widespread support for Palestinians who randomly murder Israelis; the primitive state in which women are kept in many Muslim countries; the celebration of death; the honor killings of daughters, and so much else that is terrible in significant parts of the Muslim world—knows that civilized humanity has a new evil to fight.

He argues that just as previous generations had to fight the Nazis and the communists, so this generation has to confront militant Islam. But he also notes something is dramatically different about the present Muslim threat. He says: Far fewer people believed in Nazism or in communism than believe in Islam generally or in authoritarian Islam specifically. There are one billion Muslims in the world. If just 10 percent believe in the Islam of Hamas, the Taliban, the Sudanese regime, Saudi Arabia, Wahhabism, bin Laden, Islamic Jihad, the Finley Park Mosque in London or Hizbollah—and it is inconceivable that only one of 10 Muslims supports any of these groups' ideologies—that means a true believing enemy of at least 100 million people. This very large number of people poses a threat that is unprecedented. Never has civilization has to confront such large numbers of those would wish to destroy civilization. So what is the threat in the United States? Columnist Douglas MacKinnon has some chilling statistics. While he recognizes that most Muslims in the U.S. are peace-loving, he begins to break down the percentages. He says:

[I]f we accept the estimate that there are 6 million Muslim-Americans in our country, and 99% of them are law abiding citizens who are loyal to our nation, then that means that there may be—may be—1% who might put a twisted version of Islamic extremism before the wellbeing of their fellow Americans. When you stop to think that 1% of 6 million is 60,000 individuals, that then seems like a very intimidating one percent. Let's go to the good side of extreme and say that 99.9 percent of all Muslim-Americans would never turn on their own government. That would still leave a questionable 1/10th one percent—or 6,000 potential terrorist sympathizers.

You can see that even the most conservative estimate of possible jihad warriors in this country results in a scary scenario for the future.

3

WOMEN IN ISLAM

One of the areas where Islam has had difficulty in adapting to the modern world has been in its treatment of women. While some Muslim leaders actually claim that Islam actually liberates women, contemporary examples prove otherwise. Women who lived under Taliban rule in Afghanistan or who live under Sharia law in many Muslim countries today do not enjoy equal rights.

While it is true that many Muslims do respect and honor women, it is not true that those ideas can be found in the Qur'an. Here are just a few passages that illustrate the way women are to be treated. According to the Qur'an, women are considered inferior to men: "Men have authority over women because God has made the one superior to the other" (Sura 4:34). The Qur'an also restricts a woman's testimony in court. According to Sura 2:282, her testimony is worth half as much as that of a man.

Polygamy is sanctioned in Islam, and practiced in many Muslim countries. Sura 4:3 says, "If we fear that ye shall not be able to deal justly with the orphans, marry women of your choice, two or three or four; but if we fear that ye shall not be able to deal justly with them, then only one, or a captive that your hand possess, that will be more suitable, to prevent you from doing injustice."

Women in many Muslim countries cover their faces. The justification for that can be found in the Qur'an that teaches that women must "lower their gaze and guard their modesty: that they should not display their beauty and ornaments except what must ordinarily appear thereof: that they should draw their veils over their bosoms and not display their beauty except to their husbands, their fathers" (Sura 24:31). Women in many Muslim countries cannot leave their house alone. Again, this is part of Islamic law. It states that a "husband may forbid his wife to leave the home."

It also places other requirements. For example, "a woman may not leave the city without her husband or a member of her unmarriageable kin accompanying her, unless the journey is obligatory, like the hajj. It is unlawful for her to travel otherwise, and unlawful for her husband to allow her to."

Not only was this practiced in Afghanistan under the Taliban, it is found in countries like Saudi Arabia. In that country, women cannot drive nor can they leave their home without being accompanied by a male family member. Amnesty International reports that women in Saudi Arabia "who walk unaccompanied, or are in the company of a man who is neither their husband nor close relative, are at risk of arrest on suspicion of prostitution" or other moral offenses.

CHURCH AND STATE IN ISLAM

Islam and the West differ on many fundamental issues, but one of the most significant is whether the institutions of church and state should be separated. Hundreds of years of Western tradition have demonstrated the wisdom of keeping these institutions separated and the danger that ensues when the ecclesiastical and civil institutions are melded into one.

Bernard Lewis explains that no such separation exists in Islam:

> *In [the Islamic] world, religion embraces far more than it does in the Christian or post-Christian world. We are accustomed to talking of church and state and a whole series of pairs of words that go with them–lay and ecclesiastical, secular and religious, spiritual and temporal, and so on. These pairs of words simply do not exist in classical Islamic terminology because the dichotomy that these words express is unknown.*

Since the words (and the concepts) do not exist in Islam, it becomes difficult to see how to form democracies in the Muslim world. Essential to the functioning of these governments is a belief in the separation of powers. This would not only include a horizontal separation of powers (executive, legislative, and judicial), but a religious separations of powers (ecclesiastical and civil).

Chuck Colson says that "Islam is a theocratic belief system. It believes in not just a state church, but a church state. And so, it doesn't advance like Christianity does. These are radically different views of reality."

This leads to another fundamental difference between Islam and Christianity. As we have discussed in previous articles, Islam historically has advanced by force or compulsion. Chuck Colson puts it this way: "Christianity advances by love, it advances by winning people over, it advances by the grace of God; radical Islam advances by force."

Even within Muslim countries, Islam advances by compulsion. But it is important to point out that the Qur'an (2:256) says "there is no compulsion in religion." But that really depends upon your definition of compulsion.

A closer look at Islamic law demonstrates a veiled threat that many believe is tantamount to compulsion. For example, Muhammad instructed his followers to invite non-Muslims to accept Islam before waging war against them. If they refused, warfare would follow or second class status. They would be inferiors in the Muslim social order and pay a special tax. This tax (known as the jizya) is required in Sura 9:29. If they pay it, they may live, but if they refuse to pay it, warfare will ensue.

While those of us in the West would consider this compulsion, the traditional Muslim interpretation of this would be that this would fit into the category of "no compulsion."

4

DILEMMAS OF POLITICS AND CULTURE

THE CRISIS OF PARTICIPATION

The Muslim community in the United States is also facing a crisis of participation. Is it religiously legitimate for the believer to be politically active in a system of government which is not only non-Islamic but is potentially anti-Islamic from time to time? Should a Muslim agree to vote under the United States constitution and against the background of the role of the United States' controlling if not intimidating many Muslim countries? In the 1990s alone American bombs and missiles have fallen on Iraq, Afghanistan, Sudan, and accidentally, Pakistan. We could use some of the categories of medieval Islamic jurists who divided the world between Dar el Islam (the Abode of Islam) and Dar el Harb (the Abode of War). Are Muslims in America an enclave of Dar el Islam lodged in the body politic of Dar el Harb? Where does the political participation of Dar el Islam fit into the political process of Dar el Harb? Or should we abandon altogether these medieval Islamic divisions of the world as being outdated?

Another dilemma concerns possible differences between Muslim minorities from one Western country to another. Are British Muslims in a different predicament from American Muslims? Is there a difference between Muslims voting in a Christian theocracy (like England) on one side, and Muslims voting in a secular state (like the United States), on the other?

The Head of State in England is also the Head of the Church of England. The Archbishop of Canterbury is chosen with the participation of the Prime Minister. And major doctrinal changes in the Church of England need the approval of the British Parliament either directly or by delegation through the Synod of the Church. The United States, on the other hand, is a secular state which constitutionally is supposed to favour no religion. Is it therefore more halal to participate in U.S. elections than in British elections?

In the world as it exists today, we have to allow non-Muslims to vote in every Muslim country. If non-Muslim minorities vote in Muslim societies, why should not Muslim minorities vote in non-Muslim countries? If Christians can vote in Egypt, why should not Muslims vote in the United States?

The most famous Egyptian of the 1990s was for a while Boutros Boutros-Ghali who would not have been eligible for the post of Secretary-General of the United Nations had he not had extensive political and diplomatic participation in Egypt before hand. Boutros-Ghali was and is of course a Christian.

The Deputy Prime Minister of Iraq is Tareq Aziz, another Christian. No Christian country in the West has as yet allowed a Muslim to rise to such a status. Should Muslims themselves in Christian countries prevent their own rise to power?

For 20 years Muslim Senegal had a Roman Catholic President (1960-1980)-Leopold Sedar Senghor. The percentage of Muslims in Senegal is 94%-higher than the percentage of Muslims in Egypt. Senegal is a remarkable illustration of Muslim ecumenicalism. If Muslim countries allow the participation and even empowerment of non-Muslim minorities, why should not Muslim minorities in non-Muslim countries seek participation and increasing empowerment for themselves?

On the other hand, it is possible for a Muslim to attain the highest office in the land in a country in which Muslims are a minority-provided the Muslim minority has not been politically inactive.

This happened in Malawi in May 1994 when, in the first internationally supervised election since independence thirty years earlier, the voters in Malawi elected Bakili Muluzi as their first Muslim president. According to most estimates, Muslims in Malawi are less than a third of the population. Could a Muslim president have been elected if the Muslim minority had declared themselves to be politically neutral? In Sierra Leone the numerical strength of Muslims is less clear. Are they a minority or are they over 50%? What is clear is that Sierra Leone elected its first Muslim President in 1996-Ahmed Tejan Kabba. Once again the question arises whether Sierra Leone would have had its first elected Muslim president in 1996 if the Muslims of the country had declared themselves politically neutral? (President Kabba's forunes have had ups and downs in that militarily troubled country).

The fourth largest concentration of Muslims in the world is a minority in a largely non-Muslim country in the world. This is the minority of some 100 million Muslims in the Republic of India. They are fourth numerically after the populations of Indonesia, Pakistan, and Bangladesh (others have argued that Indian Muslims are second numerically).

One of the factors which have influenced most political parties in India to be tolerant towards Muslims has been the voting leverage and participation of this 12% of the population. Had Indian Muslims opted out of politics completely Indian Muslims would have been more marginalized and perhaps even more victimized than ever.

The following distinctions need to be made concerning Muslims and U.S. laws:

1. Can Muslims live in the United States without obeying U.S. Laws?-Can they refuse to pay U.S. taxes, even if the taxes are not remotely Islamic?
2. Can Muslims become U.S. citizens without allegiance to the U.S. Constitution which is not Islamic?
3. Can Muslims insist that their money should not be used in wars against Muslim countries abroad?

Since Muslims in America cannot long endure without obeying U.S. laws, should they not try to influence the process of making those laws? Voting for Members of Congress and for the President constitutes part of the process of influencing the making of those laws-and not merely obeying the laws. Even those militant opponents of Muslim voting in U.S. elections do obey U.S. laws.

The Third domain is not merely Muslims voting but also Muslims running for office. This would be a process of Muslim empowerment. If elected, Muslims would not only be more directly affecting the making of the laws. The Muslims would also be influencing the implementation of the laws and their enforcement. Overtime the judicial and legal system of the United States would become more sensitized to the Muslim experience and related issues.

The central underlying question is that once American Muslims have recognized that they have to obey the laws of the United States, almost all of which have nothing to do with the Shari'a, the next question is whether Muslims should strategize to help influence the making of those laws and their implementation in the hope of making those laws more sensitive to the multicultural and multireligious nature of the population of the United States.

Fifthly, there is the nagging question: If Muslims cannot be voters in the United States, can they even be lawyers or legal consultants? Do opponents of Muslims voting in U.S. elections have sons or daughters training to become U.S. lawyers?

If it is haram to be a voter in a U.S. election, is it ten times haram to be trained as an expert in U.S. law and practicing it? Is a Muslim-American lawyer who is devoting his or her time defending Muslim clients committing at least a double haram?

On the other hand, if we concede that Muslims may become attorneys and lawyers in the United States, why should not Muslims become voters also? Voting is connected with law at many different stages and in many different respects.

What we have here is the complex inter-relationship between law-making (legislature), law interpretation (the judiciary), law implementation (the executive). Voting is part of the process of choosing who makes these laws, who interprets them, and who implements them. The logic of the legal process is intertwined with the logic of the electoral process.

The logic of saying that it is haram to seek to influence law-making in the United States would make it haram to have Muslim lawyers practicing under U.S. law. It would also make it close to haram to obey the laws of the land. Such advice would be dangerous indeed for a Muslim minority living almost anywhere in a primarily non-Muslim country.

The conclusion to be drawn is that it is to the unmistakable advantage (maslaha) of a Muslim minority to seek ways of influencing governance in the direction of greater enlightenment.

Muslims located in the United States have additional obligations since they are geographically located in the most powerful country in the world-with an immense capacity to either harm or benefit the rest of the ummah world-wide.

The United States can either do such positive things as helping Afghanistan get rid of Soviet occupation or do such negative things as bombing Khartoum and Tripoli when there is suspicion of so-called Sudanese and Libyan "terrorism".

The United States can either look the other way and let Iran arm Bosnian Muslims against Serbian genocide or the United States can pass illegal legislation penalizing Third countries for trading with Iran and Libya.

American Muslims need to be active enough to monitor and influence American policy not only in domestic affairs but also in foreign affairs. The self-denial of voting power by some U.S. Muslims is an exercise in political castration.

Had the United States in the 20th century had very few Jewish citizens, the history of Israel and the Middle East would have been vastly different. Without a large and powerful Jewish lobby within the United States, U.S. generosity towards Israel would probably have substantially evaporated. At the very minimum the United States would have spent less money on arming Israel, used fewer vetoes to defend Israel at the United Nations, been more attentive to Palestinian and Arab concerns, and been more publicly critical of Israeli atrocities. Jewish activism in U.S. politics produced pro-Jewish results.

American Muslims may never equal the power of the Jews in the U.S. system, but the Muslims may one day help provide some counterbalance in policy-formation. Muslim participation and empowerment within the U.S. political system is therefore vital not only for the sake of Muslims themselves but also for the sake of the wider ummah world wide, and for the sake of enriching the pluralism and global representativeness of American civilization.

THE SECRET BALLOT AND THE INFORMATION REVOLUTION

But there may be fundamental areas where Islam in America and the new information revolution need to find accommodation. These could be at the heart of any Islamic reform movement if it occurs. One area of tension concerns the relations between men and women. Will U.S. Muslims in alliance with the new technology of information fundamentally alter the gender playing field forever? The new technology is leading to shrinkage of sovereignty and the death of distance. But is the third consequence a case of privacy unveiled? On the gender question the Muslim world has alternated between two codes of conduct. One code has been to treat genders as separate but equal.

The United States once attempted to implement the Constitutional doctrine of treating whites and Blacks as separate but equal. However, by 1954 the Supreme Court was ready to conclude that separation of the races resulted in or perpetuated inequality. In the momentous decision of Brown versus the Board of Education in 1954, the U.S. Supreme Court at last rejected the doctrine of "separate but equal" for the races. Racial segregation became unconstitutional.

If "separate but equal" was untenable for races, why should the doctrine work for genders? Because genders live together in homes in a way in which races never used to do in the United States. Every man's mother is a woman. So are men's wives, daughters, and granddaughters, aunts and other female relatives. So the separation of genders is inevitably moderated by family ties. That is a qualitative difference from the separation of races. The gender doctrine of "separate but equal" could survive the new information revolution. Under the new technology the computerized hijab is at hand, women can more easily stay at home and still be equal computer workers. The distinction between home and work-place is getting abolished. U.S. Muslims may take the lead in that. Indeed husbands may also work at home alongside wives in the 21st century.

But many Muslim societies treat women as "separate and unequal". Is this a sexist code of conduct? Aspects of this are rooted in the Shari'a which made women inherit half of what men inherited, and made the testimony of women in court be worth less than that of men on some economic issues.

Such Muslim societies have assumed that there were two different doors of knowledge-one for men and one for women. Many Muslim societies had assumed that there were branches of knowledge which were not fit for women and children under 15. Partly for reasons of modesty women were spared from certain areas of know-how. Today the Taliban in Afghanistan have carried this theory of two tiers of gender knowledge to the extreme.

The new information technology is going to blow that distinction totally out of social existence. U.S. Muslims may be leading the global ummah in the new technology. More and more information may refuse to be susceptible to gender-discrimination. What men know about sex, pornography, politics and corruption may also be accessible to women through the World Wide Web, Internet and the emerging information superhighway.

In time the veil as the modesty of the face is bound to be destroyed by the new technology. Women may cover other aspects of their personality, but increasingly they will be totally available facially to the viewer through the Internet and the approaching image telephone system. The new technology will pass a death sentence on the tradition of the harem as we have known it since the Abbasid dynasty in many Muslim societies. Will U.S. Muslim women lead the way?

The traditional forms of seclusion of women will not long survive a technology in which women can declare their presence and in time assert their rights. Women voting in the U.S. will be a start. Women running for election will come a generation later. American Muslims will join forces with the new technology of information to precipitate fundamental reforms in gender relations in the Muslim world. But how should Muslims vote? For one thing Muslims should avoid the mistake which African Americans have made for much of the twentieth century-that of being predictably for one political party and having nowhere else to go. In recent decades African-American votes have been too predictably identified with the Democratic Party-with the result that neither party has tried very hard to court their vote. They have simply tried not to alienate them completely.

Muslim voters should behave differently. They should use the vote as a leverage to reward those who take Muslim concerns seriously and to punish those who ignore those concerns. In some years more Democrats may deserve Muslim support than Republicans; in other years the Republicans may turn out to be the more Muslim-friendly.

In the Congressional elections of the years 2000 and 2002 Muslims should vote candidate by candidate-and not by political party. The American Muslim Alliance has the ambition of having one Muslim senator elected by the year 2002.

Muslims in each Congressional constituency, in each Senatorial constituency should examine the candidates according to (a) their record (b) their policies and pledges (c) their degree of sensitivity to Muslim concerns at home and abroad.

At the Congressional and Senate levels in the years 2000 and 2002 Muslims should vote by candidates and not by party affiliation. What about the presidential election when it comes? Since this is a crisis of political participation, we must confront the issue head on. There will be two specific candidates close to the elections. Will one of them be more Muslim-friendly than the other?

In 1996 Bill Clinton (at least as compared with Bob Dole) had earned the vote of U.S. Muslims because he had gone further than any other president in U.S. history to give Islam some standing as an integral part of American society. But this was Clinton not as a Democrat but as a pro-Muslim initiator. He had started the process of going beyond the political convention of treating the United States as a Judeo-Christian community only. In personal behavior Clinton fell below Islamic standards of family values, but in official behavior he was a particularly ecumenical President of the United States.

Under his watch, President Clinton recognized a major Islamic institution within the U.S.-the fast of Ramadhan. He sent an open letter to believers wishing them a blessed fast. Under the Clinton watch, the White House for the first time ever celebrated Idd el Fitr to mark the end of Ramadhan at which the first lady recognized the increasing expansion of the Muslim community within the United States and wished Muslims well.

Under Clinton's watch, the United States decided to look the other way when the Islamic Republic of Iran was arming the Government of Bosnia in the face of an illegally-imposed arms embargo by the United Nations in spite of Serbian aggression.

Under Clinton's watch the first Muslim chaplains of the U.S. military were appointed-with the major participation of the American Muslim Council. Under Clinton's watch Arab and Muslim Americans met with the President of the United States and discussed issues of Arab and Muslim concern. Under Clinton's watch Muslim representatives were received by Anthony Lake of the National Security Council and explored with him the implications of U.S. policy towards Bosnia.

Indeed, under Clinton's watch enemies of Islam began to accuse the White House of extending hospitality to Hamas and socializing with mujahiddeen. Bill Clinton stuck his political neck out for Muslims of America. While in foreign policy Clinton was no less friendly to Israel than any other U.S. president, in domestic policy he was more Muslim-friendly than any other president in the history of the United States. Those Muslims who voted for him in 1996 instead of for Bob Dole might have taken some of such factors into account. To be or not to be politically active in a non-Muslim society. The burden of our analysis has been that U.S. Muslims cannot afford to be politically neutral.

In 1996 the United States made the practice of female circumcision illegal within the country. There were no Muslim protests. That silence was the right code of conduct. Female circumcision has been wrongly attributed to Islam-some Muslim countries practice it for cultural rather than religious reasons. Other Muslim countries reject it altogether. It is not surprising that U.S. Muslims did not make an issue of the banning of female circumcision.

Now that American Muslims (like the Somali Americans or Egyptian Americans) are not permitted by U.S. law to circumcise their women, why should they symbolically castrate themselves by opting out of the political process?

AMERICAN ISLAM: BETWEEN IDENTITY AND POLICY

In terms of national origins, Arab Americans have been politically active since before Israel was born. Americans of Arab origin have included Christians (such as the consumer advocate Ralph Nader) as well as the more politicized Muslim Arabs. In the struggle to prevent the partition of Palestine before 1947-8 both Christian and Muslim Arabs lobbied hard in favour of "undivided Palestine". To the present day the Arab American population in the United States is more Christian than Muslim, on balance.

But after Israel was created the "Palestinian cause" in the United States became increasingly identified with Muslims on their own. This coincided with a period of unprecedented Jewish rise in influence in the American political process-in the second half of the twentieth century.

Although the number of Arabs within the U.S. population rose from 1948 (the year of Israel's creation) to 1967 (the year of the Six-Day war), Arab impact on U.S. foreign policy probably declined during that period. This was almost certainly in direct proportion to the impressive expansion of the influence of the pro-Israeli lobby on Capitol Hill and on sections of the Federal Government during those years. Many Arab Americans also chose to keep a low profile out of fear of Zionist extremists and of other zealots of Middle Eastern politics.

What has changed in the last quarter of the twentieth century is that Arab Americans are less inhibited, feel less politically intimidated, and are more sophisticated in skills of utilizing the American political process. However, they are still subject to some of the tensions and divisions of the wider Arab world.

The foreign policy issue on which South Asian Muslims in the United States feel most strongly about is perhaps Kashmir. There is constant lobbying on Capitol Hill for either resolutions to censure India for human rights violations in Kashmir or for legislative action in search of a solution. There is also a constant flow of brochures, pamphlets, news-updating on Kashmir not only targeted at Congress, but also distributed widely to campuses, news media, and other contributors to policy-formation. Now that India and Pakistan have become nuclear powers, there is anxiety that Kashmir might become a nuclear trigger in the years ahead.

While the majority of South Asian Muslims in the United States favour self-determination for Kashmir or union with Pakistan, there is a minority of Muslim citizens of India who would rather see Kashmir remain part of India. It is worth remembering that India today has more than a 100 million Muslims (the fourth largest concentration of Muslims after Indonesia, Pakistan, and Bangladesh). Many Muslims of India are ambivalent about Kashmir. Do they want Kashmiris to have self-determination and risk depriving India of its only state with a Muslim majority? Or would they rather have Kashmir remain part of India and strengthen the plight of other Muslims in India? Muslims from India who have become U.S. citizens betray the same ambivalence about Kashmir.

However, those American Muslims who favour the status quo for Kashmir have decided to keep a low profile-especially since most of them are appalled by the human rights violations often perpetrated by the Indian troops in Kashmir. The most vocal American Muslims on Kashmir are those who favour self-determination for the embattled people of that province.

From the point of view of racial identity, the great majority of Muslims in the United States are of course people of color. Their position on apartheid in South Africa before the 1990s was almost unanimous. There was Muslim consensus that the United States should impose and maintain sanctions against the racist regime in Pretoria (as it then was). The American Muslim Council went into a kind of strategic alliance with TransAfrica, led by the African American activist Randall Robinson. TransAfrica was by far the more active U.S. organization against apartheid. But many Muslims supported Robinson. And the American Muslim Council held a major conference in the 1980s on the theme "Islam against Apartheid" with major international speakers, including Muslim activists from South Africa itself.

The United States was persuaded (especially by TransAfrica and its allies) to impose wide-ranging sanctions on the racist regime in South Africa. The sanctions lasted until after Nelson Mandella was released and the African National Congress was legalized in the 1990's. Imam Warith Dean Mohammed, the African American Sunni crusader, played an important role in consolidating the Muslim crusade against apartheid and racism.

The most race-conscious of all those who call themselves Muslims in the United States are, however, the followers of the Nation of Islam, currently led by Minister Louis Farrakhan. Foreign policy was part and parcel of the birth of the movement, for the founder was an immigrant reportedly born in Mecca, who arrived in the United States in 1931. Was Farrad Muhammad an Arab? In pigmentation he was very fair, but he identified himself with the Black people of the city of Detroit.

Farrad Muhammad disappeared without a trace in 1934. His successor as leader of the Nation of Islam was Elijah Muhammad. The foreign policy tests came with the outbreak of World War II. Elijah Muhammad enjoined his followers that as Muslims they had no obligation to fight for the flag of the United States. He was imprisoned from 1942 to 1946 because of that position.

The dilemma between Islam and the flag in the United States continued afterwards. The boxing champion Muhammed Ali, a follower of the Nation of Islam, refused in 1967 to fight for the United States in Vietnam. He was convicted and stripped of his championship in retaliation. He in turn reportedly threw away his Olympic gold medal in protest. It was not until 1971 that the Supreme Court of the United States revoked his conviction and helped to restore his championship title, by protecting his religious freedom and freedom of expression under the American Constitution. At the 1996 Olympic games in Atlanta Muhammed Ali was also ceremonially honoured with a replacement of his ostensibly "lost" Olympic medal.

I spent five hours with Minister Louis Farrakhan at his home in Chicago, Illinois, in January 1996. This was of course after the Million Man March of October 1995. Did the Million Man March have foreign policy implications? Minister Farrakhan told us that soon after the march he had received congratulations from Muamar

Qaddafy, the Head of State of Libya. Qaddafy was most impressed by the success of the march.

Farrakhan also told us about his plans to tour both the Muslim world and Africa. He started the tour the following month-stirring much debate in the United States when he was reported to have visited Iran, Iraq, Syria, and Libya, which were regarded with particular hostility by the U.S. government.

When Libyan sources reported that Muammar Qaddafy had offered Louis Farrakhan one billion dollars for his movement, and Farrakhan confirmed this on his return to the United States, there were demands in Congress that Farrakhan be compelled to register as a "foreign agent." Farrakhan retorted that he would be prepared to discuss such a possibility if several members of Congress would similarly register as agents of the state of Israel. In any case, Qaddafy's proposed one billion dollars to the Nation of Islam was for schools, clinics, and social services and not for political lobbying or political activism, Farrakhan insisted. The issue has been bogged down with legal wrangling.

When U.S. Muslims behave as Muslims (heirs of the Hijrah), and when they behave as concerned Americans (heirs of the Mayflower), they have operated under a number of paradoxes. Let us examine those paradoxes affecting codes of conduct.

MORALITY AND POLITICS

The first paradox is that while American secularism is good news for Muslims (separating church from state), American libertarianism is bad news for Islam (such as the latest American debate as to whether same-sex marriages should be legally recognized nationwide as they already are in Hawaii).

The Democratic Party in the United States is more insistent on separating church from state, including its opposition to prayer in schools. This draws some Muslim parents towards the Democrats, since the Muslim parents do not want their kids to be under peer pressure to attend Christian prayers.

On the other hand, the Republicans are stronger on traditional family values and are more opposed to sexual libertarianism. This draws many Muslims (especially immigrant Asians) to the

Republican party. Most Muslims share Republican concerns about abortion and gay rights.

The second paradox concerns the Clinton Administration. We have mentioned that while Clinton's administration had been more pro-Israel than any other U.S. administration since Lyndon Johnson, this same Clinton administration had domestically made more friendly gestures towards U.S. Muslims than any previous administration. We referred to the President's greetings to Muslims during the fast of Ramadhan in 1996. We referred to the First-Lady hosting a celebration of Idd el Fitr (the Festival of the End of Ramadhan) in the White House in April 1996 and 1998. Vice President Al Gore visited a mosque in the Fall 1995. And the first Muslim chaplain to serve the 10,000 Muslims in the US armed forces was sworn into the Air Force under Clinton's watch.

President Clinton received in the White House a delegation of Arab Americans to discuss wide ranging issues, domestic and international. We referred to the National Security Advisor, Anthony Lake, receiving a delegation of Muslims (including this author) in 1996 to discuss the ramifications of the Bosnian crisis.

The Clinton gestures towards Muslims were sufficiently high profile that a hostile article in the Wall Street Journal in March 1996 raised the spectre of "Friends of Hamas in the White House"-alleging that some of the President's Muslim guests were friends of Hamas, and supporters of the Palestinian movement. The critic in the Wall Street Journal (Steve Emerson) had a long record of hostility towards U.S. Muslims. His television programme on PBS entitled Jihad in America (1994) alleged that almost all terrorist activities by Muslims worldwide were partially funded by U.S. Muslims. President Clinton's friendly gestures to Muslims probably infuriated this self-appointed crusader of Islamophobia.

The third paradox facing U.S. Muslims is that in foreign policy the Republicans in recent U.S. history have been greater friends of Muslims than have Democrats-whereas in domestic policies the Democrats are probably more friendly to Muslims than the Republicans. We shall return to that thesis soon.

The fourth paradox concerns the two Islams in America-indigenous and immigrant. But let us first return to the first paradox. In the United States Western secularism has protected minority religious groups by insisting on separation of church and state. That is a major reason why the Jews in the United States have been among the greatest defenders of the separation of church and state. Any breach of that principle could lead to the imposition of some practices of the religious majority-like forcing Jewish children to participate in Christian prayers at school.

In discussing the role of American Muslims qua Muslims (heirs of the Hijrah), we have to look more closely at their moral concerns in relation to American culture. Curiously enough, American secularism is indeed good news for Muslims in America. The bad news is the expanding arena of American libertarianism. Secularism in the political process does indeed help to protect minority religions from the potential intrusive power of the Christian Right. On the other hand, expanding American libertarianism in such fields as sexual mores alarms both the Christian Right and Muslim traditionalists in the United States.

These moral concerns in turn have consequences on how American Muslims relate to the wider political divide between Republicans and Democrats in both foreign and domestic policies.

In the 1990s more and more American Muslims are registering to vote and seeking to influence candidates in elections. On such social issues as family values and sexual mores, Muslims often find themselves more in tune with Republican rhetoric and concerns. On the need for a more strict separation of church and state, which helps to protect religious minorities, it is the more liberal Democrats who offer a better protection to Muslims. Let us look at these contradictions more closely.

The First Amendment permits religious minorities to practice their religions in relative peace. Of course, like all doctrines, secularism has its fanatics who sometimes want to degrade the sacred rather than permitting it. But at its best a secular state is a refuge of safety for minority religions. It is in that sense that American secularism is a friend of Muslims living in the United States.

But while secularism is a divorce from formal religion, Muslims see libertarianism as a dilution of spirituality. One can be without a formal religion and still be deeply spiritual in a humanistic sense. John Stuart Mill and Bertrand Russell were without formal religion, yet each had deeply spiritual values. Albert Schweitzer, the Nobel Laureate for Peace, was at times an agnostic-but he was deeply committed to the principle of reverence for life-even protecting the lives of insects in Africa.

Religion has been declining in influence in the West since the days of the Renaissance and the Enlightenment. But it is mainly in the 20th century that spirituality in the West has taken a nose-dive. From an Islamic perspective, America has become not only less religious-but dangerously less spiritual. America has become not only more secular but dangerously more libertarian.

It is the libertarianism which is regarded as a danger to Muslims living in the Western hemisphere. There is the libertarian materialism of excessive acquisitiveness (greed), libertarian consumption (consumerism), the materialism of the flesh (excessive sexuality), the materialism of excessive self-indulgence (from alcoholism to drugs). These four forms of libertarianism could result in a hedonistic way of life, a pleasure-seeking career.

What is more, Muslim parents fear that American libertarianism is likely to influence the socialization and upbringing of the next generation of Muslim children-excessive levels of acquisitiveness, consumerism and diverse forms of sexuality.

It is because of all these considerations that Islam within the United States feels threatened less by American secularism than by American libertarianism.

IDEOLOGY AND PRAGMATISM

But there are also the political and ideological shifts in power in the Western world as a whole-between liberals and conservatives, between Tories and Socialists, between Democrats and Republicans. American Muslims have been sensitive to those shifts internationally. What does the end of the Cold War mean for the Muslim countries? In much of the Western world in recent times it is not simply a case of more conservative parties winning elections; the whole political system in France and Britain has been moving to the right. Muslims worldwide have wondered about the implications of all these developments and changes for Islam today.

American Muslim leaders follow global trends with mixed feelings. What used to be major socialist or internationalist parties have not only shrunk in support-they have also diluted their left-wing orientation. Communism is crippled. A party of the right may lose an election-as the Tory Party has done in Britain in the last General Election — but it lost to a Labour Party which is a much more conservative force today than it was thirty or fifty years ago.

Indeed, the leader of the British Labour Party had already got the party to get rid of clause 4 in its constitution-a clause which had for so long committed the party to the socialist ambition of nationalizing the means of production, distribution and exchange. In France when the late socialist President Mitterand was ailing, so was his old style of socialism. The system had not only moved to the right-it had become a little more racist. There is also more Islamophobia in France today than there has been at any other time in the 20th century. The move to the right has coincided with greater anti-Muslim and anti-immigrant sentiments.

What about the United States? Is it simply a case of the Republicans winning control of the Congress? Or are all three branches of government moving to the right with only minor variations between the two parties? Was the Clinton style of "New Democrat" a reflection of the force of conservative influence? Is the U.S. system as a whole going conservative-and how is it going to affect Muslims? Is the shift short term or long-term?

In France the move to the right has triggered off some degree of xenophobia or hostility towards foreigners. French cultural xenophobia has included Islamophobia. In Germany xenophobia has included Turkophobia, or hostility towards the Turks-which in turn has included elements of Islamophobia. Turkish houses have been fire-bombed and Turks have died at the hands of German neo-Nazis. U.S. Muslims are bracing themselves for similar chauvinism against immigrants. After the Oklahoma City bombing, there were at least 227 hate crimes against Muslims, according to the Council for American Islamic Relations. Muslims braced themselves for more hate crimes after the atrocities against the U.S. embassies in Kenya and Tanzania in 1998.

In the United States changes in regime between Republicans and Democrats has had historical paradoxes. In Middle Eastern politics Republican Administrations in the past have sometimes shown greater ability to stand up to Israel than have Democratic administrations. American Muslims have noted that.

In 1956 it was Republican President Dwight Eisenhower who insisted on a halt to the occupation of parts of Egypt by Britain, France and Israel-and compelled the Israelis to withdraw from the Sinai which they had occupied in the Suez War of 1956.

It was Republican President George Bush who put his foot down against the indirect use of American money on illegal Jewish settlements on Arab occupied lands. George Bush did lead Desert Storm against Iraq in the Gulf War of 1991-but perhaps no U.S. President (Republican or Democrat) would have permitted Iraq to annex Kuwait. What is more, a Democratic president might have authorized a march onto Baghdad.

On the other hand, it was a Democratic President Harry S. Truman who gave the U.S. green light in 1947 for the creation of the State of Israel-setting the stage for fifty years of Arab-Israeli wars, for Palestinian suffering and for mutual hatreds.

It was Democratic President Lyndon Johnson's administration which helped Israel (with logistical intelligence) win the June war of 1967 in six days which resulted in the occupation of Arab lands in Gaza, Sinai, Golan Heights, and the West Bank. It has been Democratic President Bill Clinton who came closer than any U.S. President towards giving silent legitimization to Jewish settlements in occupied Arab territories. Bill Clinton did once even consider recognizing Jerusalem as the capital of Israel. A brief temptation. The Clinton Administration was for a while more militant in trying to isolate Iran internationally than previous U.S. administrations had been since the Islamic revolution in 1979. The election of Muhammad Khatami as President of Iran in 1997 began to tip the scale. Khatami was more liberal.

It was, on the other hand, Republican Richard Nixon who took a position sympathetic to Pakistan and against India in the

Indo-Pakistani conflict in 1971 when Nixon was in power. Nixon was hated in India for it. What all this means is that in foreign policy, the Republicans have so far often been greater friends of the Muslim world than have Democrats.

But domestically the Democrats are the party of minorities and the secular state. And so although Muslims have not emerged very explicitly as a political minority, the party most likely to be sensitive to domestic diversity is the Democratic Party. If Muslims are discriminated against or harassed at home within the United States, the Democrats are more likely to come to the rescue than the Republicans.

In foreign policy, on the other hand, the Republicans so far have been greater friends of the Muslim world, than have the Democrats. The anti-terrorist legislation proposed and signed by the Clinton Administration was probably both a matter of domestic policy and foreign policy. The divide between Republicans and Democrats was therefore even.

IMMIGRANT AND HOME-GROWN

In places like Britain, France and Germany both Islam as a civilization and local Muslims as residents are widely regarded as foreign even when the Euro-Muslims are citizens of the European countries. In the United States, on the other hand, half the Muslim population will soon consist of descendants of families who have been Americans for hundreds of years. 42% of Muslims in the United States are already African Americans. This creates a different situation from that of Europe.

In Europe both Islam and Muslims may be regarded as foreign; but in the United States such an equation is increasingly difficult. Islam may be new, but its followers include millions who have been part of American history for two or three hundred years. African-American Muslim population is expanding significantly.

But even the immigrant half of the Muslim population of the United States is operating in a country of immigrants any how- unlike the immigrant Muslims of France, Britain and Germany.

In the United States it has been possible for an immigrant with a heavy foreign accent to become the most outstanding non-presidential American statesman of the second half of the 20th century-Henry Kissinger, the brilliant Jewish Secretary of State. So even the immigrant Muslims in the USA are, in that special American sense, less foreign than the Muslim immigrants in Europe. But there is no doubt of the reality that the United States faces a TALE OF TWO ISLAMS.

We define "indigenous" in the United States in this article as people who have been American for at least two centuries. We might therefore conclude that indigenous American Muslims are mainly African Americans, with a small percentage of white Americans. We regard immigrant Americans in this essay as those who have been part of American society for less than a century. Immigrant American Muslims are mainly from Asia, the Middle East and Africa in recent times. Some are from Muslim Europe.

While indigenous American Muslims are highly sensitive to issues of domestic policy in the United States, immigrant American Muslims are more sensitive to the foreign policy of the United States.

The problem of low income families among indigenous Muslims may be above the national average-this is to say, there are too many poor families. On the other hand, the proportion of families in the professional class among immigrant Muslims (teachers, lawyers, doctors, engineers and others) may be above the national average.

Indigenous Muslims (especially African Americans) tend to rebel against the mythology of the American dream as a pursuit of personal advancement in conditions of economic freedom. Immigrant Muslims, on the other hand, seem to be disproportionately persuaded that there is more opportunity than oppression in capitalism.

Indigenous American Muslims are new to Islam but old to America (though Islam did once arrive in the Americas with enslaved Africans in chains). Today African American Muslims are fully Americanized but not always fully Islamized. Warath Dean Mohammed is among those who is both fully American and fully Muslim. With immigrant Muslims the situation is the reverse. They are old to Islam but new to America. They are often substantially Islamized but not yet fully Americanized. Indigenous American Muslims are overwhelmingly unilingual-speaking only English (standard or dialect or both) though they often learn some modest Arabic for purposes of Islamic ritual. Immigrant Muslims are often bilingual and even trilingual. At home they may even speak more than one European language. Lebanese Americans may speak French, Arabic as well as English. Indigenous American Muslims are weak economically, but as African Americans they have considerable potential political leverage. After all, the population of African Americans generally is much larger than the population of the Jews of the whole world added together. And yet at the moment the influence of African Americans on US foreign policy is only a fraction of the influence of Jewish Americans. Will the difference in leverage narrow in the 21st century? Will African-American influence reflect the political importance of Islam among American Blacks?

If indigenous Americans are currently economically weak but potentially strong politically, the immigrant Muslims may be in the reverse predicament. They may be politically weak but with considerable potential for economic and professional leverage. The population of indigenous Muslims may expand as a result of the new Republican attacks on welfare, medicaid, and on the safety nets which had once been provided for the Black poor. More poor Blacks may turn to Islam. On the other hand, the population of immigrant Muslims may decline as a result of more strict laws against immigration from all parts of the world. Muslim immigration may also suffer from how the new anti-terrorist legislation is actually implemented on the ground. Individual immigration officers might be encouraged to be particularly harsh to visa candidates from the Muslim world.

But when all is said and done, the two sets of Muslims in the United States (indigenous and immigrant) are in the process of being forged into the largest Muslim nation in the special hemisphere of Christopher Columbus, the Americas. In 1492 the Islamic presence in Spain was ended. In 1492 Christopher Columbus opened up the Americas for the West. Five hundred years later an Islamic presence was trying to establish itself in the lands which Columbus helped to open up for Spain and the West.

Was history indulging her ironic sense of humour all over again? The heirs of the Hijrah became simultaneously heirs to the Mayflower.

In foreign policy the four identities of U.S. Muslims play their part. The issue of national origins, the membership of a racial group, the power of religious affiliation, and the moral concerns of U.S. Muslims as ordinary Americans-such a confluence of identities is part of the politics of pluralism, part of policy-formation in a liberal democratic order.

But in the final analysis the cultural dimension of the American Muslim experience is not simply this crisis of identity. It is also the simultaneous and interrelated crises of participation and code of conduct. It still remains a drama in three Acts. First Act: Am I an American Muslim or a Muslim American? Which comes first-and under what circumstances? Second Act: Do I accept to be a participant in the American constitutional process? Third Act: Is my code of conduct as a Muslim compatible with my code of conduct as an American? The heritage of the Hijrah and the legacy of the Mayflower are in search of a moral synthesis.

THE THREAT OF DOUBLE-CONSCIOUSNESS

Two basic challenges confronting Muslims in America inform the present essay. The first has to do with the enterprise of self-definition, that is, of defining for oneself who one is and which actions and non-actions are therefore consistent with one's choice of selfhood. The second has to do with the problem of self-determination, or how to gain the requisite control or influence over the social and political institutions that affect one's life. These challenges are intimately connected to each other. They are also connected to the issue of Muslim participation in American society, socially and politically. This latter point is obvious in the case of self-determination. It becomes equally obvious, however, in the case of self-definition, once it is recognized that the real goal of any act of self-definition is both to affirm one's subjectivity vis a vis the world around one and to gain public recognition for one's subjectivity chosen self. Self-definition, in other words, is always and fundamentally a social cum political act; it is never a purely intellectual one.

From the outset, the enterprise of Muslim self-definition is complicated by the fact of the heterogeneous make-up of the Muslim community in America. American-born converts (the majority of whom are African-Americans) are a product of American history, as are their hopes, fears, fantasies and proper ambition. They are both repelled by the American experience, by virtue of their history as a marginalized minority, and attracted to it, by the virtue of their connection to a uniquely rich Afro-American historical and cultural tradition. Their search for a boa fide Muslim identity is still in its exploratory stage. To this point, however, the record of successive turns and turnabouts has proved one thing if nothing else: Whatever this Afro-American-Muslim identity turns out to be as a final product, if it is to be life-affirming as opposed to a paralyzing agent, it will have to embrace, however discriminately, rather than ignore the reality and history of African-Americans, just as effectively as it fortifies for them the boundaries between Islam and non-Islam.

Foreign-born Muslims, on the other hand, are the heirs of a much older tradition of Muslim identity formation. For them, a basic feature of self-definition is in fact the very preservation of the cultural tradition that has been handed down to them. To be sure, they too are engaged in a process of exploration, as they seek to determine which aspects of the received tradition are essential and which coincidental. But this is done with extreme caution and in the context of a conscious rejection of the proposition that their coming to America imposes upon them any obligation to assimilate. In fact, as one observer has recently noted, coming to America is now seen by many immigrants as the greatest ensurer of the right to remain themselves!

Thus, even as the notion of an "American-Islamic" identity gains acceptance among foreign-born Muslim (and especially their children), whatever this "American-Islamic" identity turns out to be, it will have to accommodate, and in part confirm, received tradition. It will not be accorded the authority to override or negate that tradition.

As these two groups of Muslims move closer, then, to their respective choices of Islamic identity in America, one wonders if they are not at the same time moving away from each other, seeing how vastly different the sources of their respective new identities are. Both groups are engaged, meanwhile, in a battle against what W.E.B. DuBois referred to as "double-consciousness," i.e., the seemingly inescapable tendency to look at oneself through the eyes of some other, to "measure one's soul by the tape of a world that looks on in amused contempt..." DuBois saw this phenomenon as contributing to the ineffectiveness (largely perceived as weakness) among blacks, because it foisted upon them a "contradiction of double aims". The black craftsman, for example, had to struggle, on the one hand, to escape white contempt for being a mere draftsman, while, on the other hand, striving to turn his skills to the needs of his people. This, DuBois observed, could only result in making him a poor craftsman, because "he had but half a heart in either cause". This double-consciousness and contradiction of double aims are an even greater threat to the Muslim, black, white or immigrant. For the simultaneous struggle against being a Muslim along with the struggle to be a Muslim necessarily reduces the amount of energy devoted to the latter. As such, the threat of double-consciousness has a direct bearing on the matter of salvation and how successfully Muslim can live a life that earn's God's pleasure in the Hereafter! Like George Orwell's, "How many fingers am I holding up Winston?," this kind of psychological pressure can turn even the clearest Qur'anic verses into matters of doubt and speculation and even the most basic religious obligations into matters of choice. What greater threat could there be to the Muslim and Islam in America?

We are brought, then, back to the issues of self-definition and self-determination in the most serious and meaningful sense. And given that both of these are always and necessarily socio-political activities, both foreign-born and American-born Muslims are equally confronted with the question of how they should seek to influence American social and political institutions to the end of gaining public recognition and respect for themselves as Muslims and contribute to the creation of a social reality that is free of double consciousness. Whether in concert with each other, or as distinct and separate movements, American-born and foreign-born Muslims will have to think about and develop approaches to this task.

MUSLIM IDENTITY BETWEEN CULTURE AND POLITICS

No serious discussion of the role to be played by Muslims in shaping or influencing social and political institutions in America can avoid the prior question of whether it is legitimate for Muslims to participate in the social and especially the political life of a non-Muslim polity.

At the same time, I would like to warn against the all-too-common fallacy or perhaps the ruse-of over politicizing matters to the point that legislative politics (i.e., voting, nominating candidates, holding political office) emerge as the only or even the main means of affecting social and political life in America. For, legislative politics are neither the only nor in every instance the most effective means of influencing society. As such, we should be careful about how uncritically we surrender to the loaded, zero-sum proposition: Either get involved in legislative politics or forfeit the opportunity for self-definition, not to mention self-determination.

What is needed is a balanced approach in which the potential benefits, functional limitations and possible religious impediments to Muslim participation in American social and political life all receive their due. For some time now, however, the main trust of Muslim attention has been in the direction of legislative politics. Some have stressed the practical benefits of Muslims involvement. Both sides, however, seem to be fixated upon the same object: legislative politics.

In the meantime, very little attention has been paid to the functional limitations of legislative politics, or to other possible means of effecting social and political change. This, I think, is a telling oversight that provides some useful insights into some of the inadequacies of Muslim though in the West, as well as some of the obsessions and biases that tend to limit the scope of its vision. Before entering, therefore, into the main issue of Islamic law and participation in American legislative politics, I should like to register a few points about the limitations of that enterprise, with the aim of excavating a few conceptual tools that might aid us in our thinking about the proper modality of political participation and its relationship to other means of effecting social and political change.

ON THE LIMITS OF LEGISLATIVE POLITICS

I begin with an insight borrowed from the Italian neo-Marxist, Antonio Gramsci (d.19-). Gramsci had witnessed the collapse of the American economic system during the Great Depression of 1929. He also observed that despite the economic ruin that came to many among the elite, there was virtually no change in the social cum political relations among America's haves and have-nots. Whereas one would have expected the haves' loss of wealth to reduce them-socially and politically-to the status of have-nots, in the end they lost virtually nothing of their status as premier citizens who both assumed and received the right to deferential treatment. On this observation, Gramsci developed his concept of "hegemony," via which he concluded that it was not control over the means of material production that determined relations of power and authority in society but control over the means of material production that determined relations of power and authority in society but control over the means of producing and disseminating intellectual products, namely, ideas and images. It was the educational, cultural and religious institutions along with the media and entertainment industry, that held the keys to how people saw themselves and interacted with each other in society. And where there existed no challenge to the views and images created by these institutions, politics and economics would do little to change the status quo.

Gramsci's theory goes a long way in establishing the fact that he attitudes and assumptions, the stereotypes and habits of deferential or contemptuous treatment, which form the basis of how people see themselves and interact with others in society are far more the product of how effectively ideas and images are manipulated through cultural and educational institutions then they are the product of pure politics or economics. One of the most glaring confirmations of this can be gleaned from developments in the United States during the 1960s, when black cultural figures like Muhammad Ali (I am the greatest!) and the singer James Brown (Say it loud; I'm black and I'm proud!) succeeded in altering the language and categories through which white supremacy had sustained its status as normal. By smashing the boundaries between the imaginable and unimaginable, between the valued and the valueless, their contributions to the American cultural landscape paved the way for blackness to take on meanings and to occupy psychological spaces therefore unknown to it. Legislative politics would in turn confirm this transformation in the 1970s with the unprecedented proliferation of black elected officials and other beneficiaries of such government initiatives as Title and Affirmative Action.

Even the more overtly political successes of figures like Martin Luther King Jr. were ultimately indebted to developments outside the realm of legislative politics. The touch-stone of King's genius lay in his success at developing what Hobbes referred to as a political "trump-card," i.e., a legally sanctioned activity outside of legislative politics via which concessions can be forced from a government. Trumps operate outside the realm of legislative politics precisely because governmental systems are not in the business of legislating themselves out of existence. As such as long as one works within the system, change is almost always slow, almost never radical, and usually perceived as necessary to the health and survival of the system.

"Dissidents," meanwhile, who wish to bring about more fundamental change must recognize and act in accordance with one basic rule: Where there is no recognized political trump-card, clubs become trumps, and the government assumes the right to put down dissent through violence. Martin Luther King Jr. located his trump card in the ability to subject the government to public shame and embarrassment. The daily images, televised and printed, of police-dogs, billy clubs and hoses turned against peaceful, unarmed blacks literally embarrassed the United State government into instituting change.

But the secret behind King's success actually runs much deeper than this. For, shame is not a sensibility into which the sponsors of unjust social and political orders are easily coerced. How was it, in other words that actions and attitudes that had for centuries been accepted as part of the "normal" operation of the regime of white supremacy suddenly came to constitute a public embarrassment? It is here, in this new attitude toward the meaning of blackness and, concommitantly, toward the unjust treatment of blacks that we come to appreciate the aforementioned role of such cultural figures as Mohammed Ali and James Brown. If the aim of any would-be Muslim participation in U.S. legislative politics is to promote a dignified existence for Muslims in America, to contribute to the fight against the plague of double-consciousness-not to indulge inflated egos or to feign inclusion in the American melting pot-the parallel necessity of effecting cultural change in America, i.e., of changing the language and categories of thought and common experience, of developing and effectively using a Muslim trump-card, must certainly be accorded at least equal importance.

For the effectiveness of the former depends fundamentally on success in the latter. And it is here, to my mind, in the cultural realm, that Muslims face the greater challenge. For it is here, more than any place else, that essentialism and the politics of identity among Muslims (American born and immigrants) tend to obliterate the distinction between the successful indigenization of Islam or the successful appropriation of aspects of American culture-as positive achievements, and assimilation into the ways of the slavemaster/colonizer, as a proscribed capitulation to Stephen Carter's "culture of unbelief". And as long as this remains the case, there will be no unleashing of the kind of God-given talent and cultural imagination that will enable Muslims to engage in the kind of cultural production that is not doomed to be marginalized and treated as a spectacle.

In a real sense, the future of Islam in America will depend not on whether Muslims can arrive at an understanding of scripture and tradition that allows for home-mortgages or inheritance between Muslims and non-Muslims, but on whether that understanding will liberate the Muslim cultural imagination and allow it come into its own, here in America For the fact is-and every honest Muslim knows it-that one can live with a lot of broken rules of *shari'ah*. But what repentance can there be from a broken soul or psyche? And how can the latter be avoided if the world outside the *masjid* reflect nothing of the Muslim's thoughts and creative spirit? If Muslims are to establish a real existence here in America, one that will enable them not only to consume but to shape American reality, the Muslim cultural imagination will have to be liberated. Once this is done, Muslims will be able to move beyond the relatively safe arena of sports (Hakeem Olajuwan, and until recently, Mahmud 'Abd al-Ra'uf, etc.) into those of literature, poetry music, fashion design, comedy, interior decorating, etc., just as has existed throughout Islamic history, and just as exists in virtually every Muslim country in the world!

All of this has serious implications, of course, for such questions as "Muslim identity," "Islamic culture," and the legitimacy of Muslim involvement in American society as a whole. This may explain why such issues as cultural production have received such scant and inadequate attention to date. It may be that the growing consensus among Muslims on the necessity of participating in legislative politics is in the end a cop-out, a safe haven into we have begun our retreat from the more difficult task of penetrating, appropriating and redirecting American culture. Muslims may enjoy the initial warm feeling that goes along with this; but it may not be long before this cools and we are forced to acknowledge that we wet our pants! For, even the most successful incursions into American law and politics will not change the reality of what it means to be a veiled woman (or girl!) in America. And who can deny that blacks in America did more to change their reality during the 1960s, when the doors to legislative politics were virtually closed to them, than they have in the subsequent era of black political empowerment?

MUSLIMS AND AMERICAN LEGISLATIVE POLITICS

The foregoing should be understood, however, only as an attempt to point out some of the limitations of legislative politics, to insist that there is a dialectical, give-and-take relationship between culture and self-determination, that power (or politics) contributes to but does not determine the shape of society. At the same time, there are laws and policies in this country that have a real or potentially devastating effect on Muslims, practically and religiously. One need only consider, e.g., the RICO act, or the new Anti-Terrorism bill, or banking regulations, or divorce and inheritance laws; or one could look at such policies as the Immigration and Naturalization Service's use of "secret evidence" against alien Muslims, or Child Protective Services' discriminatory intervention into Muslim family life. No amount of isolation will place Muslims beyond the reach of these laws and policies. And it is only through the medium of legislative politics that laws and policies are made and unmade. On practical grounds, then, there would seem to be no question about whether Muslims should get involved in legislative politics. The question, however, is whether such involvement can be legitimized on the basic of *shari'ah*.

ISLAM AND AMERICAN LEGISLATIVE POLITICS

The question of the legitimacy of Muslim involvement in American legislative politics raises two important prior question. The first is whether or nor Muslims are permitted to live in a non-Muslim land. For, if it is not permissible for Muslims to live in a non-Muslim polity, it is a fortiori, not permissible for them to participate in its political system. The second question arises out of the assumption of a positive answer to the first. If it is permissible for Muslims to reside in a non-Muslim polity, what are the conditions and circumstances that warrant such a permission? What, if any, are the Muslims' obligations towards effecting self-determination once they have decided to live in a non-Muslim land? These two questions enjoy a rich and lively pedigree among pre-modern-and even modern-jurists. Some of them have insisted that it is not permissible for Muslims to live in a non-Muslim land, that is not permissible for Muslims even to travel to non-Muslim lands, and that it is incumbent upon those who convert to Islam in a non-Muslim land to migrate to the lands of Islam.

Others have had taken a more lenient approach, concluding that, depending on circumstances, it may not only be permissible to migrate to a non-Muslim country, it may even be forbidden to leave it! Between these two poles there is a lot of detail, much of which underscores the role played by history and experience-above and beyond interpretations of scripture-in informing the conclusions of the various schools and individuals. One thing, however, seems to emerge clearly from all of this: No school and no jurist has ever held (to my knowledge) that is permissible for Muslims to reside in a non-Muslim land and remain completely passive, doing nothing to promote the safety and welfare of the Muslims and the dignity of Islam!

This amounts, in effect, to what some jurists have construed to be a type of consensus (*ijma*) to the effect that if Muslims do decide to take up residence in a non-Muslim land they must, as a community (*ala wajh al-kifayah*), do everything that would appear necessary to ensure the safety and welfare of the Muslims and, above all, the dignity of Islam. This may or may not include participation in legislative politics. But once the permissibility of Muslim residing in a non-Muslim territory is conceded, as a matter of *shari'a*-law, as is the obligation upon those Muslims to act in a manner appropriate to their circumstances, the question of the propriety of their involvement in legislative politics becomes a question of fact that is subject to the discretionary judgments of Muslim individuals and groups. It cannot be treated as a question of law that is subject to a permanently binding assessment of *wajib* (obligatory) or haram (forbidden). This is a crucial point that is often confused in the minds of many. And since an adequate assessment of the positions taken in traditional Islamic law depends on a fair understanding of this distinction, I shall take a moment here to digress for clarification.

THE LAW-FACT DICHOTOMY IN ISLAMIC JURISPRUDENCE

In a number of his jurisprudential works, the great *Maliki* jurist, Shihab al-Din al-Qarafi (d.684/1285) takes up the issue of the distinction between jurisdiction of law and jurisdiction of fact. Basically speaking, jurisdiction of law is the authority to interpret the meaning of scripture (including *hadith*). Jurisdiction of fact, on the other hand, is the authority to determine the existence of facts. Now, it is obvious that say, a medical doctor's authority to speak on the existence of certain diseases does not render him an authority when it comes to interpreting scripture. What is equally true, however-and this was al-Qarafi's point-is that a jurist's mastery of scripture does not render him an authority when it comes to the determination of facts. According to al-Qarafi:

There is a difference between Malik's statement, Engaging in homosexual relations necessitates stoning, and his statement, "So and so committed a homosexual act." We may follow him in the first statement but not in the second. Rather, this second statement falls into the category of testimony (*shahadah*). If three other upright witnesses testify along with Malik, the ruling is established; if not, it is not. And in this regard, the testimony of any other upright witness would be absolutely equal to that of Malik. His status as a *mujtahid* would be of absolutely no consequences in this regard. Nor would the status of any of the other *mujtahids*.

When it comes, in other words, to questions of fact, i.e., Did X occur? or Does X exist?, the views of a jurist are not authoritative and should not be treated as such. Al-Qarafi indicates that many errors had been committed as a result of overlooking this distinction. As an example, he holds up the position upheld in the *Maliki* school on the status of public lands and utilities in Egypt following the coming of the Muslims.

According to Malik, agricultural lands and public works of territories conquered by force are public trusts (*waqf*) for the general benefit of the community. As such, they are exempt from private ownership. It was also Malik's view that Egypt had been conquered by force. Based on these two views, *Maliki* jurists in al-Qarafi's day upheld the ban on privately owning public utilities in Egypt. Now, according to al-Qarafi, it was proper (though not obligatory) to accept Malik's opinion regarding the status of lands conquered by force. For this was a legal interpretation, based on Malik's reading of scripture. But it was wholly improper for *Maliki* jurists to accept as authoritative Malik's opinion to the effect that Egypt (or any other territory) had been conquered by force. For, this was a question of fact of which a followers of Malik (or any historian) might have greater knowledge than Malik. The position of al-Qarafi's contemporary *Maliki* jurists on this question was thus neither correct nor permissible to follow.

If a jurist, then, states that such and such is permissible or impermissible because of the existence of this or that fact, it remains the right-indeed the responsibility-of individuals to ascertain for themselves (or through other qualified determiners of specific facts), whether or not the jurist's pronouncement of permissibility or impermissibility applies to the matter at hand. This may or may not lead to consensus within a community. But the fact remains that when it comes to observable facts, every individual Muslim is his or her own authority.

THE DISCUSSION AMONG THE SCHOOL OF LAW

We may turn now to the legal discussion among the *Sunni* schools of law on the permissibility of Muslims residing in non-Muslim lands. Of the four schools of law, the *Maliki* school is by far the strictest and least compromising on this question. We might begin, therefore, with the *Maliki* school, since any concessions or insights gained from them may be justifiably assumed to apply to the others.

The *Maliki* tradition on Muslim residence in non-Muslim territory goes all the way back to Malik himself (d.179/769). In the *Mudawwanah,* Suhnun (d.240/854) asks the long-time disciple of Malik, Ibn al-Qasim (d.190/805) if Malik disapproved of merchants travelling to non-Muslim territory for the purpose of conducting business. Ibn al-Qasim responds, "Yes, he strongly disapproved of this. And he used to say, "They should not go to their lands where they will become subject to the laws of polytheism (*ahkam al-shirk*)". Subsequent *Maliki* scholars confirm this position, and the basic prohibition on Muslims residing in non-Muslim territory is sustained in the *Maliki* school for over a millennium, right down into modern times. The great Spanish authority, Ibn Rushd (the grandfather) (d.520/1122) for example, insisted that not only was it forbidden for Muslims to travel to non-Muslim territories, but that anyone who converted to Islam in a non-Muslim land had to leave and migrate to a Muslim polity. Such a danger did Ibn Rushd consider Muslim residence in non-Muslim lands that he proposed that check-points be built on land and sea to prevent Muslims from leaving the lands of Islam for non-Muslim territories. These sentiments are repeated several centuries later in the *fatwas* of the great North African jurist, Ahmed b. Yahya al-Wansharishi (d.914/ 1508). Writing after the fall of Granada in 1492 C.E., al-Wansharishi rejects, time and again, what would seem to be even the most plausible excuses and insists categorically that the Muslims must leave Spain for Muslim-controlled territory. At one point, for example, al-Wansharisi is asked about a Muslim-controlled territory. At one point, for example, al-Wansharisi is asked about a Muslim who stayed behind in Spain and acted as an intermediary between the Christian authorities and the Muslim community, often gaining for the latter concessions that they would otherwise not have enjoyed. Al-Wansharishi rejects this as a justification and insists that this man, and all other Muslim residents of Spain, must migrate, regardless of whatever material losses they might suffer.

The great Nigerian *Maliki* jurist and reformer, *Shaykh*u Uthman b. Fudi (d. 1233 /1817) eloquently laid out his position on the matter in a well-known book entitled *Kitab bayan wujub al-hijrah ala al-ibad wa bayan wujub nasb al-imam wa iqamat al-jihad,* i.e., Clarifying the Obligation Upon the Muslims to Migrate (from the lands of unbelief) and to Install an Imam and to Prosecute the *Jihad*. Here *shaykh*u, citing several other *Maliki* authorities to authenticate his stance, insists emphatically that it is absolutely forbidden for Muslims to reside in non-Muslim territory. He states, in fact, that this is a point of consensus (*ijma*) on which no two scholars disagree. All the way down through *shaykh* Muhammad Ulaysh, who died in 1299/1882-, this uncompromising *Maliki* position is repeated with astonishing fidelity.

Again, the basic reason underlying this position was the fact that residing in non-Muslim territory would subject Muslims to the laws of the polytheist unbelievers (*ahkam al-shirk, ahkam al-mushrikin*). It is important, however, to understand exactly what this implied for these jurists. Falling under "the laws of the polytheist unbelievers" was not simply a matter of Muslims being subject to engaging in activities forbidden by Islam, e.g., certain criminal laws or certain commercial transactions, while at the same time enjoying the right to maintain their faith and their basic religious institutions. Rather, "the laws of the polytheist unbelievers" was a much broader construct that assumed, first and foremost, the precariousness if not impossibility of remaining Muslims.

This is clearly born out by the position of none other than the above-cited Ibn Rushd, who argues, for example, that it is permissible for Muslims to deal in *riba* with non-Muslims in a non-Muslim territory. Such an activity, in other words, though normally forbidden, would not constitute a violation of Islamic law for Muslims in a non-Muslim land. Thus, this could clearly not have been the object of Ibn Rushd's fear. Similarly, in the staunch *shaykh*u Uthman b. Fudi, there is a clear sense that syncretism, or the mixing between Islamic and pagan beliefs and customs, was feared to be the inevitable result of African Muslims residing in non-Muslim African lands.

This was apparently based on what *shaykh*u understood to be a cultural-political reality, namely, that where African Muslims lived under non-Muslim African rulers they generally followed the latters cultural-religious ways and customs. For this reason, even lands where the overwhelming majority was Muslim, were not considered by *shaykh*u Uthman to be Muslim lands, if the rulers were not Muslims.

Nor were lands, however, where the rulers were Muslims if the majority of the population was not. For in this case, it was feared that the Muslims would be overwhelmed by popular pagan culture. Thus, for *shaykh*u Uthman, only in lands where both the overwhelming majority and the rulers were Muslims was it permissible for Muslims to reside.

Turning to al-Wansharisi, here again there are clear signs that his thinking was informed not simply by fear of the imposition of un-Islamic laws on Muslims but by fear of the humiliation and possible forced apostacy that the Muslims might suffer at the hands of Christians. In one of his *fatwas*, for example, in which he insisted that all Muslims must leave Spain following the Christian take-over, al-Wansharishi lays down the following list of reasons:

1) that the word of Islam and the testimony of truth (*kalimat al-islam wa shahadat al-haqq*) would not be honored and respected but humiliated and debased;
2) that the prayer (*salah*) would not be openly displayed but would be subject to humiliation, being scoffed at and made fun of, which could lead to its abandonment;
3) that the *zakah* would be nullified, since there would be no Imam to collect it;
4) that the fast of *Ramadhan* would be subject to nullification, since there would be no Imam to oversee and validate its beginning and end;
5) that the *hajj* would be rendered defunct, since it would fall outside the capability of the Muslims (*li adam istita atihim*);

6) that the Muslims would suffer contempt and humiliation, while the Prophet (*alayhi's-salam*) has said, "The Muslim should not subject himself to humiliation";
7) that the Muslims would suffer ridicule of a type and magnitude that no self-respecting person would needlessly tolerate;
8) that the honor and integrity of the Muslims, and may be their person and property, would be jeopardized;
9) that the Muslims would be constantly exposed to all manners of vice, impurities (*najasat*) and religiously questionable foods.

Clearly, for scholars like Ibn Rushd, *shaykh*u Uthman, and al-Wansharisi, a world in which Muslims could live under non-Muslim rule and not be subject to official (and non-official) pressure to renounce their faith, or where the cultural affinities between the Muslims and non-Muslims did not threaten to blur the boundary between Islam and non-Islam was part of the unimaginable. Their thinking, however, was perfectly consistent with the reality of their time and place. Thus, rather than being criticized or scoffed at for being "rigid," or "reactionary," or "conservative," these scholars should be commended for being the realists that they were. Having said this much, however, rather than uncritically accepting and applying their views to present circumstances, these views should be examined in light of the above-cited distinction between law and fact.

The views of these scholars was clearly informed, if not dictated, by what they understood to be the customs and habits obtaining in non-Muslim lands in their time. This, however, is clearly a question of fact, and the only question that remains is whether contemporary Muslims should themselves to the views of these men, even if they differ with the latter in their assessment of these facts. The answer to this question is provided, once again, by the *Maliki* jurist, Shihab al-Din al-Qarafi. At one point, al-Qarafi is asked:

What is the correct view concerning those rulings found in the *madhhab* of al-Shafi, Malik and the rest, which have been deduced on the basis of habits and customs prevailing at the time these scholars reached these conclusions? When these customs change and the practice comes to indicate the opposite of what it used to, are the *fatwas* recorded in the manuals of the jurisconsults rendered thereby defunct, it becoming incumbent to issue *fatwas* based on the new custom? Or is it to be said, We are *muqallids* (lay followers). It is thus not our place to issue new rulings, as we lack the qualifications to perform *ijtihad* (independent interpretation). We issue, therefore, *fatwas* according to what we find in the books handed down on the authority of the *mujtahids*?

Al-Qarafi's response is both clear and pointed.

Holding to rulings that have been deduced on the basis of custom, even after this custom has changed, is a violation of consensus (*ijma*) and an open display of ignorance of the religion.

To acknowledge, then, that America, or any other country for that matter, is a place where Muslims enjoy constitutionally guaranteed rights to freedom of religion, protection of life and property and the opportunity to contribute to the shape of American society does not at all involve a challenge to the integrity of these *Maliki* jurists as jurists. At the same time, once the right of contemporary Muslims to assess their own reality is acknowledged, the application of these pre-modern *Maliki* views to the question of Muslims residing in modern America can be seen to be a misappropriation of an otherwise valid tradition.

Turning to the views of the remaining schools, we find a different situation. While *Maliki*-dominated territories had suffered great losses at the hands of pagans and Christians, two of the greatest Muslim communities in history, Spain and Sicily, being irretrievably lost to Christian conquerors, this differed from the situation in the East, where the *Shafi* and especially the *Hanafi* schools dominated. It is true that the Eastern lands of Islam also suffered losses at the hands of both the Mongols and the Crusaders. But in both cases, these lands were subsequently returned to Islam, through voluntary conversion in the case of the Mongols, through military re-conquest in the case of the Crusaders. During the interim, however, between the time these Eastern lands were lost to these non-Muslim conquerors and the time they were returned to Muslim control, Muslims lived, as a simple matter of fact, under non-Muslim rule, including a three-year during which there was no caliph! This did not lead, however, to any sustained syncretism or to any mass exit from Islam, and it seems that this informed the perspective of the *Shafi*, *Hanfi* and *Hanbal* jurists, just as the historical reality in the West (*al-maghrib*) informed that of the *Malikis*.

Generally speaking, for the *Shafi*'s, *Hanafi*'s and *Hanbali*'s, the operative issue is whether Muslims living in a non-Muslim polity are safe and enjoy enough freedom to practice the rudiments of their religion. Such Muslims should seek to conduct their affairs in such a way that they do not contribute to the military strength of their host-country, such that other Muslims would suffer at the latters' hands. But, unlike the *Malikis*, these three schools do not begin with the premise that it is not permissible under any circumstances for Muslims to reside in non-Muslim territory and that it is incumbent upon those who convert to Islam while in a non-Muslim country to migrate to a Muslim land. *Hanafi* jurists, for example, appear to be generally unopposed to Muslims residing in non-Muslim lands, assuming that Muslims are able to establish congregational prayers there, especially *Jumu'ah* and *Id*, fast *Ramadhan*, and they can work to procure the appointment of Muslim governors to oversee their affairs.

The *Hanabali*'s by and large hold a position similar to that of the *Hanafis*. *Shafi*'i jurists, meanwhile, take matters a step further, as is demonstrated in the position of the great Shams al-Din al-Ramli (d.1004/1596), also known as "Little al-*Shafi*'i. At one point, al-Ramli is asked about a community of Muslims residing under a Christian king who exacted taxes from them but allowed them to practice their religion, i.e., to build mosques, hold Friday prayer, fast *Ramadhan*, and generally apply the laws of Islam. Al-Ramli's questioner indicates that although this was the situation at present, there were no guarantees that this would last and that the Muslims would not subsequently come under the jurisdiction of Christian laws or pressure to apostacize. Al-Ramli's answer is that not only is it not incumbent upon these Muslims to migrate but in fact it is forbidden for them to do so, because in leaving this territory it was less likely to be guided to Islam.

In sum, the majority (i.e., three of the four schools) hold it to be permissible for Muslims to live in non-Muslim territories. This license was conditioned, however, albeit implicitly, by the assumption that these Muslims would be in a position to promote and protect their interests and that they would in fact do just that. Even among the *Maliki*'s there are signs that where this was understood to be the case, the general prohibition might be relaxed. The real issue, then, was the concrete situation of the Muslims on the ground, a situation for which the Muslims-not the non-Muslim-must assume responsibility. On this understanding, it would seem to me that there are only two tenable positions on the matter of Muslims residing in America: Either the Muslims are obligated to migrate; or they must actively pursue the welfare and dignity of Islam and the Muslim. Inaction-even inaction that hides behind rhetoric or dogmatic and uncritical appropriations of tradition-is not a justifiable choice.

MUSLIMS AND THE U.S. CONSTITUTION

The issue of the active pursuit of Muslim interests brings us finally to the question of Muslims and the U.S. Constitution, since, obviously, the constitution provides the legal framework within which any such activity will have to operate. This is a huge topic which no single essay could hope to do full justice. In the space remaining, however, I would like to direct a few remarks towards two aspects of the relationship between Muslims and the constitution. The first of these is the Muslim attitude toward accepting the provisions and advantages afforded by the Constitution. The second concerns the challenge that operating within this constitutional framework poses for Muslims.

The First Amendment of the U.S. Constitution guarantees the freedom of religion. Muslims, however, are often hesitant, if not hostile, toward accepting or acknowledging the validity of this provision. This is because such acceptance and acknowledgment raises in the minds of many Muslims the question of sovereignty and authority, what Sayyid Qutb often referred to as *al-hakimiyah*. If part of the meaning of the *shahadah* is that God and God alone has the authority to confer rights and impose obligations, then certainly a man-made constitution that does not derive its authority from God must be illegitimate, as a violation of God's rightful monopoly on authority. By the same token, any Muslim who recognizes the validity of such a constitution is guilty of attributing legal authority and sovereignty to someone other than God. To be sure, there is a certain forcefulness to this logic that renders it difficult at times to resist, at least at face-value. Closer examination, however, suggests that while this might apply to Muslims who arrogate to themselves the right to rule independent of god, this is by no means the only or even most plausible construction to be put on the relationship between Muslims and the U.S. Constitution.

To begin with, the U.S. constitution was the result of an agreement among a group of non-Muslims about how to distribute political rights and power within a non-Muslim polity. Not being Muslims, it was only natural that this agreement not be based on Islamic law. To recognize this fact, and concomitantly the validity of such an agreement, is not necessarily a recognition of the right to ignore or flaunt God's law. Rather, it is more akin to the jurists' recognition of the validity of a formerly Christian or Jewish couple's Christian or Jewish marriage even after the couple has embraced Islam.

Obviously, this marriage did not take place in accordance with Islamic law; in fact, it may have explicitly violated specific rules of *shari'ah* e.g., by not having witnesses present or including a bride-price consisting of some Islamically banned commodity, such as wine or pork. Still, the marriage of this couple is recognized by Muslim jurists as a valid marriage, both in the event that the couple remains Jews or Christian, and if they convert to Islam. Or, take the issue of buying from and selling to non-Muslims. Obviously, this entails a recognition of the property rights of these non-Muslims, since both of these transactions assumes a legal transfer of property. This obtains despite the fact that this right could not have acc to these non-Muslims on the basis of their recognition of any divine authority. And if they do not recognize God's authority, how is it that such rights accrue to them? Yet, when, shortly following the fall of Mecca, the Prophet (*alayhi's-salam*) asked Safwan b. Umayyah if he could borrow some tools and weapons and Safwan asked whether the Prophet was in fact borrowing these things or simply taking them, the Prophet (*alayhi's-salam*) responded that he was borrowing them. In other words, the Prophet acknowledged Safwan's right over his belongings. Of course, it could be argued that what is really going on here is that this right is effectively being established by God's command to the Prophet not to confiscate the Meccans' property. But if this is so, then recognition of these non-Muslims' right can in no way be seen to constitute an affront to God's monopoly as Right-Giver.

The Qur'an and *Sunnah* are full of exhortions to the Muslims to honor treaties and agreements brokered by non-Muslims. Again, however, this implies a tacit acknowledgment of the legitimacy of non-Muslims as bargaining parties. In other words, were it not legitimate for non-Muslims to broker agreements (since such agreements are neither derived from divine authority nor likely to be based on the law of Islam) it would not be legitimate, a fortiori, for Muslims to honor these very agreements. Yet, we find that even agreements to which the non-Muslims attached stipulations that appeared to curtail or infringe upon certain rights of the Muslims, as occurred, for example, in the Treaty of Hudaybiyah, where Quraysh stipulated that Muslims who leave Mecca to join the Prophet (*alayhi*'s-*salam*) at Medina must be sent back to Mecca, were honored and recognized by the Prophet as legally binding. Clearly, however, none of this in any way implied any acceptance-as a matter of conscience-of the right of non-Muslims to challenge or violate God's rightful monopoly as Law-Giver.

All of this is reminiscent of a very rich discussion in classical Islamic jurisprudence over the question of whether non-Muslims are responsible for the concrete rules (*furu*)-as opposed to the basic principles (*usul*), such as *tawhid*, the prophethood of Muhammad, belief in the Hereafter, etc.-of Islam. The well-known position of the *Hanfi* school was that they were not. This was also the view of the *Shafi*'i, Fakhr al-Din al-Razi and, with some important qualifications, the *Maliki*, Shihab al-din al-Qarafi.

On this view, contracts, property rights, etc. that non-Muslims enjoyed over each other (or with Muslims in a non-Muslim territory) were accorded full legal validity, even if they had not been carried out in accordance with the stipulations of Islamic law. Yet, none of this implied the belief on the part of these jurists that these instruments were religiously valid, and that by recognizing their legal validity, they were somehow attributing to someone other than God the right to confer legal rights in any ultimate sense.

It would seem, then, to be problematic, at the very least, to insist that Muslim recognition of the validity of the U.S. Constitution implies a violation on their part of God's rightful monopoly as Law Giver. How can a decision among non-Muslims to confer certain advantages upon Muslims be said to amount to an act of shirk?

The U.S. Constitution defines the parameters of a non-Muslim state, not a Muslim state. How can Muslims be shouldered with the responsibility for these parameters? If in the future America becomes a predominantly Muslim country (politically or numerically) then Muslims will be responsible for ensuring that its legal and political order are consistent with the dictates of Islam. In the meantime, this becomes a questionable demand at best. The kind of confusion that has been generated over this issue is, I think, another example of what happens when Muslims in the West blindly import views and ideologies from the modern Muslim world.

A more profitable approach for Muslims would be to look at the opportunities the Constitution affords them to promote their interests as Muslims and to take full advantage of those opportunities. According to the Constitution, the U.S. government cannot force a Muslim to renounce his or her faith; it cannot deny him or her the right to pray, or fast, or perform the pilgrimage; it cannot force him or her to eat pork, shave his beard or remove her hijab; it cannot deny Muslims the right to build mosques or to hold public office; it cannot deny them the right to criticize government officials and policies, including the person and the policies of the president.

The U.S. government cannot even force a Muslim to pledge allegiance to the United State! Surely it must be worth the Muslims' time and energy to ask if these (and many other) rights and opportunities should be squandered in the name of dogmatic minutae and uncritical readings of Islamic law and history, rather than turned to the benefit and welfare of Islam and the Muslims.

MUSLIMS, ISLAMIC LAW AND THE SEPARATION OF CHURCH AND STATE

The U.S. Constitution does, however, pose at least one challenge to Muslims, namely, in its insistence on the separation between religion and state. Many Muslims understand this to mean that Islamic law (or Jewish or Christian law for that matter) is, as a permanent constitutional provision, disqualified form becoming the basis of law and or public policy. Could therefore never become the law of the land. This, in their view, renders the Constitution unacceptable from their perspective as Muslims.

My understanding, however, of the so-called separation between church and state is somewhat different. On my understanding, the real challenge resides not so much in the Constitutional ban on admitting religious values and rules into the public domain but in the inability or unwillingness on the part of Muslims to articulate Islamic law in terms that show its benefit and utility to American society. The doctrine of separation between church and state in American Constitutional discourse does not means that religion can play no role in public policy, or even that religious rules cannot be applied as law. What it means is that religious rules cannot be applied simply because someone's religion says they should. Law, in other words, is conceived of as a being both secular (i.e., this-worldly) and a public trust. A such, only those laws that prove serviceable to the public here and now can qualify as law. In other words, the doctrine of separation between church and state might be likened in many ways, to use the language of Muslim jurists, to a ban on treating *mu'amalat* (matters of public utility and civil transactions) as if they were *ibadat* (matters of religious observances).

In Islamic law, there is a basic distinction between *mu'amalat* and *ibadat*. *Ibadat* are generally identified as those rules through whose application the primary benefit (*maslahah*) accrues to humans in the Hereafter, not in this world. These would include such things as prayer, fasting, pilgrimage, and the like. Mu'amalat, on the other hand, consist of those rules through whose application humans enjoy some benefit in the here-and-now, in addition to the reward they receive in the Hereafter for complying with God's command. These would include such rules as those governing sales, contracts, theft, drinking, divorce, etc. It is precisely because the worldly benefits contained in these rules are apprehensible by human reason that the Law can be extended to cover cases not explicitly addressed by scripture. This is done through the use of analogy, or *qiyas,* a basic application of *qiyas* would run something like the following. Drinking wine is forbidden; the reason (known in Arabic as the *illah*) for this is that drinking wine corrupts one's faculties for reasoning; by extending the prohibition on drinking wine to any substance that contains the *illah* of corrupting one's mind, a substance like crack-cocaine can be adjudged forbidden, even though it was not around at the time of revelation. Obviously, the key to all of this is the ability to analyze the rules of *shari'ah* in order to be able to penetrate the reason or *illah* underlying them. For without this *illah,* there can be no analogy, and numerous social and other problems would go unaddressed.

Now, all of the four *Sunni* schools of Islamic law recognize analogy as a valid mechanism for deducing the law. In addition, they all recognize that virtually all of the rules of *mu'amalat* contain *illah*s or reasons that can be known to man. Moreover, there is a general recognition of the idea that all of the *mu'amalat* are legislated for the purpose of promoting the worldly welfare and happiness (*masalih*) of man. It is because of this that Muslim jurists are able to debate the application, modification, suspension, etc. of rules of *mu'amalat* depending on whether or not the purpose, or *illah,* for which they were legislated is likely to be served. It was on this basis, for example, that Ibn Taymiyah once reportedly stopped one of his disciples from interrupting a group of Mongol Muslims who were drinking wine. Ibn Taymiyah's explanation was that the ban on wines was issued because intoxication turns people away from prayer and from the remembrance of God. But when these Mongols drink, it turns them away from looting, rape and murder.

It is precisely through this ability to penetrate and articulate the rules of Islamic law in ways that clearly define their benefit and utility to society at large that Muslims are likely to be able to influence the legal order in America. And it should be understood that once this is done, there are no Constitutional impediments to having these laws applied in the public domain.

Muslims must be vocal and confident in articulating the public utility underlying the rules on things like *riba*, adultery, theft, drinking, contracts, pre-marital sex, child-custody and even polygyny. This should all be done, however, in the context of an open acceptance of American custom (*urf*) as a legally valid source in areas where the shari'ah admits the reliance upon custom. Muslim Americans to take them. And they should be willing to recognize areas of common interest and concern.

This much said, it would be foolish to deny that the prospects for American acceptance of such institutions as stoning, or flogging or amputation are virtually nil, at least for the foreseeable future. Here, however, two things, I think, should be born in mind.

The first is that the specific punishments for criminal offenses in Islamic law are precisely the *ibadah* aspects of these rules. In other words, while many other forms of punishment (e.g., jailing, fines, public announcement) could have served the purpose of deterring from these acts, God chose these specific punishments. Since, however, there is no necessary or exclusive relationship between these punishments and deterrence, these punishment are assigned a status akin to that of ritual acts of worship. This "ritualistic" aspect is captured in the jurists' common reference to these punishments as "right of God (*huquq Allah*)".

Meanwhile, the primary *maslahah*, or worldly aim, behind these rules remains the avoidance of the harm and evil contained in the forbidden acts. Now, where there is a conflict between these two aspects of these rules, jurists differed over whether or not the rights of man (e.g., protection of property) should take precedence over the rights of God (e.g., amputation of the hand). Many, if not most, gave precedence to the rights of man.

Al-Wansharisi, for example, stated openly that if a Muslim has a choice between living in a land where there is injustice while the rights of God are observed, the Muslim should choose the land where there is injustice while the rights of God are observed, the Muslim should choose the land where there is justice. In other words, if it is not possible to ensure the rights of God, this should lead Muslims to give up on trying to ensure the Islamically sanctioned rights of man.

The second thing to keep in mind is that notions of what is cruel and unusual, of what is barbaric, of what is barbaric, of what is draconian (which is the real basis upon which America rejects these punishments) are a function of culture, not law. It is only through changes in American culture that American attitudes towards such things are likely to change. Thus, in the end, as in the beginning, we are brought face to face with the inextricable connection between American culture and Muslim self-determination. May God grant us the courage and the vision to rise to the task before us.

IDENTITY AND PARTICIPATION

The dilemmas that confront American Muslim citizens regarding political participation — identity, the if an how of participation, and the ability to influence American political and social life successfully, are not new dilemmas for religious or ethnic communities. Struggles over the meanings of secularism, libertarianism and the implications for morality, values and public conduct are also old American history. Various religious communities' approaches to political participation give us a few facets to explore. For example, the Amish and to a certain degree the Mennonites and Quakers seek to opt out of the political arena. this enables them to keep their distinctive religious and ethnic identities and perhaps even more sharply defines those identities. Unfortunately, the choice of non-participation subjects these communities to the vagaries resulting from the political and social choices of the larger community.

At the other end of the continuum sit the Christian Right and the Jewish communities. Though their impetuses for participation in the political arena arise from different spaces, both communities use their religious understandings as guidance in the arena. For the Christian Right, the United States is a Christian nation with an unparalleled Constitution that while permitting and protecting religious liberty and the rights of the individual have lost its way. Members of the various communities under the umbrella of the Christian Right assert that it is our efforts to uphold liberty and freedom that propel society toward a secularism that values only the material world and is without a moral consciousness. Members of this community seek to ignore the racial, ethnic and religious divides of the nation and assert a political platform that stands on Christian moral principles. The decade of the 90's has been a decade of success for this community. They have brought their platform to the attention of the nation and made their issues — the issues to which Americans must respond.

The Jewish community, seeks to protect itself from a seemingly endless legacy of ethnic/religious persecution. This community marshals it energies and considerable wealth to protect Jewish interests at home and abroad. Toward these ends, the Jewish community has elected officials at all levels of government, established an overwhelmingly successful series of political lobbies and large, vigilant watchdog organizations.

Unlike other minority communities such Amish, Mennonite, Mormon or Quaker communities, American Muslim citizens are not homogenous regarding race or national origins. Unlike Jews, Muslims do not have a legacy of ethnic/religious persecution that could force some cohesion of needs and unity of action at the political level. Certainly unlike the Christian Right, Muslims are not representatives of any aspect of majority religion. Media malattention to Islam and Muslims, American governmental inaction in the face of genocide against Muslims overseas, and increasing antipathy for Islam and Muslims at home as a result dictate the need for political participation.

Inside of each American Muslim community — African American and immigrant, there is a divergence of opinion on political participation whether the concern is domestic or foreign. The best recent example began with the Gulf War and the dilemma is best described in an article by Robert Dannin, "Understanding the Multi-Ethnic Dilemma of African-American Muslims." in 1990, the Muslim World League and the World Supreme Council of Masajid sought to "create worldwide consensus in favor of the Saudi-American military coalition against Iraq." In the U.S., these organizations offered material assistance to a convention of both African American and immigrant imams. In the African American Muslim community, the only obvious supporters of the offensive were the communities under Imam Warithudeen Muhammad. Most other Sunni Muslims, representing the majority, as well as the Nation of Islam, was opposed. both groups used their news organs to publicize their opinions and tried to influence the general public stance. While many immigrant organizations were also publicly opposed to the war, there was little cooperation with African American communities.

The African American Muslim community is visibly and substantially divided "over issues of national allegiance, ethnic identity, and religious orthodoxy." The immigrant American Muslim community is more obliquely though just as substantially divided over ethnic identity, national origins and multiple allegiances. For both communities however, there must be a reconciling or at least an appropriate interpretation of Islamic legal sources in order to understand the limits or extent of their political participation. But this is not the end of the complexity.

Many African American Muslims are not familiar with the various discourses on political participation in non-Muslim lands in the four accepted schools of legal thought. In this matter Professor Jackson's article is both timely and critical. He presents the divergences and convergences of the scholars regarding the political possibilities for Muslims living as minorities in non-Muslim lands. That there is more than one opinion is news for many. Whether this information will be used by leaders of communities or if it will be used at all is something only time will reveal. Nonetheless, the claims against political participation using assertions that this what Islamic law demands are considerably weakened. Interestingly, the only legal school that is against any manner of political participation is also against Muslims living under non-Muslim rule and demands that they move to Muslim lands.

Equally, many immigrant Muslims are unfamiliar with the range of legal opinions on political participation. More interesting though is the fact that many of the immigrant Muslims who oppose political participation come from countries where the legal school sanctions their immigration. Professor Mazrui addresses aspects of this issue. For some immigrants, American citizenship has not compromised allegiance to country of origin and if there is to be any political participation it should be focused on foreign policy. Unable to influence the politics of the Muslim homeland from within, has led many immigrants to form help organizations here in the U.S. The relative freedoms in the U.S. have provided the space for distant action.

African American Muslims though active in the various causes focused on Muslims in the Muslim world have not been able until recent incidents of domestic discrimination to interest immigrants in domestic issues — poverty in the inner cities, social reform, school reform, etc. Older Muslim organizations such as The Islamic Society of North America and The American Muslim Council have only very recently been forced to turn their attention to recording and challenging situations of prejudice in the workplace and the public space. The Council on American-Islamic Relations is the first organization specifically founded as a watchdog group to monitor the media and assist Muslims in asserting their rights as citizens to live and work without harassment.

I think that one question both articles lead the reader to is — what exactly do we mean by political participation. Obviously all American citizens pay taxes, which support public schools, support military excursions, and support a particular worldview that embraces all of the wonders and limitations of a largely Protestant Christian secular society. All immigrants must pledge allegiance to the flag of the United States to become citizens. This uncontested support is political. All citizens participate whether they do so enthusiastically or not in obeying the laws of the land. Is this what we mean by "political participation?" Both of these scholars assert that the major issues in the American Muslim community are those which reflect on the dilemmas of identity.

The Muslim community is just beginning the deliberations that many religious communities have had in previous decades. It is beginning discussions with issues of identity. Whether the religious affiliation or the national identity is the primary identity is of course the first question. For African Americans, the American experience, political or social is one filled with deceptions, hatreds and challenges. For immigrant Muslim Americans, the American experience has largely been a dream fulfilled but with moral compromise. Members of both groups have the same set of Islamic values and understandings of moral conduct in the public space. Both have the understanding that politics in America is not an issue of morals and values rather it is a system that responds to money and clout. Muslims observe the political clout of other minority communities such as the Jews and tend to hold this community as the model but without the needed knowledge and reflection on the social conditions that permit this situation.

Professor Mazrui contends that the Muslim community is a "Tale of Two Islams." The immigrant community has material resources but no experience while the African American community has a wealth of experience but little in the way of material resources. The former group is "Islamized but not fully Americanized" while the latter community is a "fully Americanized but not always fully Islamized." I would say that neither community is fully anything. Colonialism and slavery compromise the Islam brought by the immigrant community and persistent discriminations dilute the Americanism represented by African Americans. Both groups, like other diasporic communities do have to live in a kind of limbo with multiple allegiances and identities. But before the community can coalesce into a block of significant votes or a significant voice there is another set of concerns with which it will have to engage.

Muslims put God, community, family and other interpersonal relationships at the top of the list. A web of obligations in Islam supports this worldview. Muslims have to look further than single issues, be more demanding of those in politics for explanations of positions, and most importantly decide for themselves what is important. Following the agenda of others is not the way politics is done in the United States. Political power emerges from collective action. For Muslims this means coming together about what matters to Muslims. There are religious offices in Washington and Muslims, in order to do more than survive, must begin to vigilantly monitor the government's policy-making process just as the Protestant churches, Jews and Catholics for them.

Some Muslims will continue to debate the legitimacy of political participation forever. For those who see the necessity of this participation, a better way to expend energy is in strategies for effective advocacy. While the end product of effective advocacy may depend on favorable circumstances, leadership and increase outside antipathy toward the community, the movement toward thinking about strategies is a must. American history is one of grassroots movements than mobilize the masses. There are enough social issues to coalesce a movement around. Muslims should see themselves as capable of providing a clear voice in the face of chaos. Other religious communities have used a variety of techniques such as television and radio ministries to generate millions of letters. Muslims must build and create viable relationships with social organizations and become visible members of the larger social community. Muslims must envision themselves as having the potential to shape public opinion on issues.

The community must generate skilled national leaders who can gain and keep access to the government. Good leaders have strategic minds. They can develop attainable goals that are clearly articulated. They need to understand the nature of coalitions and the art of compromise. Islam obligates Muslims in civic responsibility and this very fact should be the starting point.

5

ISLAM AND ITS CHALLENGES IN THE MODERN WORLD

Islam today is facing challenges from within and from the wider world. The critical problems are the fundamental tensions within Islam. The attitudes and criticisms common in the outside world can be ignored as misguided or hostile, but the tensions within Islam throughout the world must be confronted. In a simple geographical sense, Islam has to come to grips with its changing centres. The religious centres define the heartland: Saudi Arabia maintains its guardianship of the shrines at Mecca and Medina, and the conduct of the hajj, against the claims of Shii Iran, the Shii tradition, and other sects disillusioned with Saudi Arabia's credentials within the ummah. Saudi Arabia enjoys much of its strength to repudiate other claims because it remains the economic centre of the ummah. It takes a combination of the incomes of Kuwait, Iraq, the United Arab Emirates, Iran and Yemen even to come close to Saudi Arabia's oil wealth.

However, this wealth is based on finite resources, and in the years to come the economic centre will shift to those parts of the Muslim world with sustainable resources and reproductive assets. West Asian financial investments recognise this long-term problem, but they remain overwhelmingly located in the Western and non-Muslim economies. The intellectual centre of Islam is Al-Azhar in Cairo. The ideas and attitudes taught here are spread throughout the ummah, particularly through the population centres of Islam: Indonesia, Pakistan, Bangladesh, India and Malaysia. The relative power of the different centres is shifting. Over time the claims on and against the heartland from and by the peripheral Muslim communities will exacerbate the tensions already present. The conservative centre will be under greater pressure from the more vigorous, prolific and liberal Muslim societies on the periphery.

Despite the ideals promoting an equitable and productive material life, the overwhelming majority of Muslims experience living standards which are hardly enviable by any standard. This frequently appears to be a greater paradox in the wealthy oil-producing Muslim countries. Where justice and brotherhood are recommended by the ideals, in such countries we see the conspicuous consumption of the very rich, the purchase of very expensive military technology and armaments, and we see the exploitation of *'guest workers'*: fellow Muslims from Palestine, Pakistan, the Philippines, among others. The plight of these groups was obvious during and after the Gulf War in 1990-1991. Unemployment of masses of people; rapid urbanisation; unbalanced development-all need to be addressed quickly by the ummah, if the ummah is to become the social force of international Islam. The wide imbalances in the distribution of incomes and wealth between Muslim societies are obvious, but since effective redistribution is not happening within most Muslim societies it is unlikely to occur to any major degree between different Muslim societies.

Development investment in Muslim countries is slow simply because investors are put off by the more extremist agitations and the perceptions in the West about Islamic legal proscriptions of such financial mechanisms as interest. Muslim investors appear quite happy to send their money into the non-Muslim economies, where greater profits are available and the political and social circumstances are much more settled. In other cases, where people are trying to help their communities they often encounter problems from unlikely sources. The Grameen Bank in Bangladesh has been lending small sums of money, mostly to rural women so that they can engage in small enterprises, but also to collective groups. The sums are small and the interest is fixed, with the principal being repaid first and the interest calculated on the diminishing principal. Twenty per cent interest per year still seems high, but it is tiny when compared with the twenty per cent per month or ten per cent per day demanded by the traditional money-lenders, or the compound interest at Bangladesh's commercial banks. The Grameen Bank lends money to people who would not be eligible in the normal commercial sense. People are helped to determine the best way to satisfy their needs and are helped by the bank's officers in the villages. The Grameen Bank goes out to its clients and it permits the good sense and honesty of its clients to prevail: it has a recovery rate of some ninety eight per cent. The bank faces conflict from the traditional money-lenders, the commercial banks which claim that the scheme is too small to create the economic growth necessary in Bangladesh, and from the Muslims who see the scheme emancipating women in the villages. The bank fulfils the ideals of Islamic thinking, but is attacked by established interest groups defending their interpretation of Islamic practice.

Economic frustration and unequal opportunities are fertile breeding grounds for dissent and protest. Equally important is the failure of most Muslim governments to confront the demands of general education. "Modernity, the circumstance of being 'modern', is, in a central sense, inescapable. It is the necessary context for every tolerably well-informed life-journey undertaken in the contemporary world." Being modern does not mean being Western but it does mean that some degree of secular knowledge will have to be given far greater prominence in Muslim epistemologies. Dr Mahathir bin Mohamed has made the point that there can be no separation between secular and religious knowledge because all knowledge, all life, is encompassed by Islam. It is interesting that so prominent and successful a Muslim leader as Dr Mahathir had to tread a fine line: advocating on the one hand an independent and progressive Muslim attitude to acquiring the widest possible knowledge, while placating the traditional sensibilities by insisting on the moral rectitude of learning as the only way to protect the faith. There are Muslim intellectuals working to understand what it means to be a Muslim in the modern world, but they do not receive the prominence given to the extremists in Western reports. Western media are more interested in the violent and emotional than they are in quiet, but deeply significant, debates about the eternal values that remain, despite the anarchic individualism of Western communities, the essence of being human. Not only are Muslim intellectuals under pressure from the conservative elements of their own societies, they are not receiving the recognition and support they deserve from the West. Yet it is at this level of ideas and reassessments that Muslim leaders will have to convert the *de facto* modernisation of their societies into general acceptance. The renaissance of *ijtihad* will be needed to reinterpret the principles of Islam, to retain the critical moral core while jettisoning the dubious accretions of traditional and worldly Muslim authorities.

The whole panoply of modern knowledge and technology is acceptable, but its Western manifestations are to be avoided if all they achieve is the perpetuation of the Muslim world's dependence on Western developments. A fundamental problem here is that which bedevils Western societies: can the use of and reliance upon new technologies alter perceptions, change desires, force social changes? Do the people who create and maintain the new technologies become the new high-priests. All knowledge and technology entail more than the physical and objective characteristics; they also contain the moral questions about how the new technologies should be used, what controls should be placed on them and who should be responsible for the implementation of the regulations. These are moral questions the simply secular authorities cannot answer, if only because utilitarian arguments lead us only to numerical quantities not qualitative priorities.

There is a very real danger involved if Muslims are not critical enough of Western world perceptions and if they take things for granted. There needs to be an increase in criticism in the light of Islam criteria. Without a heightened critical faculty Muslims are in danger of considering

"Islam as a partial view of things to be complemented by some modern deology rather than as a complete system and perspective in itself, whose very totality excludes the possibility of its becoming a mere adjective to modify some other noun which is taken almost unconsciously as central in place of Islam...He who understands the structure of Islam in its totality knows that it can never allow itself to become reduced to a mere modifier or contingency vis-a-vis a system of thought which remains independent of it or even hostile to it."

The main danger arises if Muslims accept the more extreme view of the difference of Islam and the insistence on establishing 'the third way'. If everything Western is to be discarded, then the creative and productive dynamism inherent in Islamic traditions will be suppressed yet again. Is Islamic resurgence giving enough attention to the challenges of poverty and hunger, disease and illiteracy? Have Islamic resurgents gone past, or are they still stuck on, their rhetoric regarding education and knowledge, science and technology, politics and administration, economics and management in their preferred Islamic order? To what extent have Islamists become pre-occupied with forms and symbols, rituals and practices? Do they regard laws and regulations in a static rather than a dynamic manner ? Is there a tension between the extremists' positions and the principles of the Quran and sunnah about the roles of women in society and the place of minorities in Muslim societies? Is the main problem a betrayal of the spirit of the Quran in the extremists' exclusiveness in a variety of matters ranging from charity to politics? Are the activities of extremists encouraging sectarianism in the umma through their insistence on their interpretations being the only correct ones? Have extremist views contributed to the factionalism and fragmentation of the ummah.

The moral question is at the heart of the matter. Fazlur Rahman stated the position precisely. Islam needs: "some first-class minds who can interpret the old in terms of the new as regards substance and turn the new into the service of the old as regards ideals". Can the modernists who want modernisation without Westernisation expect to realise their hopes? There is evidence enough in Western society that modernisation, with all its technological developments, has radically changed values by putting traditional attitudes under pressure and then instituting a new ethic.

Untrammelled economic growth and development has resulted in consumerism, institutionalised selfishness, ill-gotten wealth, rising expectations, laxity in sexual behaviours, the dissolution of the family, essentially independent electronic media, the influx of foreigners and foreign values, the materialism of modern science and technology and greater amounts of secularism.

In an Increasing Secular World, can Islam unite a Modern Society? Western secular politics is based on the notion that sovereignty belongs to individuals who select their governors through political consensus arrived at during free and regular elections. Islam believes, in theory at least, that sovereignty belongs only to God and that a legitimate temporal government is so only for as long as it implements God's will and the Sacred Laws. Whatever the theory asserts, the reality is that governments have to find the equilibrium that produces social prosperity and harmony under the guiding impulses of a strong moral code.

The problem is made more complex when the moral code is itself subject to sectarian divisions: between orthodox and heterodox claims to revelation and legitimacy. We have to return to the questions: whose Islam, what Islam, where and when? It is clear that in states which have declared Islam as the ideology of political order, Saudi Arabia, the Sudan, Pakistan, Iran and Afghanistan, there has been little reduction in domestic conflict or the reduction of conflict with their neighbours, Muslim or otherwise. In these states there is little real evidence of effective redistribution of wealth or substantial economic and social benefits flowing down to the general population. The benefits promised by Islam are not being realised.

In the Muslim communities with an emphasis on the secular ideology of politics, such as Turkey and Egypt, the general welfare is only slightly better, although there appears to be a greater freedom of belief and action. The majority of Muslims live under governments with a qualified acceptance of a secular ideology. These states have taken Western models for modern political and social institutions and have imbued them with a strong Islamic character. The problem remains: how does Islam deal with public morality and public order? What institutional frameworks can define, separate, and regulate private vice and public morality? What arguments can be raised in favour of, and against, the devout who insist that there exists already a definitive, well-known and comprehensive path revealed by God? In our reflections on the issues, we must remember to distinguish between the genuinely devout people and those utilising religious symbols to promote their own positions.

Political Islam is under challenge from its own rhetoric and message to be self-critical: to live up to its own standards; to live up to the principles it espouses and demands of others; to avoid and denounce excesses committed by governments and movements that identify themselves as Islamic; to take or share responsibility for the failures of Muslim societies, and not simply to blame the West for all the problems. One of the central questions will be the treatment of minorities under Islamic governments, and the behaviour of Muslim minorities in other countries. At present the political ideology of Islam cannot entertain an equal and pluralist society of Muslims and non-Muslims. This is not just a matter of tolerance: it entails the recognition in ideal and reality of the unqualified equality and citizenship rights of people of all faiths irrespective of whether they are male or female. The role and influence of political dissent, trade unions, and the media will have to be re-examined along with the social and legal issues. A new equilibrium will have to be reached between the legitimate demands of the individual and the legitimate demands of the society in which he or she lives.

In the same way, Muslim minorities will need to reach a new accommodation with the ruling groups in their countries. Indian Muslims (about one hundred millions, or twelve per cent of the population), and Muslims in the Philippines (about six millions, or eight per cent of the population), will have to control the extremist elements within their communities. The examples of Pakistan and Bangladesh are clear demonstrations that separatism is not à viable option. Religious homogeneity is no more capable of establishing a harmonious society than is the ethnic homogeneity being attempted by the Bosnian Serbs. The spread of Islamic terrorism into the emerging Muslim states in Central Asia, in Africa, as well as the sporadic outbreaks in Western countries, will need to be suppressed. At the same time the legitimate demands of Muslim minorities must be recognised by the governments of their countries. Some fifty million Chinese Muslims cannot be ignored even within a population as large as China's.

In international terms, Islamic states are increasingly significant economically, financially and politically. Across the *ummah* local interests and national politics appear to be more important than simple identification of interests based on Islamic traditions. The Islamic states antipathetic to the West (Libya, Iran, Iraq, Yemen) are balanced by those which are firmly supportive (Saudi Arabia, Pakistan, Singapore, Malaysia, Indonesia, Thailand, Philippines, Brunei). This is not to say that the states with positive relations with the West are not critical of the West. Many of the criticisms of leaders such as Dr Mahathir, Lee Kuan Yew, and Goh Chok Tong (Prime Minister of Singapore), among others, are incisive and go to the heart of many of the problems in the West.

Despite the overwhelming global influence of Western ideas, the West, of course, is not a monolithic presence. The twentieth century has proved beyond any doubt that the ideals espoused in the West do not prevent hypocritical justifications for untenable attitudes towards the rest of the world, nor do they prevent total war between European nations.

The West has to understand Islam; not because Islam is the next great threat, but because Islam contains so many ideas and moral values that the West, for all its rampant secularism, still shares. The West must also recognise the diversity of Muslim experiences across the world. Muslim societies do not only suffer from 'Islamic' problems; they suffer the same problems long familiar in the West: political, economic, ecological, social and moral development. As such, these are shared human experiences and the beneficial resolutions: in science, technology, medicine, education should also be shared equitably. If Western nations believe in the value of their defining concepts: individualism, liberalism, constitutionalism, human rights, equality, liberty, the rule of law, democracy, free markets, and the separation of church and state then they will have to be shared through sympathetic dialogue, not forced upon others. The idea of contending world views which define the good states from the bad states will have to be scrapped. It has not worked in the West's relationships with China, where the hypocrisy of the West's stance on human rights has been highlighted by the West's attitudes towards Algeria and Bosnia. Western support, especially that by the United States, for the authoritarian regimes in Saudi Arabia, Kuwait, and Pakistan while denigrating other exclusive Islamic authorities in Iran, Syria, Iraq, and the Sudan, does not generate confidence among Muslim societies around the world. Western nations supported the Mujahideen in Afghanistan, yet helped to oppress Palestinians through support for Israel. The continued existence of Israel is not negotiable, but the ways in which Western nations have treated the concerns and sensibilities of the Palestinians have not been sympathetic enough. Neither have the more aggressive Muslim attitudes helped the situation.

Western attempts to propagate ideas about Western civilisation as 'universal civilisation' have resulted in significant reactions against a new imperialism: 'cultural imperialism', 'human rights imperialism', and so on. The religious revivals and reaffirmations of local, traditional values, among the younger generations in Islamic and Hindu cultures especially, are often reactions against the insidiousness of Western cultural influences.

Just as Western societies must reassess their ideas about the superiority of their ideals, so too must Muslim societies understand that their traditions need reinterpretation. It is pointless for the ulama to keep on insisting that Islam is not simply a different tradition: it is a superior tradition. In this light Western ideas are not only inferior, they are inapplicable and irrelevant to Islam and Muslim society. At the level of ideals the arguments depend eventually on the leap of faith: whether divine authority rests in the Torah, the Bible or the Quran. People who accept the superior divinity of only one of these not only have the problem of repudiating other claims, they must also address the people who do not accept the authority of any divine revelation. It is useless to quote the authority of the Quran to people who do not accept it. The arguments have to be conducted on other levels: rational and empirical levels. Here the ideals can be seen to have been debased over the centuries by the practical realities of living. This does not mean that the ideals are worthless, but it does mean that demands for a return to the simplicity of Islamic principles must be tempered by courageous and clear-sighted analysis of the differences between the Quranic ideals and their historical development.

Islam and the West have much to offer each other. Nothing productive will develop while the dominant attitudes are those of suspicion, bigotry, and fear. Islam once played an essential role in preserving knowledge during the ignorance and barbarism of Europe's 'dark ages'.

The rediscovery and refinement of this knowledge helped to set Europe on the road to its modern dominance of science and technology. The grip of worldly and corrupted religious leaders was broken in Europe. At the same time the suppression of ijtihad and rational dissent within Islamic societies by similar sorts of rulers caused the decline of the Islamic world, permitting the Europeans to indulge in imperialism and colonialism from the eighteenth century to the mid-twentieth century. A sympathetic exchange of knowledge, flowing this time from Western societies to Islamic societies, may well revivify Islam and permit Islamic societies to enjoy a more creative and significant role in the modern world.

Simple material transfers are not enough. There has to be a reworking of the central ideas in both societies. It may seem an obvious point, but in the bigotry of the religious confrontation it is necessary to emphasise that non-Muslims must recognise as a fact God's revelation of truth to Muhammad.

If we can accept our own monotheistic traditions and the role of prophets we must recognise the genuine prophetic claims of others. We can critically examine the traditions but we must do so from recognition and knowledge not from denigration and outright rejection. Islam offers much to Western societies presently dominated by the anarchic demands of rampant 'isms': individualism, materialism, consumerism and secularism.

Islam has preserved the central position of moral values as the defining character of human society. Francis Lamand, President of the French Association 'Islam and the West', considers that: "Islam can contribute to the rebirth, in the West, of three essential values: the sense of community, in a part of the world that has become too individualistic; the sense of the sacred; and the legal sense. This can be the contribution of Islam to Western societies". In return the West has to control its arrogance and reassess its stance towards the rest of the world. The notion of there even being a 'rest of the world', from whatever perception, is something we all have to change.

ISLAM IN MODERN INDONESIA

Five Indonesians, four Americans and one Australian convened on February 7, 2002 to examine the history, the international connections and the politics of Islam in Indonesia. There was a remarkable consensus among the speakers on the key conclusions, with several of the following points being made by more than one person:

- The increase in Islamic radicalism is due basically to the "abrupt decline of central government authority together with the demoralization of the police." There is no conspiracy at the center directing radical groups but rather a breakdown in governance at the center and an inability or unwillingness to prevent the excesses of individual players.
- The vast majority of Indonesian Muslims remain tolerant and inclusive, as they have been traditionally described, and voted for secular political parties in the last elections in June 1999. Although Islamic piety has increased in recent years there has been no increase in the number of radical Muslims.
- There has always been tension between the majority view and small groups that have pushed for more orthodox, conservative, literal interpretations of Islam. These more conservative groups have been mostly indigenous although there have always been ties between Indonesian Muslims and Muslims elsewhere. These groups have had varying agendas and varying degrees of activism. International connections are not necessarily terrorist connections.
- The presence of al Qaeda in Indonesia has not been proven. However intelligence reports about the activities of individuals in various Southeast Asia countries are credible and should be investigated cooperatively among those countries.
- The Laskar Jihad is the most flamboyant and militant of the Islamic organizations. There is ample reason to presume it receives its funding from internal sources, including individuals from the former elite of the New Order who have vast sums of money at their disposal.

- The Islamic-oriented political parties are in disarray and are ineffective. There is no likelihood that any legislation would succeed in requiring Muslims to observe Islamic (Shariah) Law. There is no likelihood of Indonesia becoming an Islamic State. Islamic politics is less about doctrine than about power struggles of individuals and groups seeking to maintain their positions.
- Democratization will not proceed in Indonesia until it is actively supported by the Islamic community and until the values of democracy are explicitly articulated as compatible with Islamic doctrine.
- Civil society, however important, will not create a democracy unless it is linked to state institutions and reinforced by actions of the government.
- Despite its relatively small size, Islamic radicalism in Indonesia poses a danger because it may co-opt the moderate majority in the absence of effective counter measures.
- The United States should not over emphasize the threat of radical groups in Indonesia because it will give them the publicity they seek, enable them to play the "nationalist" card, provoke a negative reaction among moderates and increase bilateral tension.
- The best way for the United States to counter radicalism will be to continue assistance to democracy-building institutions and continue support for economic recovery.
- The United States should help the police in training to maintain law and order, and should look toward increased military to military relations within the bounds of current U.S. law.

Indonesian Islam in a World Context

Azyumardi Azra, rector of the State Institute for Islamic Studies (IAIN), said it is "simplistic" to think of Indonesian Islam as the same as Islam in the Middle East. Because of its slow, peaceful penetration over centuries, accommodating to and integrating with local beliefs and customs, and because of the less rigid structure of Indonesian traditional society (including the active role of women in public life), the conventional wisdom of Indonesian Islam as tolerant, inclusive and inherently compatible with democracy is valid.

The head of Indonesia's most venerable state institution to promote liberal Islamic studies and to integrate religious and secular education in the country, Professor Azra associated the most democratizing Muslim countries, as listed by Freedom House in New York, as being the "least Arabicized." (Freedom House listed Indonesia along with Bangladesh, Nigeria and Iran.) Nevertheless, Indonesia has experienced indigenous radical groups since independence that wanted to establish an Islamic state, the most famous being the Darul Islam, which operated from the mid 1950s until 1962. Professor Azra said that some other groups, which operated during the Soeharto period "were believed to have been engineered by certain army generals in order to discredit Islam." These radical groups failed because they were crushed by the army and also because they "failed to gain support from mainstream Muslims."

This persistent but minor thread in Indonesia's Muslim community has emerged again because of the power vacuum after the fall of Soeharto, and more recently the ouster of President Wahid (Gus Dur). Many are new groups that were unknown before, and no exact account exists, but "there are reports...their leadership have been close to certain army generals [and] some observers assert that they have been sponsored, or at least helped, by certain circles of the Indonesian military." He said it is "conspicuously clear" that these groups are led by people of Arab, particularly Yemeni, origin. He gave as examples Habib Rizq Shihab, leader of the FPI (Islamic Defense Group), Jafar Umar Thalib, leader of the Laskar Jihad, Abu Bakar Baasyir of the MMI (Indonesian Council of Jihad Fighters) and Habib Husen al-Habsyi, leader of the JAMI (Jamaah al-Ikhwan al-Muslimin Indonesia).

These groups share a literal interpretation of Islam and claim that Muslims should practice only "pure" Islam as practiced by the Prophet Muhammad and his companions, or *Salaf*. They can thus be included among Salafi activist movements that attack discotheques and other "places of violence." They also take a militant view of *jihad* as "holy war" against perceived enemies of Islam rather than the mainstream view of *jihad* as meaning "exerting oneself to the utmost" in Muslim activities, with war as a last resort.

Professor Azra listed other groups as well, in existence since the Soeharto period, that were less radical. Of these the most important is the Hizb al-Tahrir (Party of Liberation) established in Lebanon and first introduced in Indonesia in 1972. Its objective is to re-establish the Caliphate, a universal Islamic political entity, as the most effective way to achieve Muslim unity. This group has been active in mass demonstrations against the U.S. after the start of its military operations in Afghanistan. Despite increased visibility Professor Azra quoted its leader as saying the membership has not increased.

All radical groups have some connections with theological or organizational groups elsewhere, including the Middle East, but it is difficult to establish a connection with al Qaeda. According to Professor Azra, the leaders of the FPI, Laskar Jihad and JAMI have criticized Osama bin Laden.

However, the MMI, led by Abu Bakar Baasyir is known to have close links with the KMMM, Malaysian Military Muslim Group. Baasyir fled to Malaysia to escape Soeharto repression and returned after the fall of Soeharto. He is associated with the Jamaah Islamiyyah which has alleged links to al Qaeda. Professor Azra acknowledged a much deeper investigation into these links, involving all of the ASEAN governments, is needed. The increase in radicalism of these groups is basically the outcome of the "government failure to enforce the law and solve…social ills such as ethno-religious conflicts, increased crime, rampant corruption, widespread drug abuse and the like," and the "abrupt decline of central government authority together with the demoralization of the police."

Meanwhile, he said, the largest mainstream Muslim organizations, the Nahdlatul Ulama and the Muhammadiyah, have been overshadowed by media attention to radical groups. Since November, however, they have become more assertive, and have recently agreed to carry out joint activities to combat extremism. Both leaders, Hasyim Muzadi of NU and Ahmad

Syafii Maarif of Muhammadiyah, appealed to the government to take harsh measures against lawbreakers.

President Megawati, after a slow response to Muslim hardliners, is beginning to take a firmer policy.

The United States should not overemphasize the threat of radical groups, thereby giving them the publicity they seek and alienating mainstream Muslims. This excessive attention could provoke a reaction, bringing moderates closer to radicals and creating a momentum to challenge Megawati's presidency, thus adding to Indonesian political instability.

Mark Woodward, a professor of religious studies at Arizona State University and an authority on modern religion and ethnicity in Indonesia, focused his remarks on the international nature of Islam and the moderate as well as radical ties among Muslims, and the great variety of cultures within Islam.

He pointed out that although Islam originated in Arabia it is not synonymous with Arabian culture, and he quoted Gus Dur as having said "The Saudis don't understand the difference between Islam and their own culture."

Until the rise of the conservative Wahabi movement in the 18th century, Mecca was the center of a lively international congregation of scholars, including some from what is now Indonesia. He noted that the connections between the Middle East and Southeast Asia especially included Yemen, and he pointed out that not all Yemenis were necessarily radical, citing the family of Ali Alatas, former Indonesian foreign minister, as originally from Yemen.

He further noted that the well-established international connections of Indonesian Muslims include but are not limited to Saudi Arabia. Those students in various universities in Saudi Arabia lean toward the strict, literal tradition of Wahabi Islam. A large number of Indonesian students are studying Islam in Cairo, at al Azhar University. These students are mostly associated with the Nahdlatul Ulama and are associated in dialogue with leading liberal intellectuals in the Middle East. A third group studies in the United States and other Western institutions such as McGill, Australian National University and others. He noted that

Indonesia's leading moderate Islamic scholar, Nurcholish Madjid, has a PhD from the University of Chicago, as well as the conservative Muslim politician Amien Rais, chairman of the Peoples' Consultative Assembly.

Robert Hefner, a leading scholar on Indonesian Islam, has most recently conducted research on radical groups including the Laskar Jihad.

He presented a very somber view of the state of liberal Islam in Indonesia, all the more somber because he viewed Indonesia during the last years of the Soeharto New Order as one of the "most vibrant centers for new Muslim political thinking the modern world has seen." This was not just intellectuals, but a "lively coalition" linking leaders and mass-based institutions. He credited these efforts with assembling the ingredients essential to creating a lasting Muslim democracy: thoughtful articulation of policy that is justified under religious doctrine, and a link between respected intellectuals and mass-based organizations.

This promise was betrayed by events after the fall of Soeharto, he said. He cited the failure of governance as the primary cause for the rise of radical groups, and said this failure was primarily due to the lasting influence of the cronies of the old regime, who have vast sums of money at their disposal.

The coalition that brought about Soeharto's resignation quickly fell apart after his departure into diverse alliances of Islamist and secular nationalist groupings. Moreover, most of the old elite remained in positions of power. Rather than simply uniting to oppose reform, however, political elites reached out, at national and local levels, to various groupings to create expedient alliances to remain in power. In a vacuum of central power these rivalries flourished, resulting in ethnoreligious tensions and clashes. In some areas, such as Yogyakarta and East Kalimantan, these rivalries were kept within civil bounds by local governments; but in Maluku, Central Kalimantan, Poso (Central Sulawesi) and a few other regions the conflicts got out of hand. Moreover, the rival elites brought into play "another category of social actor" known since colonial times but which became more prominent at the end of the Soeharto era: the "organized political-cum-criminal syndicates known as *preman*." These gangster groups usually adopted the ideology of their patrons to assume an air of public service, and by the end of the New Order the popular ideology was Islam. This set the stage for gang warfare between Islamist, Christian and nationalist groups. It is important in evaluating events in Indonesia since September 11 not to exaggerate the strength of radical Islamism and overlook the role of "simple patronage and extralegal competition," he said.

The elections of June 1999 showed that most voters favored secular or moderate Islamist political parties, in fact by a larger majority than in the only other free and open general elections, held in 1955. "Only about 16 percent of the vote went to parties advocating (conservative Islamic) programs...as opposed to more than 40 percent in 1955."

At the same time, he said, most social indicators show that the populace is becoming more observant of Islamic customs. This increased piety has not resulted in more conservative voting. It is not Islam that is destabilizing Indonesia, he said, but "a breakdown of governance exacerbated by elite factionalism and the willingness of ...elites to take advantage of ethnoreligious tensions for the ir own purposes."

There is no conspiracy at the center to control these radical groups, he said, but rather a collapse at the center and an inability or unwillingness to prevent the excesses of individual players. In this context, Professor Hefner discussed two organizations, MMI (Indonesian Mujahidin Council) and Laskar Jihad, as "heirs to a tradition of radical politics and religion that...has always operated on the fringe of Indonesian society."

MMI was founded in August 2000 and its spiritual leader, Abu Bakar Ba'asyir, served prison time in the late 1970s for his opposition to Soeharto. He remained a strong critic of Soeharto and also of the army. Ba'asyir is accused by Malaysian and Philippine intelligence sources as leader of *Jemaah Islamiyah*, which these sources say has ties to al Qaeda. He is unlikely to have any support from the Indonesian armed forces, according to Professor Hefner.

The Laskar Jihad, on the other hand, is "long thought to enjoy the patronage of a small but significant faction of the armed forces." It grew out of a conservative religious movement founded in the early 1990s by Jafar Umar Thalib. It is distinguished from other conservative movements in the "firm belief that the United States and Israel are leading a world-wide conspiracy to destroy Islam." Jafar's fiery sermons stress the need for *jihad* to cleanse society of un-Islamic influences. Importantly also, his concepts include the stipulation that unbelievers in Indonesia must accept the role of protected minorities and not be allowed to exercise authority over Muslims. Jafar has made clear that "he believes that the equal citizenship sanctioned by the Indonesian constitution is utterly antithetical to Islam."

The possible connections between the Laskar Jihad and al Qaeda are not clear. Laskar Jihad has strongly denied receiving any funds from Osama bin Laden. However, Indonesian intelligence chief General Hendropriyono confirmed reports of al Qaeda training camps in Indonesia to assist Laskar Jihad fighters in Maluku and Central Sulawesi. Hendropriyono was strongly criticized by other conservative Muslims, for presumably looking for an excuse for action against radical Islamic groups. He subsequently backed away from his assertion. This did not illustrate the truth of the matter but instead the conflicting views among the security and political elite. In any case there is ample evidence that Laskar Jihad enjoys considerable domestic financial support, according to Hefner. He quotes a former field commander of Laskar Jihad who told him that in January 2000 Jafar "was approached" by military retirees with the message that they approved of his plans to escalate the armed campaign against Christians in Maluku. The purpose was explicitly stated: "to undermine the reform government of Abdurrahman Wahid." In fact, the Laskar Jihad was subsequently able to arm and transport its fighters from Java to Maluku without any challenge, despite the fact that President Wahid and other government leaders appealed to security officials to stop the militia from traveling.

Hefner stated that these radical groups, although operating with the collusion of certain officials, still do not represent the views of the majority, who are uneasy with violence and yearn for politics that are moderate and inclusive. However, the outcome will depend on how effective will be the efforts of President

Megawati, the mainstream Muslim leadership and moderate elements in the armed forces. They must forge a working consensus between civil society and the government to combat extremist and divisive elements.

The Politics of Islam in a Democratizing Indonesia

Ulil Abshar Abdalla is executive director of the Indonesia Conference on Religion and Peace, an organization associated with the Nahdlatul Ulama, one of the two largest Muslim organizations in Indonesia. He is cheerfully optimistic about the prospects of incorporating democratic and modernist notions, such as openness, pluralism, gender equality and the like, into the theological framework of Islam. He reiterated the point made by speakers in the first session that this explicit ideological support is necessary and that democracy will not really take root in Indonesia without the strong support of the Islamic society. Thus active efforts toward democratization are required from the moderate Muslim community.

Mr. Ulil described discussion circles, a radio talk show, a weekly newspaper column and a journal, all designed to promote dialogue among liberal (a term he acknowledges as "controversial"), moderate and radical elements of the Muslim community.

He said that radicals such as Jafar Umar Thalib and Habib Rizq are not as radical as people think, and that they seem to be amenable to these conciliation efforts. He said the Laskar Jihad was "responding" to the attack on Muslims in Maluku, and that this group as well as the Islamic Defense Group (FPI) share the notion of a nation state of Indonesia and are not pressing for an Islamic state. They believe, however, that Muslims were treated unfairly under Soeharto and want to be treated as the majority that they represent in the population.

While they wish to have *shariah* (Islamic) law implemented for Muslims, Ulil said there is no clear consensus and therefore "room for dialogue" on what *shariah* law implies.

Lies Marcoes Natsir, a researcher with the Association for the Development of Pesantren and Society (P3M), described the work of her organization to promote the rights of women in an Islamic society, a goal that is relevant because Islam prescribes relationships between men and women. She said the Western notion of Islam being repressive toward women because of such injunctions as requiring women to "wear the veil" and restricting their public role seems "peculiar to us" because the repression of women is not limited to Islam. She said it has less to do with theology than simple "male political tactics." As an example she discussed the development of ideas in Indonesia regarding the acceptability of a woman as a political leader.

A decree issued by the Nahdlatul Ulama in 1997 stating that there was no prohibition for a woman to be head of state was later retracted, she said, because the original decree was linked to the promotion of Soeharto's daughter Tutut as a potential political candidate. After Tutut's prospects dissolved with the resignation of her father and before Megawati became vice president, most Islamic organizations again rejected the idea of a woman as head of state. However, after the disillusionment with Gus Dur this opposition to Megawati declined somewhat and in August 2001 the Muhammadiyah organization decreed that there was no obstacle to a woman as head of state. At a recent Muhammadiyah Congress in Bali it was agreed that a woman may be elected as leader of that organization.

Ms. Lies described the activities of her NGO in the advocacy for women's rights within Islam, specifically in the 10,000 *pesantren* or Islamic boarding schools spread across Java and Madura, where more than 70 percent of the entire Indonesian Muslim population lives. Most of the *pesantren* are affiliated with the Nahdlatul Ulama, one of the two biggest Muslim organizations, located mostly in rural areas, and the one considered the more traditional though tolerant. Her organizatio n focuses especially on reproductive and political (both domestic and public) rights. The second largest Muslim organization, Muhammadiyah, also has a women's affiliate that has established a network of vocational education centers and programs for women in development especially in the fields of education, health and small-scale finance.

Asked whether Western pressure for human rights is helpful to organizations such as hers, Ms. Lies answered that it is "somehow bad" because it causes confrontation between Islam and the West and, she implied, complicates their efforts. Greg Fealy is a lecturer in Southeast Asian politics and history at Australian National University and a student of political parties in Indonesia. He sees today's parties as much degraded from parties that were prominent during the parliamentary democracy period of the 1950s. Taking a closer look at the leading five Islamic political parties, he finds them sorely lacking in the qualities that make an effective organization. "Islamic parties are more divided now than at any time in history since 1945," he said.

Politics of the 1950s have been "dismissed," he said, but he sees important insights in comparing political parties of that period with today:

- Individuals are more powerful now. There is something almost "cultic, iconic" about present day party leaders, who have little connection with their organizations.
- The demise of ideology. Parties in the 1950s had conferences and heated debates on particular issues. There are few party platforms today.
- Physical intimidation. No party in the 1950s had a paramilitary wing. Now every party has an auxiliary organization, from well-trained cadres to ordinary hooligans.
- Money politics. Outright buying of public or party position is much more common today. He examined the five leading Islamic political parties according to their share of the vote in the 1999 elections. They are the PKB (Gus Dur's party), with 12.6 percent of the vote, the United Development Party (PPP, the party of the vice president Hamzah Haz), 11.7 percent; the National Mandate Party (PAN, the party of Amien Rais), at 7.4 percent, Crescent Star (Bulan Bintang, the party of Yusril Mahendra), at 1.9 percent, and the Justice Party (Partai Keadilaan) at 1.7 percent.
- He chose four indicators of future effectiveness and looked at the above parties in this light. They are branch activities, leaders arising from the cadres, internal communication between the elites and the grass roots localities, and coherent party platforms. Most Islamic parties are doing poorly, according to his conclusions:

- Most are "election only" parties and are moribund at the branch level. There are a very small number of elites.
- Party cadres are not emerging. In most cases money will buy a party post, except for the Partai Keadilaan which has rigorous rules and leaders who are not wealthy.
- Communication is poor within organizations and little value is given to grassroots opinion.
- Few parties had a platform in 1999 and little work has been done since on issues. Fragmentation is a serious issue. There have been serious splits in four of the five parties, with the exception of Partai Keadilaan. Leadership has been keenly disappointing, illustrated by the disastrous performance of Gus Dur and the contradictions of Amien Rais. Ideology is "hollow."

The two most doctrinaire parties, PPP and Bulan Bintang, focus on the Jakarta Charter, a proposition that was defeated in the 1945 Constitution that held that Muslims must follow *shariah* law. However, no attempt has been made to define *shariah* law. This basic issue has not been worked out.

In answer to a question Mr. Fealy cautioned whether a reform of the electoral system would produce more coherent political parties and more accountability. He said there are "enormous barriers" to installing a district system that might require four or five years to carry out. He warned that in the end, if not properly implemented, an ineffective system might lead to violence.

As for constitutional reform, he said the core problem of government in Indonesia is not caused by a struggle between a presidential and a parliamentary system, but a lack of leaders' decisions and implementation. The problem is more cultural than constitutional, he said.

Indonesian Reactions to the September 11 Terrorist Attacks

Douglas Ramage, Representative to Indonesia, The Asia Foundation, described the reaction of Indonesians to the September 11 attacks in the United States and the subsequent sequence of events that led to a temporary rise in anti-American sentiment. The immediate Indonesian reaction was one of sympathy, he said, and was swift and spontaneous. During President Megawati's visit to the United States shortly after the attacks she expressed this sympathy and support.

However, before long there was speculation in Indonesia on why the attacks occurred, and several expressions that they were the result of a wrong-headed American policy in the Middle East.

The Indonesian media played a role in exacerbating the resulting tensions by publishing unsubstantiated speculation on the reasons for September 11 and vitriolic attacks on the U.S. It was the first evidence of the downside of the Indonesian free press, which is truly unregulated, privately owned, and for profit.

By the end of September the issue had become politicized. "It was the opening salvo of the 2004 election campaign," according to one Golkar member. President Megawati was shocked by attacks from the right on her Islamic credentials, for expressing support of the United States, and from the left from nationalists who criticized her speech in Houston, Texas inviting American business to come to Indonesia. She was considered a "lackey of the Americans" by both groups. Small radical Islamic groups demonstrated at the U.S. embassy and threatened "sweeps" of American tourists from hotels.

It was a serious matter for her. She leads a weak government and must thread her way between the nationalist left and the Islamic right. She dealt with it by a speech on the eve of a prominent Muslim holiday in which she criticized the spilling of blood to avenge the spilling of blood. Without naming names, she distanced herself from the United States and particularly from the U.S. campaign in Afghanistan, which had begun by then.

The domestic reaction to this speech was interesting. The criticism began to subside, perhaps in part due to some publicity about the joy in Afghanistan shown by those liberated from the Taliban.

Eventually public attention returned to normal preoccupations, such as local scandals and it was politics as usual. The government deployed security forces to protect the embassy, and mainstream Muslims, including the head of Muhammadiyah, shocked by the earlier vitriol, began to speak out. Pragmatic nationalism reasserted itself. Megawati has something of a Teflon quality and seems to have emerged unscathed. Most political parties are divided by internal wrangling and are unable to maintain any momentum in attacks against her. However, the criticisms of the U.S. touched a chord. Indonesian objections to U.S. Mid-East policy is widespread, and now can be freely expressed in the press. There is a genuine rejection of unilateralism. But these feelings are not strong or deep-seated, so the affair did not progress to widespread anti-Americanism.

But why were those who threatened U.S. citizens not punished? Impunity is the most intractable problem in Indonesia. No one is ever punished. It may be latent sympathy with the views articulated by radicals, or fear of further domestic consequences; but one should not underestimate the possibility of simple incompetence and weak government institutions.

Indonesian Reactions to September 11, Extremism and U.S.-Indonesian Relations

Moeslim Abdurrahman, a member of Muhammadiyah's board of directors, further described the aftermath of September 11 in Indonesia, and gave examples of some of the popular and common anti-American rhetoric that increased during this period.

He reported that in the *hudpah* (the Friday sermon after prayers in the mosques), audiences were frequently reminded to be more careful of the international conspiracy of the United States and Jews to suppress Muslim countries like Indonesia. According to this view, this conspiracy is actually behind the economic crisis, so [wealthy] Christian missionaries can benefit from poverty and convert Muslims by providing rice. He described other examples of response, some equally ominous and some quite frivolous, such as the selling of Osama bin Laden tee shirts, which, he said, did not mean support for bin Laden but was just a temporary fad. The moderates, who were mostly silent, do not have a culture of speaking out as do the radicals, he said.

This variety of Islamic reaction demonstrates that it is difficult to generalize about Islam in Indonesia. Most people are ill informed and confused about international issues like globalization and U.S. foreign policy and are still figuring out issues like the meaning of gender, democracy etc. But foreign observers should not underestimate the importance of community and the strength of civil organizations in the communitarian religion of Islam. The Muhammadiyah and the Nahdlatul Ulama have thousands of universities, hospitals, and other institutions, all outside the state. This represents a strong civil society, and in cases of local need, e.g. floods, the local communities are more effective than government.

Rizal Sukma, director of studies at the Centre for Strategic and International Studies, is a member of Muhammadiyah and comes from Aceh. He described his reactions to September 11, ranging from puzzlement that Indonesians would criticize the victims of the attack in saying it happened "because the Americans were arrogant" and anger when the U.S. responded with the bombing of Afghanistan. He was angry that, while there has been great discussion about "collateral damage" in other conflicts, i.e. the number of Palestinians killed or the number of Afghans killed, there is no interest in the number of Acehnese being killed in the current conflict there.

He said in Indonesia the reaction to September 11 is understood as a test for the Megawati government: would it stand the test of not being co-opted by the United States? This is typical of any post-colonial state, he said.

He added that the objections to the U.S. military campaign also reflect a strain of opinion opposing military force to deal with terrorism, a view that springs from Indonesian experience. (However that view disappeared with the fall of the Taliban, he said.) He said radical Islam comes from several sources in Indonesia: moral frustration, ideological fear of globalization and Western domination, a desire for a *Pax Islamica* in Indonesia, simple political opportunism, and economic and social resentments. It is a phenomenon not found outside Java, he said, and is urban-based.

Today's radicals grew up in the 1970s and 1980s, at the height of Soeharto's New Order. They are motivated by various factors, he said: the urge to taste power in the vacuum after the Soeharto regime; weak law enforcement by government; and economic hardship. There are now 40 million people unemployed, he noted, and 1.3 million internally displaced people (IDP), refugees from ethnic and religious conflicts.

The failure of military reform plays into this game, he said. The police, now in charge of internal security, claim they cannot enforce law and order because they are constrained by possible human rights violations.

What can the United States do? Rizal recommended that the U.S. should continue to assist economic development and not allow the war on terrorism to derail pro-democracy movements in Aceh, Papua and other places. Better public democracy is also needed: the U.S. is not doing much to explain in Indonesia what is going on in the United States.

Donald Emmerson, senior fellow at Standord University's Asia/Pacific Research Center, noted some provocative ambiguities and ironies in American policy.

American Activism: The upsurge in American patriotism after September 11, and the explicit pride in establishing global democratic projects, are not much different than Islamism in terms of loyal fervor and proselytization.

The notion that people everywhere can achieve self-government under the rule of law might be seen as a "hyper-Wilsonian invitation" to secession.

"Let's roll!" has been cried too many times; as if all we have to do is act. What is needed is time, for long-term solutions. American impatience will be a problem.

Leverage: It's a question whether Indonesia is better off when the U.S. wants something or when there is no immediate national motive. American indifference versus American obsession presumes an assymetrical relationship between the two countries. Indonesia needs the United States for many things. If the United States needs something from Indonesia, does that suggest Indonesia has some leverage?

Meanwhile, the U.S. "obsession" is not entirely unwarranted. The U.S. vulnerability to terrorists is a real issue. It was recently reported that 16 of 22 identified al Qaeda terrorists are still at large. Military to military relations provide a good illustration of the ambiguities of the U.S.-Indonesia relationship. Has the Bush Administration requested financial support for the Indonesian military in the draft budget for the Defense Department? If there is global authorization for the U.S. military to offer training against terrorism this can be seen as an end run around the Leahy Amendment [to the Foreign Operations Act that prohibits any aid to Indonesia's military until they redress past human rights abuses]. However, perhaps not all the outcomes from September 11 are necessarily negative. If the recent meeting in Geneva on Aceh made some progress it may be because the GAM [Acehnese Independence Movement] attended; and its attendance may be because of increased pressure for settlement after September 11. General Zinni [President Bush's special envoy for Middle East negotiations] was reported to be present at that meeting.

PROCEEDINGS

Nancy Yuan: Indonesia is the largest Muslim country in the world and has been in the news almost daily for the past several months, particularly since September 11th, in matters about Indonesia's economy, about Indonesia's democracy under President Megawati's leadership, to discuss the problems in privatization or the perceived rise of Muslim extremism. As representatives of the U.S.-Indonesia Society, the preeminent organization trying to promote understanding of Indonesia in the United States, and the Asia Foundation, which has operated and managed programs in Indonesia for nearly 50 years, we thought it an important and timely opportunity to bring some people here to talk more about the complex problems facing Indonesian Muslims today. We are very pleased to bring to you a number of experts from Indonesia, Australia as well as American experts to give a more nuanced picture of the complexities of Islam, to examine Indonesia's future, to look at U.S.-Indonesia bilateral relations and issues that concern us all.

INDONESIAN ISLAM IN A WORLD CONTEXT

Compared to Middle Eastern Islam, Indonesian Islam has a number of distinctive characteristics. By and large, Indonesian Islam is a moderate, accommodating kind of Islam, and the least

Arabicized. For these reasons, the American anthropologist Clifford Geertz loves to call Islam in Java as "religion of Java," which he adopted as the title of his acclaimed book published in 1964. The term "religion of Java" refers to Islam in Java (as in many other places in Indonesia) that has been mixed and amalgamated with ancient pre-Islamic beliefs and socio-cultural traditions. Therefore, Indonesian Islam is much less rigid than Middle Eastern Islam. Not long ago, even *Newsweek* and *Time* magazine referred to Indonesian Islam as "Islam with a smiling face" – Islam that is in many ways compatible with modernity, democracy, and pluralism.

Given these distinctive characteristics, it is not surprising if Indonesia – the largest Muslim nation in the world according to the Freedom House report "Freedom in the World 2002: The Democracy Gap" – is one of "bright spots" of democracy together with other less Arabicized Muslim countries including Bangladesh, Nigeria, and Iran. Freedom House found that while there is a democracy deficit in the Islamic Arab world – referred to as the Arabic core – democratic activity is considerable in countries with a significant Muslim population such as Albania, Bangladesh, Djibouti, the Gambia, Indonesia, Mali, Niger, Nigeria, Senegal, Sierra Leone, and Turkey.

The formation of distinctive characteristics of Indonesian Islam has a lot to do with two factors at least. First of these is the peaceful spread of Islam, which T.W. Arnold called "penetration pacifique" in his classic book, *The Preaching of Islam*. This is to say the spread of Islam was not through the use of force –from Arabia, for example – but rather by way of slow penetration over centuries and allowing for the accommodation of local beliefs and cultures. This process can also be referred to as the "indigenization" or "vernacularization" of Islam. Second, the structure of Indonesian society is very different from Middle Eastern society. For example, while Islamic Middle Eastern society is male-dominated, with women confined to the domestic sphere, Islamic Indonesian society allows for greater flexibility, and women enjoy much greater freedom.

The election of Vice President Megawati Soekarnoputri to replace the embattled President Abdurrahman Wahid on July 23,

2001, is representative of the freedom that women enjoy in Islamic Indonesia. President Megawati gained uncontested support not only from the Majelis Permusyawaratan Rakyat (MPR or Peoples' Consultative Assembly) but also from the majority of Indonesian Muslims. It is important to make it clear that large mainstream Muslim organizations such as the Nahdlatul Ulama (NU) and Muhammadiyah – which claim a membership of 40 and 35 million followers respectively — have no religious objections to Megawati as a female president. Other large regional Muslim organizations in Western and Eastern Indonesia took similar attitudes on this particular issue. A similar position was also taken by Islamic or Muslim-based parties like the PPP (Partai Persatuan Pembangunan, or United Development Party), PBB (Partai Bulan Bintang, Star and Crescent Party), PK (Partai Keadilan, Justice Party), PKB (Partai Kebangkitan Bangsa, National Awakening Party), and PAN (Partai Amanat Nasional, National Mandate Party). The PPP, which had staunchly opposed Megawati on religious grounds in the preand post-general election of 1999, later accepted Megawati as president. In fact, the national chairman of PPP, Hamzah Haz, was elected vice president during the special session of the MPR on July 24, 2001, creating a duet of leadership that consists of a secular nationalist represented by Megawati and a religious nationalist represented by Hamzah Haz.

Only a limited number of hardliner Muslim groups opposed the ascendancy of Megawati on the grounds of gender, because according to their literal understanding of Islam, Islamic law does not permit a woman to hold the highest level of leadership in a Muslim society. These groups, while losing momentum after the impeachment of President Wahid, came to the forefront in a more visible, vocal, and militant manner in the aftermath of the terrorists' attacks on the World Trade Center in New York and the Pentagon in Washington DC. Even though these groups, like the Front Pembela Islam (FPI, Islamic Defence Front), Laskar Jihad, Hizb al-Tahrir (Party of Liberation) and Majelis Mujahidin Indonesia (MMI, Indonesian Council of Jihad Fighters), exert only a limited influence among Indonesian Muslims as a whole, they try to make use of any possible issue related to Islam for their own purposes, such as to undermine President Megawati's authority. President

Megawati, however, will survive the challenge of radical political Islam because of the sustained support of mainstream Muslims.

The existence of hardliner, militant, radical, or even "fundamentalist" Muslims within Indonesian Islam that have been so visible recently and are even regarded to have kidnapped the center stage of Indonesian Islam in the aftermath of the September 11 terrorist attack, is actually not new. There were radical groups during the Soekarno and Soeharto periods that attempted to establish an Islamic state in Indonesia, and to replace Pancasila – the ideological common platform that had been accepted by virtually all Muslim as well as secular nationalist leaders. These groups were known as the DI/TII (Dar al-Islam/ Tentara Islam Indonesia, or Islamic State/the Army of Islam in Indonesia) in the 1950s. Later, during the Soeharto period, radical groups like the NII (Negara Islam Indonesia, Islamic State of Indonesia) and "Komando Jihad" Jihad Command) again attempted to establish an Islamic state in Indonesia. It is important to note that some of these radical groups during the Soeharto period were believed to have been engineered by certain army generals in order to discredit Islam. But all of these radical attempts failed not only because of the harsh and repressive measures of the Indonesian army, but also because they failed to gain support from the mainstream Muslim population.

The fall of President Soeharto after more than three decades in power, and the following political liberalization, has brought momentum to the rise of radical Muslim groups. Many of them are new, such as the Front Komunikasi Ahlu-Sunnah Wal-Jama'ah (FKASWJ) with its better known paramilitary group, the Laskar Jihad (Jihad Troops), the Front Pembela Islam (Islamic Defense Front), the Majelis Mujahidin Indonesia (Indonesian Council of Jihad Fighters), the Jamaah al-lkhwan al-Muslimin Indonesia (JAMI), and some other smaller groups. There is no accurate account of the origin and establishment of these groups, which have made their appearance since the interregnum of President BJ Habibie. There are reports that some in their leadership have been close to certain army generals; therefore some observers assert that their rise has been sponsored, or at least helped, by elements in the Indonesian military. However, what is clear is that leaders of Arab – particularly Yemeni – origin are at the helm of these groups. Habib Rizq Shihab is the leader of the FPI, Jafar Umar Thalib leads the Laskar Jihad; Abu Bakar Baasyir leads the MMI; Habib Husen al-Habsyi the Ikhwan al-Muslimin Indonesia. Even though each of these groups claims [to have] a large number of members, it is clear that their membership and influence are very limited.

Religiously speaking, thes e groups tend to adopt a literal interpretation and understanding of Islam. Furthermore, they insist that Muslims should practice only what they call the "pure" and "pristine" Islam as practiced by the Prophet Muhammad and his Companions (Sahabah, or the Salaf). Given these terms, they can be included among the Salafi movements. Based on their literal understanding of Islam and Salafi's activism, they attacked discotheques, bars, and other places they considered as "places of vice." Within this kind of Isla mic worldview they understand the concept of jihad as "holy war" against those they consider enemies of Islam and of Muslims. In fact, "jihad" means "exerting oneself to the utmost" in any kind of Muslim activities. "Jihad" as "war" is only allowed as the last resort to defend Islam and Muslims from hostile enemies.

In addition to the above-mentioned groups, there are older groups that have been in existence since the time of Soeharto, but escaped the regime's harsh measures because they made some adjustments not only politically vis-à-vis the regime, but also religiously vis-à-vis the mainstream Muslims. The most important of such groups is the Hizb al-Tahrir (Party of Liberation), which was originally established in Lebanon by Shaykh Taqi al-Din al-Nabhani, and was first introduced to Indonesia in 1972. The main objectives of the Hizb al-Tahrir are to perpetuate what it regards as the true Islamic way of life globally and, most importantly, to re-establish the *khilafah* (caliphate), a universal Islamic political entity, which is believed to be the most suitable and effective political system by which to achieve Muslim unity. To achieve these goals, the Hizb al-Tahrir seems to have little difficulty in resorting to radicalism. This is why it soon became one of the most popular movements among disenchanted students and young people, not only in the Middle East, but also among Muslim students in Western countries. After the fall of Soeharto the Indonesian Hizb al-Tahrir became more visible, assertive, and vocal in voicing its ideals; it was also very active in mass-demonstrations against the U.S. in the aftermath of September 11, and subsequent U.S. military operations in Afghanistan. Though it is more visible today, its leader told me the membership of the Hizb al-Tahrir has not increased in any significant way.

There is little doubt that the radical groups mentioned above have some theological or organizational connections with particular groups in the Middle East or elsewhere in the Muslim world. It has already been noted that the leadership of newer groups is often of Middle Eastern origin and tends to be Middle-Eastern oriented in their ideology. Older groups such as the Indonesian Hizb al-Tahrir did in fact originate in the Middle East. It is difficult, however, to ascertain their possible connection with Osama bin Laden or al Qaeda. The leaders of FPI, Laskar Jihad and JAMI have denied any connection with Osama bin Laden or al Qaeda. In fact many leaders of these groups are very critical of Osama bin Laden whom they accuse of being *Kharijites* (*Kharijites* are those Muslims who seceded from the *ummah* or Muslim community).

The MMI, centered in a village in Surakarta, Central Java, has been accused of having connection with the al Qaeda. The group is led by Abu Bakar Baasyir, a religious teacher who is also the head of the al-Mukmin Pesantren and is known to have close links with the Kumpulan Muslim Militan Malaysia (KMMM, Malaysian Militant Muslim Group). In the late 1980s he went to Malaysia to escape Soeharto's repressive measures because of his illegal activities against the Indonesian government. He returned to Indonesia only after the fall of Soeharto while maintaining, it seems, his contacts with his Malaysian counterparts. Later he was also associated with the Jamaah Islamiyah, which authorities think has cells operating in Malaysia, Singapore and Indonesia. Some of these groups have been allegedly linked with al Qaeda after the arrest of Fathur Rahmah al-Ghozi by the Philippino police on January 15. When questioned by Indonesian police, Abu Bakar Baasyir denied the allegation that he is the leader of the al Qaeda-linked Jamaah Islamiyah network. Indonesian authorities and police have maintained that both al-Ghozi and Baasyir have no links to al Qaeda; but they promise to investigate further. Therefore, a much deeper investigation involving ASEAN governments is needed to clarify the matter. Discussions about terrorism instigated by President Megawati's recent tour to ASEAN member states must be followed by concrete plans to stop and defeat terrorists with global connections.

The increased radicalism of the groups mentioned above undoubtedly has a lot to do with the government failure to enforce the law and solve a number of acute social ills such as continued ethnoreligious conflicts, marked increase of crimes, rampant corruption at every level of society, and more widespread drug abuse. The abrupt decline of central government authority together with the demoralization of the police force have permitted these groups to take law into their own hands. Therefore, one important key to solving the rise of radicalism is restoring government authority and restrengthening law enforcement agencies.

In response to the apparent rise of radical groups, the two largest mainstream Muslim organizations – Nahdlatul Ulama and Muhammadiyah – have voiced their objection to radical ways. But their voices do not seem to have been strong enough, or seem to have been overlooked by the media, which seem to have a greater interest in radical groups. But since last November the two organizations have paid more serious attention to the impacts of Muslim hardliners upon the image of Indonesian Islam. They admit that the image of Indonesian Islam has worsened following the massive demonstrations against the U.S. in the aftermath of the U.S. military operation in Afghanistan. Therefore, leaders of both organizations have agreed that they will again project an image of Islam as calm and protecting of other people and other religions. The national leaders of the NU and Muhammadiyah, Hasyim Muzadi and Ahmad Syafii Ma'arif respectively, say that the image of Islam has been politicized by certain radical groups; such radicalism represents political influences rather than Islamic thinking. Therefore both organizations plan to carry out a series of activities to tackle extremism through open dialogues, joint programs and other activities. Both have also appealed to the Indonesian government to take harsh measures against groups that break the law. Syafii warns that if stern measures are not taken against radical groups, laxity could pave the way for increased radicalism.

Given the strong position taken by the mainstream Muslim organizations, it is very hard to imagine that Indonesia could become a hotbed of "Talibanism." This does not mean dismissing the possibility of the existence of radical Islam in Indonesian. It is clear that, as in any other religion, some forms of radicalism will continue to exist among Muslims in Indonesia. But, given the stronger position of mainstream Muslim organizations, the influence of radical groups can be contained. For this reason they will fail to have any significant impact to change the peaceful nature of Islam in Indonesia.

President Megawati is expected to rebuild Indonesian political stability as well as to lead the country to economic recovery. The expectation seemed to be fulfilled by the Megawati presidency until the September 11 tragedy and the subsequent U.S. military operation in Afghanistan. Massive demonstrations and the threat of Muslim hardliners targeting foreigners have hurt prospects for political stability and economic recovery. President Megawati's slow response has only worsened the political and economic situation. President Megawati's subsequent tougher and firmer policy towards hardliner Muslims has helped the government to restore its credibility. The key here is that the Indonesian government should consolidate its policy at both the domestic and international levels, to make it possible for President Megawati to silence skepticism and criticism originating from the government's indecisive and slow response.

The U.S. should adopt a very cautious policy regarding Muslim radicalism in Indonesia. Americans should not overemphasize the threat of these radical groups, since it could give them more publicity, which they seek. As clear from above, the majority of Indonesian Muslims does not have a great deal of sympathy for the radicalism expressed by some of their co-religionists. But American overreaction would increase uneasiness towards the U.S. among mainstream Muslims, and could end up alienating even the moderate Muslims. And this is really what the radicals are looking for, that is to bring the moderates into their fold.

Furthermore, it could again give momentum for the radicals to challenge the Megawati presidency, creating Indonesian political instability.

Further strengthening and empowerment of democratic elements within mainstream Indonesian Islam is one of the ways to address radicalism. It is the responsibility of all of us to enhance Indonesia's nascent democracy. Given the numerical majority of Muslims, this could be done through mainstream Islamic institutions and organizations that have committed themselves to the ideals of building Islamic civility, democracy, plurality, tolerance, respect for human rights, and peaceful co-existence among various groups. For example, in 2000, sponsored by the Asia Foundation, the State Institute/University for Islamic Studies (IAIN/UIN) Jakarta launched a new course on "Civic Education" for its new students and student leaders. Through the "Civic Education" course, students are introduced to the idea and practice of Islamic civility in relation to democracy, pluralism and other related subjects. The program is preparing for nationwide implementation in 13 other IAINs and 33 Islamic colleges (STAINs). We hope that through these and other similar programs, Indonesians will make sure democracy is the "only game in town."

Mark Woodward: I want to do two things in the next few minutes. One of them is to offer some background and the other is to talk about some contacts between Indonesia and the Middle East that do not have the radical connotations that often are assumed in the media. There's often an assumption that we can think of Islam in terms of a center and a periphery, and that the further away from Arabia you get, the less Islamic things are. That is perhaps something that some Saudis like to believe. Former President of Indonesia Abdurrahman Wahid once told me that the problem with Saudis is that they do not know the difference between Islam and their own culture. And I think that that has a profound implication.

Actually we can go back as far as the eighteenth century and see that the Muslim world was and remains a very interconnected system. When you look at the community of Islamic scholars in Mecca in the eighteenth century and until the Wahabis assumed control of the area, it was a genuine global community. It was a community in which one found Arab-Persians, Africans, Indonesians (who were that time called the "Jawa"), serving both as students and teachers. Some of the real luminaries of the Islamic theological tradition in the eighteenth and nineteenth centuries were in fact from Southeast Asia. Some of their work still circulates widely in Arabic in the Middle East. One that comes to mind is *Nawawi al Bantani*.

These individuals wrote in Arabic which meant that many of us did not become familiar with their work and that many in the Arabic-speaking world were probably not certain of the ethnicity of the authors. But then Islam has always made it clear that ethnicity or race are not significant issues. This tradition of connections with the Middle East also took the form of a lot of movement back and forth, particularly between Yemen and Southeast Asia. The Yemeni communities in Java and other parts of Indonesia are centuries old and while it is true that the leadership of some of the current radical groups is Yemeni, former foreign minister, Ali Alatas, is also of Yemeni origin. So I think that ethnic origin does not necessarily translate into theological orientation.

Similarly, the Sufi orders play a very significant role in traditional Southeas t Asian Islam. They are international in scope. The most important Sufi order in Indonesia is the *Nakshabandhis*, a genuinely global order. One of the most important *Nakshabandhis* sheikhs in the world is currently based in California and maintains a most wonderful website for anyone who wants to check it out. The spiritual center of the *Nakshabandhi* order is in Uzbekistan. The founder of the order is buried in Samarkand. So there again there is an old and well established global connection. It goes everywhere from Central Asia to California to *pesantren* in East Java.

There are a couple of new developments, really post-World-War Two developments that I think are extraordinarily significant. Over the last fifty years and increasingly moving into the present there are a very significant number of Indonesian students studying Islam, Islamic history, Islamic theology, in three major world areas. One of them is in Cairo at Al-Azhar University, the most prominent among these students are affiliated with Nahdlatul Ulama, the traditionalist Javanese-based religious organization, formerly headed by Abdurrahman Wahid. They also maintain a very extensive web page. If you read Indonesian you can get several hundred emails from them a day. That is a very active group and they are very much in dialogue with liberal intellectual Islamists from the Middle East: people like Hassan Hanafi for example who is constantly in trouble with the Egyptian radicals. Another group includes students in various Islamic universities in Saudi Arabia. Needless to say, as students in Saudi Arabia they receive an education that is much more oriented towards a Wahabi formulation of Islam. (This is a very strict literalistic understanding of Islam.)

The third area with a large numb er of Indonesian students, and here we are really talking about the people who are the Islamic leaders of the future, are the United States and Europe. We have a significant number of these people among us today, people who have very solid traditional Islamic education as young folk in Indonesia and who have gone on to obtain Ph.Ds from institutions like McGill, UCLA, University of Chicago, Australian National University, and so on. Within this group there are a lot of theological divergences. Nurcholish Madjid, who is probably the leading liberal intellectual in Indonesia today and Amien Rais, who one can never tell whether he is a democrat or a radical (it depends on whom he is talking to and in what language) are both Ph.D. level graduates of the University of Chicago, and were there at the same time.

So you can't necessarily assume from where someone was educated, exactly what his theoretical or political orientation is going to be. I do not think it can be assumed that if there's a connection with the Middle East, that must mean trouble! It's not necessarily true.

Middle Eastern Islam is not all radical; that's just what we hear about on the news, and Islam is a genuinely global community. Consequently, wherever you go in the Muslim world, you can find close to the full spectrum of Islamic thinking on theological issues, on social issues, on political issues.

Robert Hefner: (His remarks were taken from the following paper, first published in the *Van Zorge Report*, Indonesia)

INDONESIAN ISLAM AT THE CROSSROADS

For students of comparative Muslim politics, the end of the twentieth century was marked by especially interesting developments in two countries, Iran and Indonesia. Iran is important because it is the only country in the Muslim world to have gone through the full process of an Islamic revolution, the establishment of an Islamic republic, and the postrevolutionary maturation of that polity. The third of these phases has proved to be the most revealing. The Islamic Republic managed to expand higher education and create a new Muslim middle class. The election of the reform President Khatami in May 1997 demonstrated, however, that the youth wing of this new middle class has grown deeply disaffected with the reigning conservative interpretation of Muslim politics. The children of the revolution seem more interested in the creation of a civil society with real intellectual, social, and political pluralism than they do the old shibboleths of ulama leadership. Architect of the revolutionary purges at the University of Teheran in the mid-1980s, Abdolkarim Soroush's evolution from Islamist radical to a courageous spokesperson for democracy and secular freedom provides just one of the many indices of this breathtaking, if still unfinished, transformation.

When, a few years from now, historians of Muslim politics look back at the end of the twentieth century, Indonesia probably deserves to be given pride of place on par with that of Iran. Indonesia is a Sunni country, vastly poorer and less educated than the Iran of 1979 or today. Nonetheless, in the final years of the Soeharto era, this country created a movement for a democratic reorientation of Muslim political thinking that, after Iran, was arguably the Muslim world's most vibrant. The democracy movement that toppled President Soeharto in May 1998 was, of course, a multireligious coalition that included Christians and secular nationalists in its ranks.

Among its core theorists, however, was a diverse group of intellectuals interested in devising good Islamic grounds for pluralism, democracy, tolerance, and civil society. Although hardnosed political observers may sniff at such things, a vital ingredient in Muslim politics is that political initiatives must be justified in relation to divine injunctions and religious commentaries. Indonesia in the 1990s had an efflorescence of just such thinking on matters of democracy and pluralism. Moreover, unlike the similar efforts made by Muslim intellectuals in Egypt, Morocco, or Syria, this reorientation of Muslim politics wasn't just the work of a few ivory tower intellectuals. On the contrary, the initiative showed one of the key features political theorists like Guillermo O'Donnell and Philippe Schmitter identify as vital for a successful transition from authoritarian rule: a coalitional structure linking "exemplary individuals" and intellectuals to mass based organizations in society. Measured according to its intellectual vitality and prospective mass base, Indonesia in the late 1990s was one of the most vibrant centers for new Muslim political thinking the modern world has seen.

Sadly, Indonesia's great achievement may never get the credit it deserves because the movement for democratic Muslim politics was quickly overtaken by events on the ground anything but civil or democratic. As I know from recent conversations with Middle Eastern intellectuals, the violence in Maluku and the rise of radical Islamist paramilitaries have greatly tarnished Indonesia' s reputation as a center of civil-pluralist Islam. Almost no Muslim intellectual in the Middle East thinks of Indonesia in these terms today. Far too pessimistically, I believe, most instead wonder whether this country is not descending into neofundamentalist vigilantism.

In this paper I want to offer a few preliminary reflections on recent developments in Indonesian Muslim politics, and explore what they might tell us about the future. Despite some contrary reports in the Western media, the center of cultural gravity among Indonesian Muslims remains, I believe, predominantly moderate. However, to borrow a phrase from the California political sociologist Peter Evans, the challenge of "scaling up" the qualities of moderation and civility in Muslim society into effective democratic governance has proved far greater than most observers realized several years ago. To understand why this has proved to be the case, we need to reflect on Muslim politics in the final years of the Soeharto regime and the first years of the post-Soeharto era.

AMPLIFYING THE UNCIVIL

In their *Transitions from Authoritarian Rule,* Guillermo O'Donnell and Philippe Schmitter have noted that some post-authoritarian transitions are greatly assisted by a "popular upsurge" in which interest groups in society put aside differences of ethnicity, religion, and class and rally to the idea that they are a people united by a common interest in democratic reform. In the case of post-Soeharto Indonesia, the chances for such an upsurge were greatly diminished by the fact that, rather than strengthening the public consensus on the terms of the nation, in its final years the Soeharto regime greatly exacerbated ideological disagreement.

It is this unfortunate legacy that was so starkly apparent in the speed with which the coalition that had united to oust Soeharto in May 1998 broke down into warring ideological camps after the president resigned. The primary line of ideological divide pitted an alliance of Islamist groupings interested in heightening Islam's role in the state against an equally diverse array of actors intent on maintaining state structures of a more multireligious or "secular nationalist" sort. The election of Abdurrahman Wahid to the presidency in October 1999 briefly raised hopes that this great divide might yet be bridged and the process of political reform restarted. Rather than diminishing, however, the gap between these two camps only widened. The reasons for this are many, but certainly one influence was that Wahid himself misperceived the strength of his support and undertook initiatives (opening relations with Israel, lifting the ban on the Indonesian Communist Party) offensive to the centrist and conservative wings of the Muslim camp. By the end of his presidency in July 2001, whatever had remained of the coalition that had swept Wahid to power lay in ruins. The failure of the reform coalition to hold together is related to a second feature of the post-Soeharto transition. It is that, aside from Soeharto and a few of his closest allies, most of the old regime remained in place after the president's departure. Kees van Dijk is guilty of only a small measure of hyperbole when he observed, "The 'Reformation Order' which had come into being was not much more than the New Order minus the Soeharto family" (*A Country in Despair,* p. 298). While continuity of this sort might lead some political observers to speculate that old regime stalwarts would unite against the forces of reform, what happened in fact was not nearly so simple. Old regime holdovers did obstruct portions of the reform program, but they were far from united in their efforts or ideological vision. At both the national and local level, political elites responded to the vacuum created by Soeharto' s departure by reaching out to groupings in society in an effort to mobilize popular support against rivals. In some parts of the country, such as Yogyakarta and East Kalimantan, local government demonstrated great skill at keeping this patronage-cum-ideological competition within civil bounds. In Maluku, Central Kalimantan, Poso, and a few other regions, however, the rivalry got quickly out of hand, with some claimants mobilizing support by deliberately exacerbating ethnoreligious tensions. In some of the most serious conflicts, this populist sectarianism was made even worse by rival elites' reliance on another category of social actor that had come to prominence during the Soeharto era: the organized political-cum-criminal syndicates known as *preman*. Gangsterism in the New Order had always tended to display an ideological face, and it oriented that face to whatever was the reigning ideology in the regime. Gangs did this in large part to give themselves an air of public-service respectability. Whereas the dominant gang groups in the early New Order were nationalist, by the end of the New Order period some of the largest groups adopted an Islamist garb. Turf wars were common, however, and in a few parts of the country they pitted Islamist gangs against Christian and nationalist groups. Where, as in Maluku or Poso, political rivalries were exacerbated by this flammable mixture of elite factionalism, extra-legal gangsterism, and ethnoreligious tensions, the result could be deadly indeed.

Any effort to assess the situation of Islam in post-Soeharto Indonesia must begin with this background of elite factionalism and populist sectarianism. One reason it is important to do so is that, in the aftermath of September 11, 2001, foreign observers unfamiliar with Indonesia have sometimes exaggerated the strength of radical Islamism in the country and, conversely, overlooked the role of simple patronage and extralegal competition in exacerbating social tensions. The elections of June 1999 revealed quite clearly that the appeal of even a moderatelyconservative

Islamism, defined, for example, by the ambition to apply Islamic law to the Muslim populace, has declined since the 1950s. Only about 16% of the vote went to parties advocating programs of this sort, as opposed to more than 40% in 1955. At the same time, however, most other social indicators suggest that the country's Muslim majority is considerably more conscientious about the conduct of confessional duties than it was a generation or two ago. This suggests that it is not piety or Islamization that presents a destabilizing challenge in today's Indonesia, but a breakdown of governance exacerbated by elite factionalism and the willingness of some national and local elites to take advantage of ethnoreligious tensions for their own purposes. It is this larger political crisis that has allowed a small, conservative segment of the Muslim community to exercise an influence vastly out of proportion with its representation in society.

To appreciate how this state of affairs came to be, it is helpful to recall that in its last years the New Order was not the Soehartoist monolith that many foreign academics had long imagined. From 1990 on, the ruling party and the military were plagued by bitter factional divides between those eager to play the Islamist card and those (also mostly Muslim) inclined to support policies of a multireligious or secular nationalist sort. True to his habit of playing rival claimants to power against each other, President Soeharto took advantage of this rivalry, using the socalled green or "Islamist" generals to counter the influence of the "red" or secular nationalist generals, and preventing both groups from posing a serious challenge to his rule. In retrospect, it appears that the distinction between red and green generals had as much to do with simple rivalry for power and patronage as it did deep-seated differences of religion or ideology. Once the most prominent of the green generals, Lieutenant General Prabowo Subianto, was removed from office after May 1998, several of the leading red or nationalist generals established close ties with hardline Islamists like the Islamic Defenders Front (Front Pembela Islam).

Whatever the generals' precise rationale, the impact of these rivalries on the fortunes of the conservative Islamist community was striking. From 1994 on, Soeharto and his aides provided extensive funding and tactical support to what had previously been a largely ineffectual assortment of hardline Islamists. Rather than scaling up Indonesia's movement for a civic-pluralist Islam, Soeharto and his aides pushed the movement back, relying on Islamist hardliners for help in the effort. The pattern continued in the post-Soeharto period, with several members of the oldregime elite establishing close ties with paramilitary groups like the Islamic Defenders Front and, more recently, the Laskar Jihad.

From the beginning, the turn to radical Islamism inspired controversy in civilian political circles, including the ruling party, Golkar. Although for most of its history Golkar had been a broad alliance that included Christians and secular nationalists as well as pious Muslims, in 1994 President Soeharto awarded control of the party's powerful "strategy bureau" (Litbang Golkar) to hardliners who had close ties to the green faction in the armed forces and who shared their patrons' interest in exploiting conservative Islamism for their own ends. In collaboration with these commanders, the strategy bureau helped craft many of the fiercely anti-Chinese, anti-Christian, and anti-American propaganda tracts issued during the last months of Soeharto rule. Booklets like the "Conspiracy to Overthrow Soeharto" described an evil conspiracy in which the U.S., the Vatican, Israel's Mossad, abangan Javanese (i.e. nominal Muslims), and Chinese Indonesians engineered the 1997-1998 financial crisis so as to drive Soeharto from power. Distributed in conservative Islamist circles just weeks prior to the riots of May 13-14, 1998, the book ended by calling for enemies of Islam to be driven from Indonesia once and for all, hinting the Chinese might be especially deserving of such drastic treatment.

The man who directed the Litbang Golkar during this period retired temporarily from national politics after Soeharto ' s resignation. He resurfaced just a few months into the Habibie administration, however, when he was appointed to the Council of Indonesian Islamic Scholars (Majelis Ulama Indonesia). From there, he provided behind-the-scene support for the effort to unseat Abdurrahman Wahid. From early 2000 to today, he has acted as a behind-the-scene mediator between the Council and paramilitary groupings like the Laskar Jihad. In early October 2001, as the United States threatened to launch strikes against Afghanistan, this same gentleman was one of the key figures behind the MUI appeal calling for jihad against the United States and a severing of diplomatic relations. All this shows that, although Soeharto is gone, the Islamist card is still being played as forcefully as ever.

UNCIVIL ISLAM

These examples show that a small but influential group of Muslim leaders have helped to provide legitimacy and tactical support for the activities of radical Islamist groupings, even though the majority of Muslims may have little sympathy for their actions. However much they might benefit from strategic patronage, however, it is important not to see groups like the Islamic Defenders Front or, especially, the Laskar Jihad as mere creations of an all-controlling elite. After all, a key feature of the post-Soeharto period is that there is no all-powerful party or political leadership comparable to that of the Soeharto regime. Rather than diminishing trawling expeditions into the Islamist community like those begun in the late Soeharto period, however, the weakening and fractionalization of state power appears to have increased their incidence. It is also important to recognize that, however small their representation in Muslim society, groups like the Laskar Jihad and Majelis Mujahidin are heirs to a tradition of radical politics and religion in the Muslim community that, although suppressed in the first years of the Soeharto era, has always operated on the fringe of Indonesian society. Founded in August 2000 with the aim of struggling for the implementation of Islamic law, the Indonesian Mujahidin Council (Majelis Mujahidin Indonesia) includes among its senior leadership figures earlier associated with the Darul Islam, a movement that declared an Islamic state and then did battle with the forces of the republic from 1948-1962. The movement's spiritual leader, Abu Bakar Ba'asyir-a man whom Malaysian and Philippines intelligence have recently claimed is the leader of the Jemaah Islamiyah, which these intelligence services claim has ties with the al Qaeda-served prison time in the late 1970s for his opposition to Soeharto politics and the Pancasila. When, in the mid-1990s, hardline Islamists in groups like KISDI and the Dewan Dakwah Islamiyah Indonesia reconciled with President Soeharto and joined him in attacking the democracy movement, Ba' asyir and his associated remained unreconstructed critics of Soeharto and the armed forces. This legacy explains in part why Ba' asyir and the Majelis Mujahidin Indonesia have not enjoyed the cordial reception some green officers in the armed forces have offered other neofundamentalist groupings.

The Laskar Jihad is one of the radical Islamist organizations long thought to enjoy the patronage of a small but significant faction of the armed forces. The Laskar Jihad grew out of a conservative religious movement founded in the early 1990s by a (now) 40-year-old Arab Indonesian, Jafar Umar Thalib. Jafar identifies his followers as "Salafy," a reference to a long-established movement in Islam, often associated with Saudi Wahhabism, that aims to model profession of the faith on the example of the first generation of followers of the Prophet. However, in the form promoted by Jafar, the movement is best understood as neofundamentalist or "neo-Salafy," because it emphasizes ultraconservative concerns not associated with earlier variants of Salafism, not least of those practiced in Saudi Arabia. One such emphasis is the firm belief that the United States and Israel are leading a world-wide conspiracy to destroy Islam.

Jafar Umar Thalib began his career studying in a conservative modernist religious school in Bangil, East Java in 1981. Unhappy with the apolitical nature of his instruction, he soon traveled to Jakarta to study at the Saudi-sponsored Institute for Islamic and Arabic Studies. In the capital, Jafar became active in student groups opposed to the secular nationalis t policies of the Soeharto regime. Awarded a scholarship by the conservative Indonesian Council for Islamic Predication (DDII), Jafar traveled in 1986 to Saudi Arabia for further religious study. Again impatient with the apolitical nature of his lessons, he left for Afghanistan in 1987 under the auspices of the Saudi-sponsored Muslim World League. In Afghanistan, he met briefly with Osama bin Laden, but opted to join with a faction of the mujahidin with ties to the Saudis rather than Osama. In 1989, Jafar returned to Indonesia, accepting a teaching post at a conservative Islamic school in Salatiga, Central Java. Eager to make a name for himself, in 1994 he founded a religious school twelve miles north of the city of Yogyakarta in south-central Java.

From the beginning Jafar's proselytization was distinctive in that it was primarily directed not at the Muslim community as a whole, but at university students in the exact sciences and professions. Students with these backgrounds, Jafar explained to me in August 2001, appreciate the "precision" of Islamic law. In this respect they differ from students in the social sciences and humanities, whose studies, Jafar observed, leave them "only more confused."

From the beginning of his career, Jafar's proselytization efforts were also distinctive in the way in which they combined old predication techniques, like the use of public rallies, with new technologies, such as the internet and electronic publishing. In sermons whose fiery cadences and emotionalism violate almost everything Western scholars associate with Javanese self-expression, Jafar hammers away at his themes of the failures of secular nationalism, the perfidy of infidels (especially Christians), and, most important, the need for Muslims to wage jihad. Jihad is required, Jafar emphasizes, so as to cleanse society of un-Islamic influences and to bring God's law into daily life. It is also needed to insure that unbelievers understand that their proper status in society must be that of protected minorities (*dhimmi*). A concept from classical Islamic politics, *dhimmi*-hood stipulates that non-Muslims not be allowed to exercise authority over Muslims. Unlike most of the Indonesian Muslim leadership, Jafar makes clear that he believes that the equal citizenship sanctioned by the Indonesian constitution is utterly antithetical to Islam.

Recently some Indonesian analysts have speculated that the Laskar Jihad may have ties to bin Laden's al Qaeda. In interviews with journalists, Jafar has admitted that he has been visited several times by al Qaeda representatives, as recently, even, as May of 2001. Jafar denies reports, however, that al Qaeda fighters have recently traveled to Maluku to join the battle against Christians. He and his spokespersons were outraged when, in late September, Al Chaider, a prominent militant from a more moderate wing of another radical organization, the Darul Islam, claimed that bin Laden agents had supplied the Laskar with $240,000 and several dozen Arab fighters. Laskar officials issued an immediate and threatening denial.

The issue of al Qaeda links did not end there, however. In late fall, 2001, Western journalists traveling in Sulawesi reported seeing Afghan and Arab fighters. On December 12, 2001, Indonesia's intelligence chief, Lt. General Abdullah Hendropriyono confirmed these reports, commenting that A1-Qaeda had established a training camp in Indonesia and was assisting jihad fighters in Maluku and Central Sulawesi. The next day the minister of defense, Matori Abdul Djalil, publicly announced that he had "full confidençe" in the validity of Hendropriyono's comments. Court documents provided to Indonesian authorities, and related to the arrest in November of A1-Qaeda agents in Spain, also seemed to confirm the allegations. The documents included photographs and written reports of what were said to be A1-Qaeda camps in Indonesia.

Furious at Hendropriyono's charges, conservative Muslims, including the secretary of the Indonesian Council of Scholars (the same man who had helped coordinate the Council's call for jihad against the U.S.), accused Hendropriyono of being "one sided" and doing the bidding of the United States in making these accusations. No doubt Hendropriyono and Matori had hoped that their appeals might rally sentiment among the military, police, and political elite for action against radical Islamic groups. The outcome of the effort provides a revealing insight into the state of opinion among the security and political elite. With the exception of Matori, virtually no one backed up Hendropriyono's remarks. Faced with fierce criticism and little elite support, Hendropriyono backed away from his charge three days after first making it. He claimed that he had been "misunderstood," and insisted he had never said al Qaeda had a cell in Indonesia or that the Laskar Jihad was linked to it. His formal retraction was given prominent billing on the lead page of the Laskar Jihad's web site.

Although his lieutenants expressed enthusiasm for Osama bin Laden in several interviews they gave in 2000, since September 11,2001 Jafar has gone to great lengths to condemn the radical leader. The grounds on which he has done so, however, are revealing. Where Jafar and his followers have taken greatest exception with bin Laden is, not on the question of the mass killing of innocents in the United States, but on bin Laden's opposition to Saudi Arabia. For Jafar, bin Laden's opposition to a state that enforces Islamic law marks him as a "Khawarij" rebel. The phrase refers to the "exiters" who dissented from the followers of Ali at the end of the seventh century C.E. and promoted what has come to be regarded as a rebellious and ultra-egalitarian Islam unacceptable to the Sunni mainstream.

Whatever his Middle Eastern connections, it is clear that there are sound political reasons for Jafar to repudiate al Qaeda. Since its establishment in early 2000, the Laskar Jihad has been vitally dependent on domestic backers. Jafar is an astute politician and in private conversations has made clear that he is keenly aware that, without this assistance, he would not have been able to catapult his once-marginal organization onto the national stage. A former field commander of the Laskar Jihad, whom I interviewed in August 2001 after he withdrew from the organization, provided a sense of just how some of this old regime support has been arranged. The commander explained that Jafar was approached in January 2000 by military retirees with the message that they approved of his plans to escalate the armed campaign against Christians in Maluku. These agents made clear that they were willing to support Jafar's Maluku campaign, not to punish Christians, but to undermine the reform government of Abdurrahman Wahid. Jakartan Muslim activists provided additional details on these elite linkages. They noted, for example, that a leading businessman with close ties to ex-president Soeharto in 1998 coordinated a vast flow of funds and arms to the jihad forces after February 2000.

Tactical support of this sort was what allowed the Laskar Jihad to brandish weapons in the capital in April 2000, and then travel across Java from Bogor to Surabaya without once encountering so much as a single challenge to their movements –despite the fact that the president, minister of defense, and governor of Maluku province had all appealed to security officials to stop the militia from traveling to Maluku. Notwithstanding these appeals, the militants made their way unimpeded across Java; at times, eyewitnesses report, they even received security escorts. In Surabaya, the fighters boarded stateowned ferries for Maluku. Upon their arrival in Maluku, the fighters were escorted into the city and provided with weapons. A similar tactical collaboration between factions of the political elite and radical Islamists has been evident in some of the "anti-vice" campaigns launched by hardline Islamists since 1999. In Surakarta in August 2001, a former leader of a hardline group who had grown disenchanted with the campaign when it targeted democracy activists told me, "The whole strategy to use the Islamists to attack places of immorality and the democracy movement wasn't something simply tolerated by security officials. It was designed by district officials in a series of meetings I attended during early 2001. The meetings involved the military, Golkar officials, and members of the PPP [the Islamic party]. The campaign's purpose was to mobilize conservative Islamists and destroy the last remnants of support for Abdurrahman Wahid and the democracy movement."

CONCLUSION

One could multiply these examples, but they all provide us with insights into the question posed at the beginning of this report, as to how radical groupings with a relatively small social base have managed to loom so large in recent months. The answer recalls an insight into transitions from authoritarian rule offered by the California political sociologist, Peter Evans.

Evans has observed that for a transition to succeed it is not enough that there be a democratic majority or vibrant civil society. For a transition to move forward, civil and democratic precedents in society have to be "scaled up" into governmental institutions capable of defending freedoms and promoting democratic habits in state and society alike. It is this type of democratic synergy that has proved so elusive in post-Soeharto Indonesia. Rather than building on already available resources in the Muslim community for democracy and pluralism, certain leaders have helped to give paramilitary extremists an influence vastly out of proportion with their numbers in society.

However, the contest for the hearts and minds of Indonesian Muslims is far from over. The majority of Indonesian Muslims are moderate; many support democracy and look with sympathy to the West. Despite the confusion in their leadership, a clear majority among Muslims are also uneasy with the jihadi violence in Maluku and yearn for a politics that is moderate and inclusive. The U.S. campaign against al Qaeda may yet give the conservatives additional ammunition to use against their moderate rivals, particularly if the United States extends its campaign into Iraq. Short of such drastic measures, however, the impact of the American-led effort need not be fatal.

Ultimately, however, the question of whether the tide of sectarian violence can be turned will depend on the efforts of Megawati and the mainstream Muslim leadership, as well as moderate elements in the armed forces. After the divide-and-conquer chaos of the Soeharto era, it is too early to expect a deep consensus among national and regional elites on the terms for citizenship and nation. But a working agreement to stop the violence and curb those leaders exploiting crude ethnoreligious hatreds seems still possible. Only through the forging of a new working consensus of this sort can Indonesia be pulled back from the political and economic abyss it now faces. In these days of somber developments, the good news is that there are signs that, motivated by the mixture of love of country and devotion to the truest ideals of their religion, some in the Muslim community are yet determined to make just such an effort.

Discussion

Joel Kuipers, The George Washington University: I'm intrigued by the comments about the association between literalist interpretations of Islam and political radicalism of different kinds. Those are two different ideas but they do seem to be associated in various contexts and one of my questions is, what is the association that you see between these two ideas, and is it always the case in Indonesia; and second, do literalist interpretations of Islam in Indonesia always signal a more Middle Eastern orientation or are there specifically literalistic interpretations of Islam that challenge more Middle Eastern approaches?

Azra: What we refer to as radical groups should not be understood as monolithic. In fact they have different understandings as far as politics is concerned, for instance the Hizb al-Tahrir has a very literal understanding at the theological level and the literal understanding has been translated into political fields also. As I mentioned in my paper, the Hizb al-Tahrir for instance, aims at establishing the caliphate, because according to their understanding of Islam, the caliphate is the most appropriate and the most suitable political system for Muslims. Because of their literal understanding of Islam, they consider it obligatory for Muslims to establish an Islamic state in the form of the caliphate or *khilafah*. But other groups like the Laskar Jihad for instance, do not have a clear agenda for establishing particular Islamic political entities like the caliphate. In fact, certain forms of Islamic political entities are almost absent, in the discourse of Laskar Jihad. [Thus, radical groups are not always literalists.]

Of course they are insistent on the implementation of the *shariah* [Islamic law]. So there are a lot of different opinions about the Islamic state. But other more Salafis, or let's say more radical groups like the *Kharijites* I mentioned in my paper, also have a very distinctive political view, for example, that it is obligatory for Muslims to establish an Islamic state based on a particular *ayat*, a particular verse of the Koran that states "*mahukmah ilallah,*" there is no law, there is no state, except the state that is based on the injunction of God himself. Therefore, they consider that Muslims who oppose the establishment of the Islamic state, those who follow laws that have not originated from God, are included amongst the unbelievers. This is the most radical interpretation of the literal understanding of Islam when translated it into political views.

Woodward: I'd like to pick up on those things. The distinction between neo-*kharijites* and people who are *salafis* is extremely important. The *Kharijite* movement dates back to the first centuries of Islam. *Kharijites* maintain that anyone who does not accept their understanding of Islam is called a *munafik* or a hypocrite, meaning someone who pretends to be a Muslim but who is working for the destruction of Islam. Now simply because someone is a *salafi* does not mean that he should fall into that category. Muhammadiyah is a very good example of an organization that has this very narrow and strict understanding of Islamic morality and conduct but does not fall into this category of renouncing everyone else as worse than unbelievers. The other thing is that the politicization of Islam is not restricted to people who hold this narrow legalistic *salafi* view. My favorite example of that is a group that did not get very many votes in the last election. It is called the Peace and Love Party. The Peace and Love Party is the political branch of the *Nakshabandhi* Sufi order. They have a very Islamist, although Sufi-Islamist, perspective on Indonesia's problems: If everyone would say enough prayers, the problem would go away. The Indonesian or Arabic term here is *doa*, or supplication. That is also the politicization of Islam, but the politicization of a very different kind of Islam.

Walter Engelen, Maluku Watch Network: Do you think there is a correlation between state-supported Islam and radicalism? In the last years of Soeharto he created ICMI (Association of Indonesian Muslim Intellectuals), which was led by Habibie. It [radicalism] started then. Since 1945-1967 only two churches were burned but from 1967-1998, 400 churches were burned. Maluku is basically the latest in this process of radicalism. Also, from the end of the 1980s Muslim society has become more conservative. Muslim scholars get more funds from the government than the Christians. So my question is, do you think it is really a process?

Hefner: I think if we look at the results of the national elections; if we look at the leadership of organizations like the Nahdlatul Ulama and Muhammadiyah; and if we look at the IAIN and other major Muslim educational institutions, it becomes very difficult to support the thesis that the Muslim community as a whole in Indonesia has become more conservative. Nor has it become necessarily more liberal or civil-democratic, the term I prefer, although that is the general process. What has happened instead is that there has been a great pluralization of Islam in society. There has been a great Islamic resurgence but the fact that there has been an Islamic resurgence should never be equated with a trend towards a more conservative understanding of Islam.

The formation of ICMI was all part of an effort, on the part of President Soeharto and several others, to respond to what they saw as this great wave of Islamic resurgence sweeping across Indonesia and to use it for their own ends. They never quite succeeded in that regard. ICMI, at least a small but a significant, morally significant and intellectually significant wing of it, continues to display a considerable amount of independence, not least of all through the work of Moeslim Abdurrahman here or Nurcholish Madjid.

So when we get to the question of Maluku, I think it's best to see the crisis of Maluku not as something that's the result of a general trend of conservative Islamization in society, but a breakdown in governance. And a radical mobilization, both at the local level and at the national level, among rival political elites who respond to the vacuum of power left in the aftermath of Soeharto's departure. I end by just making this observation, because we are in the United States and perhaps there has been much more discussion of the violence in Maluku as it has been conducted by Muslims. We have to remember however, that at the beginning of the Maluku conflict, the side, if we want to use that phrase, that suffered most, that experienced the most casualties, was the Muslim side. And there were Christian Jihadis or Christian holy war fighters, who really were just like some of the hard-line Islamist groups, who were using religion as a cloak to advance political, economic in some instances, as well as religious interests. They engaged in violence such as that we saw in North Halmahera at the end of 1999; violence that was truly horrific, and when publicized in the media, needless to say, put wind in the sails of groups like the Laskar Jihad, who were able to assert that this required a strong response from Muslim organizations since the government was not acting.

Donald Emmerson, Stanford University: Recasting the previous proceedings in abstract form, my question is: what things are broken and what sort of fixability and priorities do you see here? I'm not suggesting that you select one and reject the others; I'm interested in the relative order of priority which of course has policy implications.

Here are some candidate propositions. Number one, what's broken is the theology; that is to say there is an urgent need for theological reform with regard to the content and interpretation of Islam. Number two, Islam is not broken, it's a matter of sociology. (This might be termed, the Hefner hypothesis.) It's a question of scaling up, of trying to encourage voluntarism and associational activity at the local level into larger forms, institutions that can maintain stability and accountability. Three, it's a matter of intelligence. Now none of you has said this, but one possible interpretation is you don't need to fix society, you don't need to fix Islam, you need to fix a couple of individuals by arresting them. That is to say, it is a matter of security and everything else is pretty much okay. Number four, it's a matter of governance: unless you have a functioning democracy these problems are only going to get worse. Fifth and last, is a thesis that hasn't been mentioned at all, which is the economic explanation. As long as you have 13% shrinkage in the GDP as you did in 1998, that should be the focus of any effort to redress the situation.

Again I'm asking for relative priority.

Azra: I think the most important priority now is to restore the authority of the government, to strengthen the government. Because much of the problem, including the ethno-religious conflict that has been mentioned, originated from the failure of the government to enforce law and order. So we see conflict, the violence, not only takes place in Maluku, but also for instance in Borneo and Kalimantan, not only between Muslims and Christians but also among Muslims themselves.

We know that the violence in Kalimantan for instance, involves the Madurese who are Muslims, and the Malays as well as the Dayaks who are also Muslims. So I think one of the most important keys is to restore the government authority as well as the police because I think one of the problems in Indonesia today is the demoralization of the police force. We know the military, the armed forces, and the police have been a target of reforms, a target of *reformasi* because both of them have been held responsible for corruption, misgovernment, KKN (corruption, collusion and nepotism), and all ills in Indonesian society during Soeharto's time. So I think this is one of the most important priorities.

The second priority is the acceleration of the democratization process. Acceleration of the democratization process because we have to admit that Indonesia as a whole has very little experience in democracy. Many people, including of course young people, have a very obscure idea of the ideals and practice of democracy. I think in this regard Muslim organizations like Muhammadiyah and NU, as well as education institutions like mine, the Institution for Islamic Studies, can make a contribution on this. For instance, a civic education program for students is important because today many people including of course students have some kind of political disorientation because they have a very obscure idea of democracy.

The third priority is the economic recovery. Two years ago, I attended a democracy forum in the U.S.. In that forum one of the most important conclusions was that in order for a state or country in transition to be more democratic there are at least three pillars that should be established. The first one is strong government. Strong government does not necessarily mean an oppressive government. Strong government is a government that is able to protect democratic rights of its citizens. The second is a strong economy and the third is a strong civil society. Again one of the most important priorities is to restore civil society in Indonesia. In the last three years many civil society organizations including NU and Muhammadiyah have had some kind of disorientation. NU has been pulled into political crisis especially during the presidency of Abdurrahman Wahid. And of course Muhammadiyah has been pulled into Amien Rais' political game. Now we have to restore their former status.

Hefner: My own position is not that sociology and local society or the synergy between state and society is all that there is. Every transition from authoritarian rule and every culture and civilization's democratization requires that there be a scaling up of intellectual organizations as well as society organizations. What John Locke did was itself a vital part of providing a kind of intellectual legitimacy for a Christian embrace of the English system of the time. We take that for granted and we no longer perhaps need John Locke or whoever you prefer as the intellectual legitimator of the idea of democracy and human rights. But every civilization has to grapple with the terms or the grounds for providing a legitimating rationale for equality and tolerance. And in this instance, that task of providing just those intellectual terms is a vital ingredient of the Muslim tradition. And it means that some of the framework for scaling up intellectually the grounds for democratization in a Muslim society anywhere (I'm not speaking here with any specific reference to Indonesia), may vary.

As I said in the forum I would expect for an Islamic democracy not to be so much liberal in the classic early twentieth century civil democratic sense but to have more of a "communitarian" sense. Emphasizing, as American democracy did in de Toqueville's days, that a concern for sustaining certain shared public values must also be a key part of democracy. We in the West, or at least in the post 1960s West, have pulled back a bit from that commitment but there is an effort still on the part of some people to do that in the West. But in any case we shouldn't be surprised in Indonesia if the emphasis is on a kind of "communitarian" response, to the idea that morals and public ethics must be a subject of public political concern. Those issues may loom large in the intellectual scaling up of Muslim democratic tradition and I think that is what we are seeing in Indonesia and it is also what we are seeing attempted on the part of leadership in Iran.

So in response to your question the options you present are not mutually exclusive. The critical thing is not democratization of Islam but the transition from authoritarianism to the creation of a healthy civil democratic synergy between state and society. For that to take place it requires good governance and probably also the arrest of a few people. And the fact that a few of those people have not been arrested provides one of the clearest indications that the government itself does not yet have the consensus that is required to take those actions. And that is one of the most serious problems in Indonesia today because it provides the kind of opportunity and imbalance that I described in my paper, an imbalance where in reality a small portion of the Muslim community where (a very un-Islamic metaphor) the tail is able to wag the dog. (Maaf) Sorry. As to U.S. policy and what this means I think that democratization is always enduringly and necessarily incremental. You take advantage of every opportunity you can. You don't think that simply the establishment of formal elections is the only way. So for U.S. policy what this means, I would hope, we intervene at every point where we can have effective leverage, leverage that creates a kind of positive synergy between state and civil society that Indonesia so desperately requires. That may mean some kind of revisitation of relations between the U.S. and the armed forces but I'm going to defer on that to other persons and another moment.

Woodward: It is the case that domestication of democracy and the articulation of democratic values within an Islamic framework is a necessary condition for a successful democratic transition. I think that work has already largely been accomplished in the writings of people like Gus Dur, Nurcholish Madjid, and a whole host of the other younger Muslim intellectuals. That being said, I think the intellectual foundation is there. I think the problem is that Indonesia is caught in an enormous paradox that two things are required-economic recovery and political stability. As I see it the paradox is we are not going to have economic recovery until we have political stability and we are not going to have political stability until we have economic recovery. So in terms of policy implications it is not that there has to be an emphasis on civil society and democratic institutions, but there has got to be very real and serious attention paid to reviving the economy and dramatically improving the living status of all those people who have suffered so much during the last few years.

A person from the Poso Watch Network: A former Kuwait minister stated that a small group of radicals hijacked Kuwaiti policy. It is pretty much what is happening in Indonesia now. In fact the demise of the great moderate President Wahid was created by the strategy of small groups. My question is if these groups are so insignificant when do you think Indonesia can start addressing the refugee problem? Many of the non-Muslim refugees fled after all of the jihad movements. So, when is Indonesia likely to address the refugee question?

Hefner: Unfortunately the answer to that very important and urgent question will depend upon the resolution of certain problems of governance and in particular the re-establishment of a nationally coordinated system of local government across the whole of Eastern Indonesia. You don't have that now. Indeed, as we saw most dramatically illustrated in the North Maluku and Halmahera regions, you have still fierce rivalries between different elite coalitions, making the kinds of trolling expeditions that I referred to very briefly in my paper: expeditions into society exploiting ethno-religious divisions to recruit followers. Let us remember that much of the violence in North Maluku was in its inception not Christian versus Muslim, but a certain segment of the Muslim community against a Christian –Muslim coalition. And it was only as a result of great efforts of certain hard-liners on both sides that it crystallized into a clear Christian-Muslim conflict. So the answer to the question goes back once again to the resolution of the crisis of government and the recreation of that vital synergy that you need between state and society. And you need to give up on this romantic 1990s idea that all you need to make democracy work is a strong civil society. For there to be a strong civil society you need an effective government as well.

Azra: I think some progress has been achieved by the Indonesian government in the last several weeks. In the case of violence in Poso, Central Sulawesi for instance, the conflicting parties have achieved the Malino agreement in South Sulawesi. All of the conflicting parties meet with some government ministers and they achieved some ways to resolve the conflict and violence in Central Sulawesi. Of course the resolution of such conflict not only in Poso but in Maluku needs several faces. The most important thing is to stop violence in a decisive manner among conflicting parties. The second is the social and economic rehabilitation of the area, because one of the most important sources of the conflict is economic competition between the local Christians or local Muslims with the immigrants who are very aggressive in economic enterprises. That is the case in Maluku. I think the conflict environment originated from economic and political reasons: economic competition between local Christians and Buginese or Makassar people who happen to be Muslim. And of course the second reason is a political struggle between the rising Muslim population contesting the domination of the Christian political position in Maluku. So the root causes of the conflict are mainly economic and political, and religion came only later as the rallying point for the conflicting parties to face each other. Important steps that can give us hope have been taken by the government. Last week the conflicting parties in Ambon have been brought also by the government to the negotiating table, also in Malino, to resolve the Maluku and Ambon violence. Alasdair Bowie, The George Washington

University: In the forward to Bob Hefner's well-read book *Civil Islam* he refers to his discomfort about addressing a gathering of NU youths about events that occurred many decades before. Those events in 1965-66 involved the active participation of Muslim groups in the widespread violence following the coup attempt. The reason Bob Hefner was anxious was because he thought he was going to be raked over the coals by these active NU youth for identifying the role of Muslims in that violence. It turned out to be quite the contrary. In fact these youths were very much interested in his work in exposing the fact that Islamic groups were manipulated and used in this process of perpetuating widespread violence. My question is, is it the case today that there is growing outrage among NU youth or other so called mainstream Islamic groups about the fact that Indonesian Islam is being characterized in radical terms, or is it going to take us several decades more before we can look back on that and see outrage emerge?

Hefner: The evidence is that many in the leadership of the Muslim community and indeed in all of the mainstream leaders are deeply upset and concerned about the portrayal of Islam in the Western media, but not merely blaming the Western media for that, but recognizing that the rise of groups like Front Pembela Islam and the Laskar Jihad has tarnished not only the reputation but the hard-fought achievements of the Muslim community and leadership from the late 1980s to today. There is that concern. This concern was illustrated by a meeting of NU leaders which took place in early December, in which they resolved they wanted to make a protracted effort to take action against Islamic radicals in part to repair this tarnished image. Now this much said at the elite level I would have to say that I have been greatly saddened to see how effective the propaganda of the hard-liners has been in convincing not merely a handful of the people but a significant percentage of the Muslim community and perhaps, most importantly, a significant percentage of the rank and file of the Muhammadiyah that indeed there is a Christian conspiracy at the very least within Indonesia and perhaps with international support; some would say with direct international support from the United States. This impression has filtered out into the community and I have been startled in Yogyakarta and Solo to find very ordinary Muslims, moderate people, who state in a very matter of fact way that the crisis in Maluku was provoked by Christians and the government did nothing. "Of course Wahid sympathized with them and so of course we had to take action." This is saddening. While it is a serious setback for the Muslim community we should not exaggerate it. It again reflects a failure of the government to defend ordinary citizens. Christians and Muslims, both sides have suffered horrendous losses. Given the failure of the government to address what is clearly a pressing need and in these circumstances of economic crisis, we shouldn't be surprised that conspiracy stories of these sorts begin to find some credibility. To respond to your question in brief, I don't think it is going to take decades but it is going to take a resolution of what remains the most vexing crisis in Indonesia, which is not a crisis in the Muslim community, but a crisis in governance that is having an impact on an effectively mobilized and well financed wing of the Muslim community.

THE POLITICS OF ISLAM IN A DEMOCRATIZING INDONESIA

Ulil Abshar Abdalla: My focus in this session is the role of Islam in consolidating democracy in Indonesia, keeping in mind that the challenge of consolidating democracy in Indonesia should be directed at three main areas: the economy, the political and the social environments. Keeping this in mind I will confine my presentation to how Islam can play a role in consolidating political democracy in Indonesia.

The most challenging role to be played by Islam is how to give legitimacy to democracy within the theological framework of Islam. I strongly believe democracy in Indonesia will not be strengthened or take a strong root without strong support from the Islamic society. Thus I believe the interpretational effort to Islamic teaching is one of the big challenges to be accomplished by Muslim intellectuals.

In my work in the field I have seen these efforts by Muslim intellectuals especially in my organization, NU. I work for the Department of Research and Human Research Development of NU and I've been working for years promoting modern notions of human rights, democracy and gender equality from an Islamic theological perspective. Some of the work I've done is related to promoting the ideas of pluralism and democracy among the traditional Islamic leaders. As you know most members of NU are based in villages and the leadership is run by traditional Muslim leaders or *kyai*. The character of NU society is based on the patron-client relationship in the sense that the leadership plays a very important role in shaping the minds of their followers. This is how we can explain how the former chairman of NU, President Wahid, played a very important role in strengthening the democratic position and mentality within the NU membership.

In Jakarta my colleagues and I organize many courses and *halaika*, religious circles, devoted to introducing modern notions of democracy and human rights within an Islamic theological framework. It is interesting that this effort is accepted by the NU leadership and the discussion about democracy, human rights and the like is very vibrant among the NU leadership. One of the most important issues is gender equality. My colleagues in NU provide a new interpretation to classical Islamic teaching about the role of women in society within a new gender framework. Two months ago one of the most important women's organizations in Jakarta launched a book that revises and reinterprets the classical books on the role of women in Islam. They call it *Kitab Kuning*, Yellow Book, and it is very popular in Muslim society. This book is on the role of women in Islam. Of course the content of the book is very conservative but it is very influential among the Muslim society in Indonesia. Our work is to provide a new interpretation on the role of women in Islam according to the new issue of gender equality. In my organization we are working to build a network of liberal Islam. This is a tricky and controversial term but a liberal interpretation of Islam is very crucial and instrumental in strengthening the ideas of democracy within Muslim society. I'm running a weekly talk show in Jakarta, which is broadcasted to 20 private stations across the country and is also syndicated and published in nearly 15 publications around the country. One example of our work a weekly column in *Jawa Pos*, among the most popular dailies in Eastern Indonesia. The column discusses the tendency among Muslim society towards piousness but at the same time a tendency towards exclusionism. We call it more pious but less tolerant. This is one issue that we have written about that is causing controversy among Muslims in Jakarta. Another publication we have is a journal called *Afkar*. The latest edition is on the education of pluralist Islam, an issue that is very hotly discussed among Muslim intellectuals. There is a tendency to believe that Muslim education has recently been hijacked by radical groups to serve a very narrowminded Islam that is very exclusive and spewing hatred towards other groups. But as these examples prove that is just not true.

A key point I would like to emphasize is that interpretation of Islam is playing a very important role in strengthening democracy amongst Muslims. Of course there are many factors that are needed for recovery in Indonesia, such as the economy and the political situation. But I think the most challenging factors are related to the interpretation of Islam. The battle now within the Muslim society is the battle of mind and interpretation. The issue of pluralism is not an issue of Muslim society against the society outside. Pluralism is an issue within the Muslim society. It is an issue of how Muslims win the minds and hearts of the people in the direction of a more pluralist Islam. I think the hope of pluralist Islam, moderate Islam in my country is very high. In this sense I do believe that due to the economic crisis there are emerging a growing number of radical groups in the country. I believe this is just a temporary situation. The radical groups are not rooted in the minds of society. The orientation of mainstream Muslims is still towards pluralistic Islam. With a strong civilian government and with law enforcement I believe in the near future these radical groups could be moderated.

I believe there is room for liberal, moderate and radical groups. I do not believe the door of dialogue is shut. The door is still open. I agree with Bob Hefner's presentation earlier that figures like Jafar Umar Thalib, the chairman of Laskar Jihad, or Habib Riziq, chairman of the Islamic Defense Group (FPI) are not as radical as people think. I met with Jafar Umar Thalib a few weeks ago at a panel presentation and it was surprising that he spoke very eloquently about the urgency of dialogue among Christians and Muslims including quoting some Koranic verses about the imperative of these dialogues, referring to the same verses that are often quoted by Nurcholish Madjid and Abdurrahman Wahid. It is curious that a person perceived as a symbol of hatred against

Christians in Ambon and Poso is talking very eloquently about dialogue. Of course we could say that this is not a genuine position or standpoint of people like Jafar Umar Thalib. But my conviction is that he is just responding to the temporary situation. The very existence of Laskar Jihad does not signal a permanent situation within the Muslim society. It is just a temporary situation. The argument of figures like Jafar Umar Thalib is that Muslims in Maluku and Poso were under attack by the Christians. As long as Muslims are under attack we have an obligation according to our religion to defend their rights.

These are the arguments. Of course we can dispute whether the Muslims are really under attack. But I think this argument is completely understandable. The ideology of jihad is not a genuine ideology for this group. It is only a temporary notion or ideology for this group to cope with a temporary situation. It is very surprising that groups like Laskar Jihad and *Front Pembela Islam* (FPI) share the idea of the nation state of Indonesia. In all my frequent encounters with these groups I didn't find any notion of their desire for an Islamic state in Indonesia. They agree that Indonesia is a country for all. The only thing that they emphasis is Muslims as the majority have rights to be treated as such. They perceive the Muslim majority as having been treated unfairly during the New Order regime. So what they demand is only to give the Muslims their rights as the majority people. Part of the right they demand is the implementation of Islamic law (*shariah*). I think this issue is debatable and there is room for debate on this issue. Again and again the people in Laskar Jihad and FPI say Islamic *shariah* is an obligation for Muslims but that there is room for debate on the extent to which Islamic *shariah* should be implemented in Indonesia. I do not think the situation is as gloomy as people think outside Indonesia. I believe this group is just a product of a temporary situation. It is not permanent. With greater freedom and strong democratic institutions I believe this group will wither away sooner or later.

Lies Marcoes Natsir: In my opinion, talking about women in Islam is more than relevant not only because Islam is a religion with very significant detail in formulating and prescribing relations between men and women, the social positions of men and women, but also because in a society like Indonesia that considers religion an essential component of life, a woman's position in Islam can be used as a barometer of the Islamic value of democracy.

In the western media Islam is often stereotyped as a repressive and oppressive religion. To prove this point, sometimes women's conditions in certain situations under so-called Islamic rule are described without any understanding of the context in which the situation is happening. Through the media we are often tainted with images, for instance, of women forced to wear the veil, the *hijab* or the *jalabah*, or *abayah*, or descriptions of restrictions of women in the public sphere. For us in Indonesia, this image is very strange. I'm not saying that women's situation in Indonesia is better than in other Islamic countries. But like other women in Islamic countries, it might also be said of women in the Hindu religion, in India, or women in Buddhist China, Vietnam or Thailand, or even a Catholic for instance in the Philippines or Ghana. The greatest problems for women in Indonesia are related to the lack of education, a lack of social and economic resources and a lack of political power. These problems arise in Indonesia for several reasons including a male bias in the interpretation of religion that is the source of our ideas on the role of men and women.

I wish to share with you what Muslim women are doing in Indonesia in the development of the awareness and public discourse about women's rights and what precisely the issues are that are relevant and exist in Indonesia today. For more than ten years, I have been working for an NGO called P3M, the Indonesian Society for *Pesantren* and Community Development. As Pak Azyumardi already mentioned a *pesantren* is a traditional Islamic boarding school. There are more than 10,000 *pesantren* in Indonesia. Most of the *pesantren* are located in rural areas in Java and Madura where more than 70% of the entire Indonesian Muslim population lives. Normally a *pesantren* is led by a *kyai* but recently there are some *pesantren* led by an *ibu kyai*. An *ibu kyai* is the wife or the daughter of a *kyai*. In Indonesia, we consider the *pesantren* as the subculture of Islam. In the *pesantren* we find a unique cultural atmosphere created over long periods of interaction and interconnection between Islamic teachings, Javanese feudal and hierarchical systems, Hindu *ashram* educational systems as well as the traditions of agrarian society. As for the political and social organization, most of the Javanese *pesantren* are affiliated with NU. This is easy to understand because NU was established by a *kyai*, a traditional Islamic leader in the *pesantren* society. NU was therefore also established as a vehicle for political aspirations of the *kyai*.

Our main activities in the advocacy of women's rights in Islam include reproductive rights and political rights in both the domestic and public spheres. The advocacy of reproductive rights within Islam in Indonesia is contextually relevant not only because Indonesia has the highest incidence of maternal mortality in Asia but also because ninety percent of Indonesia's 200 million inhabitants are Muslim. So the ideas of the Islamic community and its leaders are particularly relevant when addressing a woman's well being. This is especially true today due to the increasing politicization of Islam and the fact that religious leaders play an increasing role in influencing government policies and programs. This is more or less the arena in which Islamic women activists have to play.

After ten years of raising the general awareness about Muslim women issues through workshops, seminars, and distributing books and publications, we began to wonder to what extent we had had an impact upon the dominant discourse regarding women's rule and the position in the *pesantren* as well as in the larger NU circle. We conducted several studies to determine the impact of our work. In my opinion the female leadership issues within Islam in Indonesia are relevant today because not only do we have a female president, but there are new developments related to female leadership within Islam. For instance, two weeks ago, the Muhammadiyah Congress in Bali came up with a very progressive decree that women could be elected into leadership positions. Normally women could only be elected as a wing of Muhammadiyah in Asia but now Muhammadiyah has decided that females could be elected as Muhammadiyah leaders.

If you look at the historical background of the issue of female leadership we see that the theological discussion concerning female political leadership in Indonesia developed after two women came to the political forefront. They were Mbak Tutut (Siti Hardiyanti Indra Rukmana) and Ibu Megawati. At the time, Tutut, the eldest daughter of Soeharto, was representing the ruling party, Golkar, while Megawati was representing the opposition party, PDI, and was supported by the masses of ordinary people. Before that the discussion concerning female leadership according to Islamic teaching in Indonesia was only held within the context of theological discussions. The issue of female leadership received serious attention also after NU held its national congress of ulama, *Munas Ulama* in Lombok in 1997. At this *Munas,* NU issued a very progressive *fatwa* declaring that there was no religious prohibition against women assuming the position of head of state. However, this progressive *fatwa* seemed to be nullified a year later by the Congress of Indonesian Ulema (KUI) in which NU also played a great role in addition to other Islamic organizations such as Muhammadiyah as well as some fundamentalist organizations. This KUI recommended that women should not be permitted to become head of state because according to the majority of the opinion in Islam, it's against Islamic teaching. What is more interesting is that before Megawati became part of the government as a vice president of Abdurrahman Wahid, the majority of Indonesian Islamic politicians, mostly men, flatly rejected the idea of a woman as head of state, but later they seemed to be of a different opinion. This became clear after one of the Muhammadiyah leaders encountered Megawati and declared that according to Muhammadiyah's views there is no restriction in Islam against women being leaders. This declaration was then followed by a statement made by several other Islamic organizations in *Al-Azhar* mosque in Jakarta in February 2001 which said that it is not prohibited within Islam to have a woman as head of state.

So what was the background for these contradictory *fatwa?* One may be struck by the significant role NU played in the political game relating to women's leadership. The context of the Lombok *fatwa* must have been linked to Golkar's hidden campaign to promote Tutut as the presidential candidate. At the time Gus Dur said Tutut would be the leader for the future. The KUI statement appears to have been related to inhibiting Megawati's progress in her presidential nomination whereas the *Al-Ashar* Mosque declaration was related to Indonesian political parties in their efforts to support Megawati and to undermine Abdurrahman Wahid's position as the president. From this it becomes clear that NU, Muhammadiyah and other Islamic political organizations created a case of political bargaining by providing religious support for the possibility of a woman head of state in one moment and withholding it in the next. Through their claim that they have legitimacy to talk about *fatwa,* they were capable for providing religious support either for or against the idea of a woman head of state. In conclusion I would like to say that the issue of female political leadership within Islam in an Indonesian context does not have much to do with religious judgments, the *halal* and *haram,* but rather male Islamic political interests. This shows us that as long as Muslim women have no power and legitimacy to talk about their position within Islam, they will remain in subordinate positions in society. They will remain an object of regulation.

I wish to discuss a few activities conducted by Islamic women to develop their rights. The older Islamic organizations that are most active in rural areas are affiliated with NU. Another organization is ICI, the women's organization affiliated with Muhammadiyah. ICI have organized a variety of religious activities but they have also set up a limited number of programs for women in development, mostly in the fields of education, health and smallscale finance. In the field of formal education however, ICI has established a relatively wide network of vocational education centers and claims to have a large number of members. *Fatayat* is regarded by NU as an organization for young Muslim women with an estimated 6 million members and seems to offer more progressive schemes and programs. Since 1997 *fatayat* has included in its traditional activities, like health and nutrition, the advocacy of women in empowerment issues and women's political participation. New women's organizations have also developed within the past few years such as *Forum Kajian Kitab Klasik Islam* that Ulil mentioned before, Forum for the Study for Classical Islamic Texts. This group was established in Jakarta in 1997 by a number of progressive men and women activists, Islamic and religious specialists as well as sociologists, anthropologists, gender-specialists and other professionals, attempting to formulate reinterpretation of the classical Islamic texts pertaining to the right and responsibility of men and women, through study group discussions.

The massive riots in Jakarta in May 1998 were followed by acts of sexual violence against women, in particular Chinese women. This development resulted in the establishment of the *Sutra Women's Organization,* to focus specifically on the issue of violence against women. *Sauda Puan Amal Hayati* is one of the women's Muslim organizations advocating women's rights within Islam and to reduce violence against women. The aim uniting all these new organizations is women empowerment and the advocacy of women's rights within Islam and within the context of Islamic teaching. This has come to include addressing a number of complex and sensitive issues such as abortion. Efforts have also been made to formulate less gender-bias and less discrimination in the interpretation of religion. This example illustrates the great differences that exist between the stereotype of women in Islam and the reality of many Islamic women in Indonesia today.

Greg Fealy: I want to talk largely about Indonesian and Islamic political parties and I speak here as a political historian and one who has done quite a bit of research on the 1950s when Indonesia had its first encounter with parliamentary democracy. This is a rather unfashionable area and indeed a lot of Indonesians tend to be dismissive or disdainful of this period of Indonesian history, but I think some interesting lessons can be learned about Indonesia's current experience with democracy. I will mention three brief conclusions that one might draw in comparing democracy, particularly the function of political parties now in Indonesia, to the 1950s. The first is that individuals are far more dominant now than they were in the 1950s. Megawati, Amien Rais, and Abdurrahman Wahid dominate their respective parties. Their ability to dictate terms to those parties has no parallel in the 1950s. There were important figures in the 1950s but they were not people who could bend an entire party to their will. There's something cultic and iconic in the status that those three have within their respective parties. The second element is the demise of ideology. This is not of course unique to Indonesia, but I think it's more graphically illustrated in Indonesia than in many other countries. Every major party in the 1950s had its ideology. Party conferences were dominated by very intense ideological debates. There was a lot of space in party publications given to discussion of ideological issues. We see very little of this in the 1990s.

The third factor is the far greater presence of "money politics", to coin the popular Indonesian term, the purchasing of positions and influence between parties, and also physical intimidation. To my knowledge, no 1950s political party had a paramilitary wing. Virtually every major Indonesian party today has a paramilitary wing, the membership of which can range from people who are very committed, well-trained cadre to people who are no better than thugs and semi-criminals. Unfortunately it tends to be more of the hooligan element which is evident in some of the larger parties such as the PDIP.

There was far less purchasing of positions in the 1950s than there is now.

I mention these things to give some sort of context in which we might see the performance of Indonesian Islamic political parties since the fall of Soeharto. Exactly how many Islamic political parties there are depends on how tightly you wish to define the term. There are parties that have Islam as their formal basis; you might call them formalist parties. There are also parties that are based on Pancasila, the quasisecular national ideology, but whose support base comes overwhelmingly from the Islamic community.

I'm going to concentrate on the five main Islamic political parties: The National Awakening Party of Abdurrahman Wahid, or PKB (Partai Kebangkitan Bangsa); the PPP or United Development Party led by the current vice president Hamzah Haz; Amien Rais's National Mandate Party or PAN; and the current justice minister, Yusril Ihza Mahendra, heading the fourth largest party, Bulan Bintang or Crescent and Star Party; and last is the Justice Party or Partai Keadilan. Of these, PKB, Gus Dur's party, got the largest vote in the 1999 elections, about 12.6%, the PPP 11.7%, PAN 7.4%, the Crescent Star Party 1.9% and PK, the Justice Party, 1.7%. So it's quite a substantial block of the vote.

I want to look at these five parties in terms of what we would expect them to be doing in a consolidating democracy. Of course political parties are a vital part of consolidating a democracy. I'm looking at a number of indicators to tell us whether the state of these Islamic parties is healthy or not, whether they're going to be able to contribute in a positive way to the democratization process. I have four indicators I would like to share. First is rising levels of branch activity and participation of members in party affairs. The second would be a systematic cadreization process taking place within these parties which would allow the most talented and committed of the members to rise to leadership positions. The third indicator would be improved internal communications and decisionmaking processes of party leaders informing

grassroots members of their policy positions and decisions, and the members giving their input to this process; a two-way communication between the party elite and the grassroots. A fourth indicator would be the development of well thought out and detailed policy platforms, if not ideological platforms. Unfortunately the answers to these indicators when looking at Islamic parties is they are doing rather poorly. In fact this is going to be a somewhat pessimistic presentation, at least looking at short-term factors.

On the first factor, branch level activity, a great many political parties are moribund at the branch level. These parties are showing indications of being only election parties. They gear up for the quinquinneal elections and in between times there is minimal branch activity. This means a small number of elite are able to control the affairs of the party.

The second element, of cadreization, is also not promising. Promotions and advancement are more often based upon access to money and patronage. You can be very bright, very hardworking but if you don't have a lot of money to buy support or a very powerful patron in the organization you are unlikely to go very far at all. The only exception to this is the Justice Party, the Partai Keadilan, which is a genuine cadre party. It has very rigorous rules which apply to advancement of people from within its ranks and it has some very impressive people at the top who are not wealthy and who have not pulled clientelist strings to get where they are.

Third, internal communications within the parties are very poor, there is little flow of paperwork, there is little use of electronic media to communicate decisions down to the grassroots. Indeed there is little interest in what grassroots opinion is among party leadership. If one looked at recent party congresses and national conferences, they have been very tightly staged, managed events creating very little substantive debate on key policy issues. The last element, well thought out policy platforms: very few parties had detailed policy platforms in the 1999 elections, and there has been very little work done in any of the parties since then to develop a sophisticated set of policies.

The Islamic political parties are ripe with clientelism, inclined towards populism and also shot through with corruption. We are not seeing Islamic political parties which are more cohesive, and which are more effective at aggregating, expressing and protecting community and national interests. The only party which might be an exception to this is the Justice Party but this is a very small party. It has seven seats in the parliament of 500 people.

I want to look at three particular issues with regard to these Islamic parties. First is their fragmentation, second is their leadership problems, and the third is their stance on ideology. The first, fragmentation: four of the five parties are beset with serious internal divisions. In the case of PKB, Gus Dur's party, there is now a breakaway party – not strictly speaking a breakaway party, it legally is PKB – led by the current defense minister Matori Abdul Djalil. And it is quite likely that Gus Dur's version of PKB would have to bear another name in the next election, a slightly altered name such as PKB-Struggle or something like that. But Matori's version will be the party that probably struggles in the polls. But in any case, that's quite a serious split within PKB. Perhaps the most serious split of all is within the PPP. Recently PPP, a reform PPP, P3 Reformasi, was formed by the most popular preacher in Indonesia, Zainuddin MZ, the nearest thing Indonesia has to a televangelist. He's a rather shallow political leader I suspect, but he's a very effective communicator. He is very effective at using the electronic media and has wide grassroots support across Indonesia in the Islamic community. So that poses very serious threat to the second most important party in the ruling coalition.

The Crescent Star Party, the Bulan Bintang Party of Yusril Ihza Mahendra, had a serious split in its congress in 2000. And I suspect there're more splits on the way. Yusril himself is both feared and loathed by many of the executive members and many branches in the party. But he maintains an iron grip over the functioning of the party. Last of all there's Amien Rais's PAN. We saw the defection of a number of so-called secular Muslim politicians and non-Muslim politicians a number of months ago, including Faisal Basri and Bara Hasibuan. There may well be more defections on the way as PAN comes to terms with just how Islamic or open it's going to be in its ideology.

The interesting thing in all these splits is that personalities feature more prominently than policy or ideological debates. The worrying thing about this fragmentation is that it greatly reduces the effectiveness of the parties in the national, provincial and in the local political sphere. It means they are concentrating on internal splits rather than concentrating on larger macro policy issues. A number of commentators have also pointed out that the proliferation of splits within parties also reduces their effectiveness to provide a counter-opposition to a number of other forces in the political system, be it the military or bureaucracy.

I think it's safe to conclude from this that Indonesian politics, Islamic politics, is more divided now than at any time in Indonesia's political history since 1945. Indeed, when the government called on Islamic parties to form in 1949 after the War of Independence, all Islamic groups agreed to form just one political party. You might compare that with the 21 political parties that contested the last election, and there may well be more that try to contest the next election.

Second, I want to look at elements of leadership and my theme here is how disappointing key Islamic political leaders have been, people who were standard-bearers for the reform process. Now I'm not judging them as disappointing here in any normative sense or imposing my own agenda on them. Merely a matter of measuring how they have lived up to the claims that they were making in the pre-Soeharto, or immediate post-Soeharto era. The first one to look at is Abdurrahman Wahid himself. He was the great hope of Islamic democratization in the 1980s and the 1990s. I don't want to dwell much on his presidency. I think most of you are aware of what a shambolic affair it was.

But I want to comment on his role within PKB. I really have come to view him as the main obstacle to internal reform within PKB and PKB becoming an internally democratic party. He is constantly undermining democratic processes in the party by dictating terms at party meetings and hand-picking the people he wants for key roles. This is very disappointing for a man who spent much of the 1980s talking about how he was trying to *mendewasakan nahdliyyin*, how he was trying to encourage NU members to be mature about the decisions they made, informing them and allowing them to make their own decisions. Instead he has constantly preempted those decisions, those democratic processes within PKB.

And more than any other party, arguably even Mega's PDI-P, this has become Gus Dur's party, where virtually nothing can get through without his approval. I think the gap between his rhetoric and action, which was pretty large during his presidency, is even more yawning if you look at what's happening within PKB. Similarly with Amien Rais, the great chameleon of Indonesian politics, we can see someone who can at one time be statesman-like, a leader, an eloquent advocate for reform and pluralism, and at other times can be sectarian, anti-Semitic, anti-Chinese, anti-Western and can be very bigoted.

But since late 1998 Amien has cast his lot with the pluralists and he set PAN up as an open party. It's a party which all Indonesians are welcome to join. He made sure in the early stages of PAN that there were always non-Muslims, not only on the boards, the national level, but also on the local level. Now after PAN's disappointing electoral performance in 1999, Amien has pursued this with less rigor. There's only one of the 34-35 PAN members of the parliament who is a non-Muslim. Most of them are from a Muhammadiyah background, an organization that Amien Rais used to head. Many of the local boards now have either driven out or sidelined non-Muslims in their ranks. So what started off as an open, pluralist party is now increasingly becoming more of a Muhammadiyah party. Many people within PAN who championed this sort of openness feel betrayed by Amien Rais's more recent actions.

I could talk about other parties, but I won't. I just wanted to mention something about ideology because there has been some talk about this and Ulil mentioned the Islamic state issue. For the more doctrinaire Islamic parties such as PPP and Bulan Bintang, the great cause in the last few years has been the so-called Jakarta Charter. The Jakarta Charter is made up of seven key words that would in effect oblige Muslims to implement *shariah,* Islamic law. This is a long constitutional debate in Indonesian history which goes back to the formation of the state. These two parties have been championing the return of the Jakarta Charter to the Constitution, in particular Section 29 of the Constitution.

It's interesting to look in some detail at how this is taking place. In the case of Bulan Bintang, the Crescent Star party, this has been a long-held position. This is a very doctrinaire party and I think it's a very sincere wish they have. In the case of the United Development Party I think it's somewhat more cynical. But they're championing this for all that they're worth.

The interesting thing is to look at the intellectual activity underlining this political campaign and this is very hollow indeed. There are very few texts where people spell out in any detail how they intend to implement this. Even within parties there is an avoidance of detailed examination about how this might be implemented in practice. For example, in the Crescent Star party you'll find probably about half of the board members are adamant that any *shariah* rule should oblige Muslim women to wear headdress, to wear the *jilbab.*

But the party chairman and more than a few of the party leaders adamantly think that this should not be included. Even this basic issue has not been threshed out within the party, and yet they are proposing to put in the Constitution something that has not been thoroughly worked out in detail. So there is something hollow about this ideological debate. There is something symbolic about the Jakarta Charter but as a prescription for how Muslims should lead their life, it is very disappointing for people who claim to be ideological Muslims not to have pursued this in greater detail.

In closing, it's too early to say whether some of these problems may be resolved by the 2004 election. In the post-2004 election we may see some genuine consolidation, but unfortunately we don't have many case studies to compare with. We could look at Turkey, for example, and see some of these elements appearing after a couple of coups and they still have not been resolved. They have been followed by subsequent military coups. So at the moment, it's very fluid and hazardous in Indonesia. It is difficult to guess how things might be resolved, because it is also partly dependent on how and what legislative changes come about in parliament.

But, despite the widespread media coverage particularly in the West about rising fundamentalism, the evidence from the 1999 election is that about three quarters of Muslims voted for pluralist parties. This is not just those people that voted for the five parties I mentioned earlier. Looking at the vote for a party such as Golkar, it's likely as far as I can work out, the single largest block of modernist votes went to Golkar. If you look where the vote came from this is where modernist leanings are strong. And Golkar is not, by most definitions, an Islamic party. The great majority of Indonesian Muslims, people who according to their citizenship cards profess Islamic faith, a great majority of them voted for parties that were not formalist in their Islamic beliefs or had Islamic agendas. And despite the publicity given to Laskar Jihad, there's little to suggest that those more Islamic parties have increased in support to a great extent. For example, the last two attempts to get the Jakarta Charter raised in the People's Consultative Assembly have been defeated by large majorities. So the picture I'm painting for these Islamic parties in the short-term is not particularly bright. The closing point I might make is about the importance here of NGOs, of the press and the various other liberal organizations, and intellectuals who provide a critique of this process. There are sections in the press that are now making a specialization of this. The journal *GAMMA* is doing a very good job of exposing corruption and double standards within the political parties and the like. *Tempo and Gatra* are also doing a good job of this as well as NGOs that are doing research into political parties. I think this is very important if we are to have some sort of corrective influence on the clientelism that we see emerging or being strengthened within political parities at the moment.

Session II Discussion

Robert Barry, former ambassador to Indonesia: Much of what Greg Fealy was talking about sounds a lot like the former Yugoslavia. I have an assertion to make, which is you can never get to more competent governance, or to a civil society, within the framework of the existing electoral system in Indonesia. And failing reform of the electoral system and the constitutional structure which creates it, we're going to continue in a cycle of one-man parties, fractionalization and lack of responsiveness. I ask particularly Greg Fealy to respond to this. **Fealy:** That's an interesting question you raised about the electoral system and whether this will have a debilitating effect on the consolidation of democracy and civil society. I can understand why people would believe that to be the case. And I think your reference to the electoral system implies that until Indonesia gets a district system you will not have proper accountability, and under this awkward mixture between the district and proportional systems that we have now, that it still gives too much power to the regional and in particular, national boards of the party. I accept that point entirely and I think the current hybrid system has failed to provide a measure of district representation which was originally intended. There is a particular problem here, namely: it will require enormous effort to install a district system.

To draw up the boundaries and to get the parties geared up for district systems, this is not something that can take place within a period of 4 to 5 years, or so I have been informed by electoral specialists including by the KPU, the Indonesian electoral commission. There's also the accompanying issue of what happens if the electoral system isn't properly implemented at a time when there is great tension and a lot of conflict in the country. An ineffective introduction of the district system could lead to an increased level of violence. This is not an argument I'm necessarily drawn to but I can understand why people see this as a legitimate reason to maintain the present system, as cumbersome as it is, for the short term.

As to the Constitution you're making reference to the need for Constitutional change, and I gather this is a reference to whether they should have a parliamentary or presidential system in Indonesia. At the moment they have something of a hybrid system, and the pendulum has swung toward a parliamentary system with the last two constitutional changes that have taken place. Gus Dur used to make a lot of noise about how he was frustrated with parliament and that Indonesia wasn't a pure presidential system.

But I certainly don't think Indonesia ever had a purely presidential system. Most of the problems he faced, Mega is also complaining about, including an obstructive parliament. Most of the core problems of government lay elsewhere. Parliament contributed to those, but those are not the reason that Gus Dur and his government failed on so many fronts. And they are also not the reason why this present government is performing so poorly. Many of the issues come back to the inability of ministers to make decisions, of the cabinet to function effectively, or the bureaucracy to implement the decisions that have been made. I'm not convinced that swinging the balance back to the presidency, back towards the executive, or indeed going to a full parliamentary system would necessarily change consolidation of democracy. It's more about how those in the executive government are functioning. I have lots of qualms with the way parliament is functioning as well and I think that's another reason to be rather depressed at recent trends. But I don't think it's a constitutional setting as such, it's something that comes back to culture and political culture, the openness of it and balancing between various forces. Dennis Halpin, House International Relations

Committee: My question is for Dr. Marcoes Natsir, as a Islamic woman involved in working for gender equality, I have a question about recent issues with the Taliban, the liberation of Afghanistan and the [American] president's statements in the State of the Union address. The West has a long history of being pushy in advocating cultural, political and religious values in other cultures. When Western political leaders make comments about women's rights in the universal issue of human rights, is this helpful or counterproductive to your work? Does it help you or does it seem like interference?

Natsir: I think the majority of wo men organizations in Indonesia including women Moslem activists are against the ideas of the Taliban because they tend to marginalize the space for woman in the public sphere. This is contrary to experience in Indonesia. Traditionally Indonesians have had wide room for woman in the public sphere. Regarding the context of *jilbab* we have a different interpretations about that. I do not believe the *jilbab* is associated with radicalism, or what happened in Afghanistan. In Indonesia we use *jilbab* as part of the fashion. We also see it used as a symbol of freedom for woman. But if you look at the historical background of the emerging of the *jilbab* you will see it began after the revolution in Iran. But then contextually it became very different, in particular after the daughter of Soeharto, Tutut wore the *jilbab* after she went to Mecca. Since then the *jilbab* has become very fashionable for middle-class women, in particular among the civil servants. So it's completely different. But indeed sometimes there are political forces that drive the wearing of the *jilbab*, for instance, Partai Keadilan, those women always wear the *jilbab*. With regard to the Western pressure I would say it has a negative influence on our work because it creates a situation of confrontation between the West and the East, and Islam and the West. But this may be in part because we make gender analysis based on tools from the West.

Abdalla: I have a point to add about the Western image and the Taliban's treatment of women. Talibanism in general is not popular among Muslims in Indonesia. We view their treatment of women as quite strange. On several occasions the chairman of one of the most important Islamic parties, the Justice Party, has said that the party supports the right of women to participate in the public sphere. And they demonstrate this by having a woman represent their party in parliament. And from my conversation with the leadership of Laskar Jihad and FPI, there is no evidence that women should be prevented from participating in the public sphere. So I think Talibanism is quite peculiar to the Afghanistan social context.

America: My question is for Ulil and Lies Marcoes. You said you're promoting a modern notion of human rights and democracy and its interpretation in Islam. How do you define modern? Is it based on Western values, or Islamic? I think Islam defines everything clearly, not just socially, politically, and economically but everything.

You were also saying that you were promoting gender equality. Where do you see gender inequality in Islam? If you are promoting gender equality does that mean there is gender inequality?

Abdalla: The first question about how you define modernity and how you reconcile Islam and modernity. A lot of Muslim intellectuals believe that there are a lot of things in common between Islam and modern notions of democracy. Only a few Muslims believe there is a complete contradiction between democracy and Islam. One such group is *Hizb al-Tahrir,* mentioned by Bob Hefner. *Hizb al-Tahrir* is a small group which is of the opinion that democracy is totally un-Islamic because democracy is based on the belief that sovereignty rests with the people while Islam is based on the belief that sovereignty rests with God. So it is inconceivable that Islam and democracy could be reconciled. Please recall that this is a small group who are not very influential. I think the majority of the Muslim intellectuals believe there are universal values shared by Islam and modern notions of democracy. I do not think the question how you define modernity is relevant because there are commonalties and universal values that are shared by Islam and modern values. Of course there are some values in modern democracy that are not supported by Islam, but I think in general, Islam and democracy are not contradictions.

Natsir: Within Islam women in Indonesia don't bother with equality and equity. What we are trying to do is to talk about gender and justice within Islam because the value of Islam in particular within the *shariah* law within the *fiqh* is very gender-biased. That is why we are trying to develop our interpretation based on female perspectives and experiences. I think this is the difference between the ideas of gender in the West and in Indonesia, particularly among Moslem activists.

Rick Kraince, Ohio University: I have a question for Ulil and this relates to Laskar Jihad. Ulil, you mentioned that you are involved in a newspaper syndication and radio effort which promotes civil democracy through an Islamic framework. I also notice recently that some of the Islamic journals have reacted to some of this discourse that you've been involved with. And in fact I see that the Laskar Jihad journal mentions that you had said that in person Jafar was quite congenial and talking about interreligious dialogue and I'm wondering what about the rhetoric he presents to his groups out in Poso and Ambon. Have you looked at that and I'm wondering what their reaction is to your work?

Abdalla: Regarding the reaction to moderate Islam project in Indonesia, it is true that recently there has been harsh criticism of my projects to promote liberal Islam and moderate pluralist Islam. But as I mentioned before I'm optimis tic that there are tendencies toward moderation because there is space for dialogues. I think the key element in overcoming this confrontation is to increase communication between pluralist Islam and radical Islam. I was very happy when some people from these radical groups came to invite me to attend their meeting and share with them some of my ideas. This is very important in moderating the ideas because some points are not clear for these people. For example the issue of the implementation of Islamic *shariah*. I say to people that I do not oppose Islamic *shariah*, what I oppose is the classical or conservative notion of Islamic *shariah* which in some ways is in contradiction with some of the modern notions of human rights. For example, freedom of expression and freedom of thinking are very crucial because some people still believe in the classical notion of apostasy. That is, people who think contrary to orthodox Islam could be accused of being apostate and the penalty is death. This is crucial for pluralist societies like Indonesia so I think if we can clarify some point in Islamic *shariah*, I think we can convince these people that we need a new interpretation of Islamic *shariah* in a different context.

LUNCH SESSION

Doug Ramage: I will be speaking about U.S.-Indonesia relations but in a very narrow context. One thing that has been of greatest concern to Americans and to a lot of our Indonesian friends since September 11 has been the perceived rise of anti-Americanism in Indonesia. I want to address that and somehow account for that and offer some tentative conclusions about what it's meant and how serious it was, or is. My talk is really structured around three broad questions. Why was there seemingly a rapid rise in anti-American sentiment in Indonesia following the September 11 terrorist attacks on the United States? And what, if anything, did this apparent rise in anti-American sentiment have to do with Islam? I'm speaking of the events in Indonesia which filled the press with anti-American rhetoric, threats to harm Americans including Ambassador Gelbard, threats to expel Americans from Indonesia and a general domination of public debate, particularly in the print media, by apparently radical or extremist Islamic organizations. Does all this depict an Indonesia no longer hospitable to Americans or an Indonesian Muslim community seemingly arrayed against the United States or American interests?

Before I get into that in somewhat clinical detail, and before I pose a few tentative answers to those questions, let me recount the immediate reaction to September 11 in Indonesia. Immediately after the September 11 attacks on the United States, Indonesians responded with enormous sympathy and shock and conveyed their condolences to Americans wherever they may be, to private American businesses, to the American Embassy, to the Ambassador, to American institutions including the Ford Foundation, the Asia Foundation and others. In fact, it was a swift and spontaneous response from many Indonesians. The first person to contact the Asia Foundation was in fact Malik Musa, the head of the Muhammadiyah Youth Organization in Aceh, an individual who himself has suffered greatly in the violence and terrorism in his homeland of Aceh for months and years. Many others called, sent e-mails, even dropped by our foundation's office in Jakarta just to say they cared or were thinking about Americans.

But then something else happened. And that was Indonesian speculation on why the September 11 attacks on United States occurred. And much of the early analysis of the press focused on what is generally believed in Indonesia to be America's wrong-headed and deeply flawed foreign policy in the Middle East. And while Indonesians were already moving on to such analysis of what the context may have been by say September 14, 15 or 16, the American community was still in a state of shock and mourning.

The American community was not necessarily prepared to listen to an analysis of how wrong or flawed our foreign policy was.

Accentuating the problem was often the gross misunderstanding of the United States which became so evident after September 11. Almost unknown to Indonesians was any information about the growth and vitality of Islam in the United States, the diversity and vibrancy of religious life in our own country, thus leading many Indonesians to believe the statement of a prominent Indonesian who said that the attacks occurred, and I quote "because America hates Muslims and demonizes Islam."

As this analysis regarding the U.S. foreign policy began to come out, Americans began to believe Indonesians were not reacting with sufficient public expressions of grief or solidarity with the Americans and this was compared very quickly and unfavorably to American friends elsewhere in Southeast Asia, to the Philippines, to Thailand, and around the world. So what emerged then by the second week or so after the attack, is what I now see as a real grief gap between Americans and Indonesians. I think many people in the American community began to feel that Indonesians didn't fully empathize because they had moved on to this analysis of why they think this happened. There were plenty of comparison in private and a bit of lamenting about why Indonesians didn't sound more like Gloria Arroyo, or Surin Pitsuan of Thailand or Tony Blair or Schroeder in Europe.

One of the things we can't underestimate in the post September 11 period is the role of a free press in Indonesia. The press in fact had a field day printing the most virulent attacks on the U.S. by the most minor or marginal figures in the Muslim community, accounts of the most conspiratorial nature. One of the notions repeated often was the bizarre contention that the United States or Israel attacked the World Trade Centers themselves so that they could forever blame it on Islam and demonize Muslims. This was repeated not only in the electronic press but on websites and throughout the papers and so on. I think what also can't be overemphasized was that Americans had never seen a down side to Indonesia's free press. The Indonesian media is now among the most free and open and most dynamic in all of Asia. And that has been a consistent trend since the fall of Soeharto and the beginning of the democratization process since 1998. It is also entirely privately owned and for profit. For the dozens of newspapers, weeklies, tabloids, newspaper syndicates and half dozen or more private television stations it was advertising gold to capture the most readers or audience with the most sensationalist, outrageous coverage possible.

Yet as weeks passed and we approached the end of September it also became clear the attacks were no longer viewed in terms of U.S. foreign policy problems. They had become domesticized. By late September early October when President Megawati returned to Indonesia from a two week trip to the U.S. and Japan what had become the order of the day was the manipulation of the attacks and Indonesia's initial response to it as a way to attack Megawati or tear down her government or question her leadership. By the time she returned to Indonesia in late September domestic political imperatives and maneuvering had taken over completely. Indeed, the single most important factor in the degree to which anti-Americanism was being exploited was to destabilized Megawati's government. I believe she was bewildered by the severity of these attacks when she returned to Indonesia.

Illustrating this was a comment from a very senior Golkar politician who told me that the Septemb er 11 tragedy "is the opening salvo of Indonesia's 2004 presidential campaign." Now how are the September 11 terrorist attacks on the U.S. used and by whom? As many of you know while Megawati was here in Washington, DC she gave an extremely well received speech at a USINDO event, and she had a good reception here and a meeting with President Bush in the White House. When she came back to Indonesia she was attacked from the right and the left.

The Islamic right used the tragedy to attack Megawati's Islamic credentials, something that has come up again and again in her career. Her visit with President Bush, in which she pledged general support and sympathy to the U.S., was interpreted in the Indonesian press as her having betrayed Islam. By portraying Megawati as close to Americans some of her political opponents hoped this would weaken her appeal to the Muslim masses, who supposedly associated America as being against Islam. On the other hand the nationalist left attacked her for selling out the country because of her appeal to American investors at the Houston energy conference she attended where she also gave an extremely well received speech pledging the openness of Indonesia's economy and basically saying 'Indonesia is open for business and you all should come.' That was also very sharply attacked by the secular nationalist left in Indonesia. At a time when Americans were wondering why Indonesia was not joining in a very public way the war on terrorism, the press was attacking her quite viciously by depicting her as having an American heart. I recall two editions of *Rakyat Merdeka*, the number two best selling paper in the country. The first was a photo of President Megawati meeting President Bush in the White House. The paper's caption decried this as betraying Islam. The second in early October showed a cartoon of Megawati with her heart revealed as the stars and stripes rather than the red and white flag of Indonesia. I think this is probably not known to most of us, that she was quite seriously attacked for being a lackey of the Americans and being to pro-American.

So why did all this matter and why did this seem to paralyze her in terms of what she could do vis-à-vis a war on terrorism? Primarily because Megawati leads a weak coalition government. She had chosen to bring the Muslim parties into governing with her by choosing Hamzah Haz as her vice president. Within her own secular nationalistic party she must contend with the nationalist left which is concerned with issues of economic nationalism and preventing foreign intervention in Indonesia's economy. She was trying to balance all of these issues. Thus I believe her domestic room for expressing support to the U.S. was very limited.

Now, how did she eventually deal with the criticism against her post September 11? Eventually she made a speech on the eve of a prominent Muslim holiday in which she criticized the spilling of blood to avenge the spilling of blood. This was not particularly well received by Americans but the impact of her speech was very interesting domestically. It gave cover to those who otherwise more or less prepared to defend her and it pointed once again to her renewed Islamic credentials. As soon as this speech was over many prominent leaders said "She is a national leader and she cares about the *ummat*," and following this speech some of the more strident criticism did begin to fall off. If we run down a number of the expressions of Anti-Americanism we can come to a number of conclusions. First, anti-Americanism initially related to Indonesian rejection of U.S. foreign policy in the Middle East. As in the Gulf War this is occasionally expressed in the street and press, the difference being that during the Gulf War Indonesia did not have a free press so exp ressions were very tightly controlled by the Soeharto regime. On the other hand, because the Palestinian cause is not something that is felt deeply and daily by Indonesians, such concerns, though widespread, are not very deep seated and they are rarely expressed. In other words, dislike of this particular dimension of U.S. foreign policy in the Middle East does not animate the general world view of Indonesians or leaders to a significant degree. But because there is a perception that somehow our foreign policy brought on the September 11 attacks it was of course extremely uncomfortable from an American point of view.

There is also a broader issue on Indonesian foreign policy. There is genuine rejection of unilaterism in international affairs by any of the major powers. There is a constitutional mandate in Indonesia to maintain an independent and active foreign policy. I think this also informs their immediate rejection of the American campaign in Afghanistan. But reiterating something which has been said this morning, rejection of U.S. foreign policy in the Middle East does not translate and has not translated into widespread hostility to America per se, or is a motivating force for widespread Muslim activism or protest. In other words, there is very little traction in the street. Politics in Indonesia remains primarily animated by local and national concerns, and very rarely in recent years has been directed at the United States. This does not at all mean that we shouldn't be concerned about small, particularly violent radical groups and individuals; but in this case they do not represent a nationwide trend or momentum, in my view, in Indonesia.

Returning to the free press, in fact there was a combination of an extremely free press with vibrant Islamic politics in a democratizing Indonesia which changed the equation entirely. I think a lot of Americans and foreigners who have spent a lot of time in Indonesia weren't really used to this and it was misinterpreted by some outsiders. The press' representation of the masses was misrepresented. There were never more than a few thousand people who protested in the street. And I think we can quickly see, in October and November, evidence of the shallowness of this anti-American feeling. The Afghanis tan campaign was suddenly replaced in the press by the Akbar Tanjung, Golkar scandal that has been the main media issue since. Then there was also the apprehension of Tommy Soeharto which took over the front pages and pushed Afghanistan and anti-Americanism definitely off the front pages and out of the papers entirely after mid November.

Eventually you had the expression of natural interests prevailing over other interests. This is a growing refrain, most articulately annunciated by Syafii Ma'arif, head of Muhammadiyah, but also by Hashim Muzadi of Nahdlatul Ulama. Beginning in mid-November their interests had to do with reform of governance or with getting the economy going. And the basic argument became 'Why are you all worried about these things in Afghanistan when they really don't concern the daily lives of ordinary Indonesians?'

But how do we account for what was extremely appropriate American concern with those people who threatened to "sweep" or expel Americans from Indonesia, and then were not punished? There was a lot of concern that the laws against these things were not applied in this case.

I think the single most important intractable problem in Indonesia is impunity and that the court system does not work. They basically don't work for anybody, whether you're threatening Americans or whether you're waging a holy war inside Indonesia; whether you're a corporate criminal or guilty of gross human rights violations in East Timor. The judiciary doesn't work for anyone, so I don't think there is special protection offered to those threatening Americans. When you combine this long-standing institutionalized impunity with the domestic political risks that Megawati associated (and perhaps exaggerated) with any potential crackdown on political expressions of Islam, which of course would remind Indonesians of the battle days of Soeharto when legitimate Islamic expressions of politics were demonized, we can begin to get a picture of the constraints which were operating in the post-September 11 period.

Having said all that, it's also important to note a couple of things that were not visible at all. The government, albeit in a very tardy fashion, nonetheless eventually deployed significant police resources to protect Americans and American institutions in Indonesia. USAID contract workers working in Central Java, American companies including foundations, our own foundation, suddenly had police protection that appeared out of nowhere. The order had come from the top and there was no public acknowledgement of this. The government didn't brag about this, in fact didn't say anything about this, which might have been also their mistake, but by mid-October we were feeling we had a better security.

Is there a silver lining in any of this? I think what shocked a lot of the mainstream Muslim organizations was the rapidity with which extremists came to dominate the press after September 11, including, but not limited to those expressions of anti-Americanism. This eventually galvanized mainstream Muslims to set into motion some extraordinary efforts to reclaim debate over Islam and Indonesia and to restate Islam as a force for pragmatic nationalism. This is in the message of Hashim Muzadi of Nahdlatul Ulama and this has been the message of Syafii Ma'arif as well since mid November and gaining momentum since last month. This represents a change in the discourse. Even some of the more militant groups are now saying, 'We do believe in equal rights for women and we're also in favor of interfaith dialogue and democracy.' I think this indicates a more balanced dialogue which we didn't see in September and October, but is coming back into the foreground.

Lunch Session Discussion

Q: Are Indonesian objections to U.S. foreign policy or Middle East policy? I recall one of Gus Dur's first policy statements having to do with Israel and the negative reaction to this in Indonesia.

Ramage: The issue is very much the Middle Eastern aspect of U.S. foreign policy that's been contentious in Indonesia. For decades Indonesia has had a very consistent position on the Middle

East and on the Palestinians' right to self-determination. That is what people are particularly focused on post-September 11. But it was there before September 11. We saw a bit of it during the Gulf War but it was not as noticeable because of the controls on the press and the different nature of the Gulf War as opposed to the campaign in Afghanistan.

You have referred to Gus Dur's attempt when he became president to begin the process of extending some kind of diplomatic recognition to Israel. This has actually been a principal point of Gus Dur. For at least 15 years he has argued that Indonesia should treat Israel as a normal country and should recognize it. It was one of the first initiatives he pushed as president and he was attacked quite strongly from Muslim groups and Islamic politicians. Many people thought it was unnecessary, in terms of how weak his presidency was, to spend valuable political capital on that particular issue. It represented what Gus Dur had been talking about for many, many years but it hurt him badly politically and domestically.

Ann Willner: There is a difference today in the attitude of Indonesia towards Israel in terms of expression of policy and behavior. When I was in Indonesia in the 1950s and 1960s some elements of the Masyumi party were interested in developing cooperatives and they were quite interested in the successful cooperatives system in Israel. I knew a couple of the leaders of the Nahdlatul Ulama and they were also interested in knowing more about Israel. I don't think the attitude was uniformly hostile. Certainly for some of the Islamic leaders and scholars it required a public attitude somewhat different from their private attitudes.

Ramage: I agree with you.

Ron Palmer, The George Washington University: I have been trying to gauge just how much change there has been in Islamic politics since September 11 and how one ought to think about it.

Ramage: Ultimately September 11 did not have a lot to do with domestic political politics. President Megawati still has a Teflon-like quality and she has managed to deflect some of these attacks on her. In some cases potential or real opposition parties to her are hopelessly divided. I think that it's kind of getting back to politics as normal. Post September 11 was something of an aberration domestically, though it quite severely strained U.S.-Indonesian relations.

Paul Cleveland, USINDO: I would like you to extend your comments about anti-American feeling, that is attitudes towards the United States, in the light of the search for the al Qaeda. There is a considerable amount of feeling among the Indonesian elite that perhaps we are being a little bit too obsessive or assiduous about that. Can you comment?

Ramage: I do not know what lasting impact this is going to have. Indonesians clearly perceive that the United States now has a checklist and that we're paying very close attention to particular issues. The danger is that Indonesians might continue to respond that it's business as usual, and that they will address these issues on their own terms, their own time and in their own way. The foreign minister said something to that effect. He is very eloquent and effective, and articulates Indonesia's foreign policy positions well. But I do not think that is accepted as readily by the United States and I worry that Indonesia – unlike Malaysia, which is not nearly as free and open a society as Indonesia – has not adjusted itself to new global realities and there is a sense of missing some of the important benchmarks that the United States is looking for. Whether or not these are fair benchmarks I'm not sure but nonetheless they are being set down.

Barbara Harvey, retired Foreign Service: In early December there was not much reporting and even now it is still under-reported in the Indonesia press about the reaction of the Afghanistan people who were liberated from Taliban rule. I remember asking an old friend who was a senior editor about this and he said "We are all afraid of being portrayed as anti-Islamic." Now, has that atmosphere changed, or is there still a feeling among some of the more moderate or mainstream press that they might be attacked for being anti-Islamic?

Ramage: Actually, since Decemb er I am struck by how quickly many people have changed their tune on the Taliban. There began to appear in late November, early December, a couple of references in the Indonesian press that Indonesia in fact had never recognized the Taliban government. Indonesian citizens were not aware of this at all. In fact there were also stories that the government of Rabani had maintained an embassy in Jakarta staffed by a chargé d'affaires to the present time. There was a letter in *Suara Pembaruan* which said basically "So you mean that the government which has just been defeated by the Americans is the government we never liked anyway?"

It is hard to overestimate the impact on Indonesians of the treatment of women in particular. This had a very sobering effect on the discussion of Afghanistan and very quickly a notion that this was a government upholding Islam was not backed. Looking back it is remarkable how often the Indonesian press, television, newspapers and magazines reprinted the photographs of the lines of people having beards shaved and pictures of women taking off their head covers. The press loved those images. They loved the anti-American images in September and October and they loved those images also and those pictures got played up as prominently as they did in *Time* magazine or *Newsweek*.

Audie Onibala, Poso Watch Network: You mentioned earlier the vibrant press in Indonesia. However I just spoke with a leading journalist from Indonesia who mentioned that no one dared to criticize the radical movement if he wanted to stay in business. In the old days if you criticized Soeharto they would take away your license. But now if you criticize the radical movement they will take your life. The only press that is willing to speak up in Indonesia now is the one from Manado which is mostly a Christian area.

Ramage: I think you have just touched on something that illustrates the changing dynamics of the press in Indonesia since 1998. The greatest threat to press freedom in Indonesia today does not emanate from the state or from the security forces. It does not come in the form of a telephone call in the middle of the night. It comes from within and amongst the community itself. It tends to fall on the issue of reporting on extremists or violent expressions of Islam or violence masquerading under the banner of Islam. Reporting on that has at times been responded to by people like the Front Pembela Islam [Indonesian Defense Front], marching to a newspaper demanding that it make a retraction, or attacking a radio station, in one case in Solo about a year and a half ago. There is concern about this and you are absolutely right. But it doesn't cancel out the fact that you do have this enormously vibrant press. There are weak points and that's absolutely one of them, and compared to pre-1998 there is absolutely no comparison whatsoever in terms of what the press covers: the investigations into corruption, investigations into problems in governance; and the detailed accounts of human rights violations by senior military officers. But there is a reluctance to report on some of the issues related to the activities of Laskar Jihad.

Robert Pringle, retired Foreign Service: Do we have what is normally referred to as a public diplomacy problem in Indonesia? Or, given the parameters of U.S. policy which are not going to change much, do we just have to ride this one out as opposed to trying to handle it better somehow?

Ramage: I believe that these issues are not easily addressed. The U.S. Embassy has worked extremely hard trying to release press statements and trying to release alternative information out in the press. The U.S. Embassy website in Jakarta is very good. The problem is that Indonesia has one of the lowest internet connectivity rates in the world so not a lot of people are reading the terrific material that the embassy is putting on the website. But in large measure there is no short term response. There is a long term dimension which President Bush and others have begun to address more globally. James Smith, Republican Conference, office of

Congressman J.C. Watts: Could you tell us more about some of the challenges that we face in Indonesia in the war on terrorism in terms of cracking down on any al Qaeda elements that may or may not be there, or cracking down on financial networks that traffic through Indonesia. How is Indonesia doing on implementing UN Security Council resolutions since September 11?

Ramage: What I feel most keenly is the complete absence of reliable information. This is not a dodge to your question but I have to say I don't know. I have not seen any compelling evidence yet, and I don't think a lot of Indonesians have either, which points definitively to concrete linkages to al Qaeda. But there's a lot of circumstantial evidence that there are individuals involved. The *Washington Post* has done some good reporting. I certainly don't have access to information which allows me to respond well to your question. So I would rather not characterize how Indonesia is making progress in terms of UN Resolutions and so on.

Mark Woodward: I want to amplify something that Doug said, namely that this virulent anti-American rhetoric is nothing new. Papers like *Media Dakwa* have been writing about CIA, Mossad, and Chinese conspiracies to destroy Islam for years. There may have been a temporary upsurge in this. But it is fundamentally nothing new and it's wise to hear what Gus Dur had to say about these people. I once asked him, "These people are so crazy, why don't you just ban them?" He replied, "Nobody listens to them seriously anyway and if we let them talk, we know where they are."

Donald Weatherbee, the University of South

Carolina: This morning the last comment Professor Hefner made in his prepared remarks was that they ought to arrest some of the more radical, violenceprone Islamicists. The question is why haven't they made arrests? Mark's comment may be partially correct, but I don't think that's fully explanatory as to why they haven't. Is it simply incompetence on the part of the authorities, i.e. the crisis of governance? Is it some latent sympathies in some of the attitudes articulated by the radicals? Or is it simply fear of domestic consequences which have already been threatened if actions should be taken? What is causing the immobility of the government at this time?

Ramage: Why aren't people arrested, and in particular those violent elements? I think it is part of each of the issues you mentioned. We shouldn't underestimate incompetence, we shouldn't underestimate weak institutions. Back in October I would have liked to see them arresting people who were threatening the lives of Americans. But what kept bringing me back is that no one gets arrested in Indonesia. If one gets arrested they get released, or they get questioned, but they are not getting convicted for anything. It points to the extraordinary governance challenge.

With a few exceptions, I do not think people who are Islamic that might be implicated or guilty of committing crimes in the name of Islam are necessarily being extended special protection by the state. I think that they too are caught up in the overall culture of impunity in Indonesia. It comes back to Megawati and her lack of leadership in terms of rule of law. She is trying to balance this very weak coalition she has and she is very sensitive to spending some of her political capital on these issues in a way which might get her accused of being anti-Islam, or not a good Muslim herself.

SESSION III-Indonesian Reactions to the September 11 Terrorist Attacks, Extremism and U.S.-Indonesia Relations

Moeslim Abdurrahman: I think Douglas covered well the complexities of the relationship between Indonesian Muslims and the United States. I will share some of my personal observations of how Indonesian Muslims reacted to September 11. Among many Muslims in Indonesia for a long time there has been the widely held belief that there was an international conspiracy among the Christian Americans and Jews from Israel and the Chinese, trying to stir up trouble among the Muslim countries including Indonesia.

One week after September 11, I had my Friday prayers at a small mosque in the South Jakarta suburbs. I listened to the Islamic preacher, and he reminded the audience to be more careful about the international conspiracy. According to the preacher right now it is evident that the United States has conspired with the Jews and the international Christians to suppress Muslim countries like Indonesia. This helped to explain why the economic crisis is getting worse. It becomes easier for Christian missionaries to give rice to the poor people, and they will in turn be comforted by Christianity. This is the popular sort of Islamic rhetoric during Friday prayers and Muslims listen carefully. Many still view the United States as a very dangerous enemy because U.S. foreign policy is biased in its treatment of Palestinian affairs. This kind of popular Islamic logic has become more and more popular after September 11. I will give you another example of why the reaction seems ambiguous. One week after September 11 there were radical Islamic groups in Indonesia attempting to harass Westerners and threatening to conduct sweepings of foreigners and especially Americans in hotels and other establishments. These sweepings seemed very threatening. Even the McDonald's on Jalan Thamrin witnessed this threat of sweeping. The owner of McDonald's responded by making the establishment more Taliban friendly by hanging an Osama poster inside to make consumers feel secure.

And also, at that time, something incredible was the production of Osama T-shirts. The phenomena where you see young Indonesians wearing Osama Bin Laden T-shirts does not indicate their ideological support for Osama or the ideology of Talibanism. In my opinion it has more to do with the fact that after the fall of Soeharto the young generation was left without a role model. I still remember when we had an Islamic Iranian revolution and among University students they were waving banners with the image of the Ayatollah Khomeini without any intention to support the Islamic revolution, but to show that they were more militant and ideological Islamists than others. These are two examples reflecting the emotion that the young generation shares after September 11.

Another example that I will give you is an illustration of what I call the untreatable media in Indonesia. It is true that one week after September 11 everybody complained that Muslim scholars educated in the United States like Nurcholish Madjid, Azyuma rdi Azra, Syafii Ma'arif, and perhaps myself, did not say anything about the tragedy. The media covered the Front Pembela Islam sitting in the front of the U.S. Embassy condemning the Americans. I met with some of the Muslim student activists and I asked, "Why don't you join with the Front Pembela Islam?" They told me they complain about the double standard of U.S. foreign policy but they cannot join the Laskar Jihad because they refuse to wear the turban, an Arab symbol that is typical among Muslim radical groups. So for me there is still a distinction between the student opinions and their support of groups like Front Pembela Islam because there is a social class distinction between university students and the social origin of the Muslim group of radicals who protest against the United States by sitting in front of the U.S. Embassy.

We need to remember there are a variety of reactions to September 11 in Indonesia and there are nuances of Islamic aspiration. I think it is difficult to make generalizations about Islam in Indonesia. There is also an uncritical media that often fails to cover both sides of the story between radical Islam and moderate Islam.

Recently we organized a small conference in Jakarta and invited Syafii Ma'arif and some of the Islamic leaders like Ulil Abshar Abdalla from the young generation. Pak Syafii made a good statement at this conference. He warned Muslims in Indonesia not to idolize the Taliban in Indonesia because if they knew the meaning and practice of Talibanism in Afghanistan they would see that it is so different and dangerous not only for the non-Muslim community but within the Muslim community itself. But the media failed to cover the statement by Pak Syafii in this conference.

This is a good example of why sometimes we still have uneven media coverage of both sides between the radical aspirations and also Islamic moderates. Lastly, I will give you the last of my personal experiences, I am working with the Muhammadiyah and within the Muhammadiyah we have the Muhammadiyah Teenager Association, what we call *Ikatan Remajah Muhammadiyah*. Many in this grouping were confused about the United States. They asked me whether they should boycott American products. They decided to boycott Coca-Cola. I told them it is also a double standard if they boycott Coca-Cola because Coca-Cola is not really an American product. Coca-Cola is produced in Indonesia with Indonesian capital and by Indonesian workers. I told them to think more seriously about American funding. If they choose to boycott Coca-Cola why don't they also refuse American aid. Ultimately they decided to boycott Coca-Cola but not on religious grounds. They joined with NGOs protesting global economic capitalism. If you try to understand and interpret what Indonesian Islam is you have to get more specific.

When everything is generalized it is very dangerous. It is a gross generalization to say that Indonesian Islam right now has a connection with al Qaeda. The majority of people are still trying to figure out the meaning of Islam; the meaning of gender according to Islam; the meaning of democracy according to Islam. The whole history of Islam, like other religions, is part of human interpretation. So Muslims in Indonesia, even NU and Muhammadiyah, are trying to interpret Islam in the new challenges in the world today.

This morning we heard about the unique aspects of Islam in Indonesia, particularly the social, educational, and cultural functions of Islam which are quite different from the Middle East. The Muhammadiyah and the NU have many universities, hospitals, and social projects outside of the state. Muslim civil society in Indonesia is very strong. People in the United States need to understand the problem in Indonesia is how to help the Muslim community strengthen civil society right now, to revive the notion that Islamic solidarity is part of what we call the core of the civil society. We demonstrated this recently when the government responded miserably during disastrous flooding in parts of the country. The government bureaucracy did not provide any assistance to the people. So for me, it is better if we have bridges to more understanding between society and society. How to re-educate the Muslim community in Indonesian and American society so that in the future we have trust to work together to establish what we call the new civilized global community. Otherwise we are destined to the continued clashing of civilizations.

Rizal Sukma: Doug Ramage basically described the Indonesian responses to September 11 very accurately. But there are a few other issues I would like to add. As an Indonesian I have multiple identities. I was puzzled at how Indonesians reacted immediately after September 11. Yet in some ways the reactions were understandable. If we look at comments made by academics and scholars and the so called hard-liners, one of the arguments put forward was that the U.S. is arrogant. I was puzzled by this kind of comment pointing blame on the victims. This attitude was prevalent shortly after the terrorist attacks.

As an Acehnese I fully understand this reaction of blaming the victims because that happened to me. When the police burned the village where my grandmother lived in Aceh, my family complained about it and the police said, "We didn't burn your grandmother's house. We burned only one house but the wind was strong and burned your grandmother's house."

As an Acehnese I was also angry when the U.S. initiated the military campaign in Afghanistan. Many people became angry and objected to the collateral damage. Yet, no one raised the issue regarding Aceh. In one conference when I raised the question how many Afghan civilians died in the military campaign almost everybody came up with the exact numbers. But when I asked how many Acehnese died in 2001, not one knew the number and I'm sure even today not many people in Indonesia know for sure how many Acehnese died in the violence during January 2002 alone. But they are quick to react when Palestinians get shot in the West Bank. For the record 238 Acehnese died during the month of January this year.

Back to reactions to September 11. Especially in Jakarta reactions were directed to test the fragility of Megawati's government at the time. You can see how the attitude of the government shifted from being nervous and uneasy to ambiguity. That also reflects the very difficult position in which Megawati found herself. She was walking a tightrope trying to find balance between supporting the war on terrorism, but at the same time not to be seen as acting under American pressure. I think that is very typical of any post-colonial state in Asia and also in Africa and, to a lesser degree, in Latin America. When the U.S. started the military campaign there was some kind of anonymous criticism of the use of military force in dealing with global issues like the threat of international terrorism. Many people questioned the efficacy of the use of military force in dealing with terrorism. Many also argued that since international terrorism is a global problem then a global force is needed through a global institution like the United Nations. Soon after the Taliban was removed this view dissipated.

I have been asked to address the forms and expressions of militancy and radicalism in Indonesia. Radicalism is caused by four factors. The first cause is moral frustration. The government and/or the security apparatus is basically incapable of dealing with illegal activities like gambling. This leads to moral frustration and people justify taking matters into their own hands. Another factor is ideological obsession that can lead to a war of ideas. Ulil Abshar Abdalla addressed this issue where basically there is a fear of globalization and also a fear of Western domination. There are some in Indonesia who are seeking to establish some kind of Pan Islam movement. Many also see that as an expression of nostalgia, of idealizing the glorious past. The third form of radicalism is basically political extortion. I think Bob Hefner already addressed the issue where political extortion is involved in this kind of activity or movement. The fourth is also a form of economic and social resentment rooted in the socioeconomic disparities made worse by the economic crisis that hit the country in 1997.

It is also quite clear to me that radicalism is primarily based in Java and is urban based. It's only in Jakarta, Yogyakarta and Solo. There is not much to be found outside Java.

If you are familiar with Jack Schneider's study *From Fortune to Violence* it is clear that militant politics resulted from the sudden collapse of the authoritarian regime of Soeharto and the newfound openness that followed. Those who engage in militant or radical politics are generations who grew up in the late 1970s and 1980s. That was the period where the New Order was at the height of its power and exercised tight political control over any form of expression of political Islam. When the country moved toward democracy I suspect that some of these people basically did not realize that we had already moved toward democracy and they became obsessed with expressing their political interests.

There was some kind of need to taste power suddenly dispersed all over the country with the collapse of the authoritarian regime. It also emerged because of the political game. There was great political struggle among the elite and among the military generals in the country.

Another cause of radicalism and militancy is the very weak, almost non-existent, law enforcement. I do not need to go into detail here.

Finally, the continuing economic hardship since the economic crisis in 1997 has left around 14 million people unemployed. There are 1.3 million internally displaced persons still living in refugee camps. Not only the Christians in the Moluccas; at least 400,000 Madurese who fled Kalimantan are still stuck on the small island of Buton.

How is militant politics expressed? It was and still is expressed in three forms. First, it is expressed against fellow Muslims. And this signifies that this militancy is basically an intra-religious problem. Second, it is expressed against the symbols of globalization: prosperity and what some militants see as moral decadence. This is why there are raids on bars, entertainment centers and so on. Finally, it is expressed against the U.S. If you look carefully at all those issues being raised on the street, the issues are mainly against the U.S. They basically complain about the U.S. military campaign in Afghanistan, and the possible U.S. military campaign in Iraq. But no one questions Russian campaigns in Chechnya; no one questions the Chinese campaign in Xinjiang; no one questions the Burmese campaign against Rohinya Muslims in Burma; no one even complains about the military atrocities in Aceh, or in any other part of Indonesia. It may have something to do with what Ambassador Skip Boyce calls the "David and Goliath" mentality in this context.

I want to comment on domestic impacts and how the use of anti-terrorist rhetoric may have significant consequences for Indonesia. I think we should be very careful here because this issue can be used by national governments, including the Indonesian government, to derail the process of democracy and the attempt to uphold human rights. The signs that this is happening are already there. Indonesia's new anti-terror bill might derail the democratization process.

The anti-terrorist rhetoric is being used for domestic political purposes as well. With regard to Aceh there is a tendency to portray Acehnese as a bunch of al Qaeda sympathizers trying to bring suffering upon Indonesia. It has also been used to justify crackdowns on pro-democracy forces in Jakarta. The United States should look very carefully at the role of the military and the issue of military reform. I have the impression that it seems the military or the police are playing this game saying "We are weak as a result of military sanctions the United States imposed on us and that's why we cannot deal with the terrorism issue. If you want us to deal with those terrorists, resume the IMET, resume the foreign assistance, resume the selling of these lethal weapons." That kind of possibility is not inconceivable because in some other countries that resumption of support of foreign militaries has occurred. In fact, there has been a lot of talk about how U.S.-Indonesia military-military relations might be improved in the post-September 11 period. How do we deal with these issues? What can the United States do? Earlier I mentioned there were four forms of militant politics. The first three actually reflect issues that are basically intrareligious. In that context I do believe that should be worked out amongst Muslims themselves. The Muhammadiyah and Nahdlatul Ulama have already made attempts.

On militancy as a form of economic resentment, there I think the United States can and must play a role to help. However, it is ultimately the government of Indonesia that is solely responsible for whether Indonesia can move toward economic recovery. The IMF has provided a very detailed plan of action that we should follow and yet economic reforms have stalled. Perhaps the IMF now regrets ever getting involved in Indonesia because the Indonesians are very bad students.

We should be careful not to allow the war on terrorism to take us off the transition path toward democracy. If we circumvent the Leahy Amendment and the United States begins selling lethal weapons to the military, can we be sure that those weapons will be used in order to combat terrorism? Will the weapons be used to suppress pro-democracy forces? Will the weapons be used to suppress the Papuan independence movement? Will the weapons be used to kill as many Acehnese as possible?

If the United States wants to pressure the government of Indonesia to do more in this area, do it through back-door diplomacy, because megaphone diplomacy will only make matters worse. There are problems with American public diplomacy. Since the fall of Soeharto the focus of many American institutions has been how to help Indonesia to democratize. Little attention has been paid to initiatives aimed at providing information to Indonesians about what is going on in the United States. What is the rationale for particular policies? I think there is a need to revitalize the role of the United States Information Service in Indonesia.

Finally, I think Americans need to understand that at the moment Indonesia is still unsettled with the past, confused with the present, and uncertain about its future. That is a very lethal combination for a very fragile democracy.

Donald K. Emmerson: I'd like to talk about the multiple usefulness of five things: introspection, leverage, activism, personality and impatience. And I would like to end with a few specifics. My hotel is two blocks away on sixteenth street. This morning when I walked down I passed six large American flags. That's unremarkable in the aftermath of what happened on September 11. And yet in another respect it is very remarkable indeed. Let me say something at the risk of being massively misunderstood. I do not think there's quite as much difference between Islamism and Americanism as many Americans might think. Both of them have universal pretensions. Now you could argue that Islamism is focused on the *shariah,* on Islamic law, and there's no counterpart on the side of Americanism. Tell that to Johnny Lumintang who discovered when he visited the United States that he was on the receiving end of a legal document which I think is going to be a disincentive for him to return to the United States. Indeed arguably there are interest groups that are dedicated to extending, shall we say, versions of American law worldwide. It's hard for me to find the equivalent of the resurrection of the caliphate, but in a universal, democratized polity, it's perhaps not completely off the mark to suggest that the United States would play a kind of lynchpin or keystone role. And again lest you think that I'm veering too far away from actual policy, remember the pride with which Madeleine Albright presided over the birth of the community of democracies. Think of the number of efforts underway funded by the United States, by American taxpayers, to establish some kind of global, democratic governance. And I cannot resist in this context, to mention a request for appropriations from Congress submitted by an unnamed agency.

Quote: "The challenge of democratization in the Moslem world is rooted in the worldwide interests and moral concerns of the United States." That's a remarkable statement. Here we have the melding of *realpolitik* and *moralpolitik.* We have the remarkable assertion that the interests of humanity are identical with the national interest of the United States. That is a presumptuous remark. Next quote, "The cancer of breakdown in any country can metastasize to other parts of the global body politic and thus constitutes a danger to international peace and security." What an extraordinarily wide open door for American intervention. Amazing. Here's another one, "People everywhere..." That's all of us, that's the entire human race, right? "People everywhere, regardless of their religion or culture, can achieve self government under the rule of law." Is this a kind of hyper-Wilsonian invitation to secession? Next quote, "The universal aspiration for democracy is the banner under which this battle for the defense of our national interest can be most effectively waged, and it is also the banner under which we have always proudly marched." There is a sense in which too many truths are being held as too self-evident, if I may paraphrase. The motto "Let's Roll!" which had extraordinarily heroic meaning inside the fuselage of United Airlines flight 93 has been replayed so many times and in so many policy contexts that it's almost as if we don't have to think anymore. All we have to do is *roll*.

I'm wondering in this context how the conclusions reached by Greg Fealy earlier today shape up against the democratizing agenda of the United States. You will recall that he said the five Islamic parties he was dealing with were organizationally fragmented, ineptly led, and ideologically vague. Now being a political scientist, from a standpoint of civic education and the formation of superior political parties, which presumably would be an essential ingredient to a successful democracy, which would of course then reflect the national interest of the United States in the universal aspiration of all human beings, one could argue that in the conclusions reached by Prof. Fealy is a magnificent agenda for an American activist foreign policy. That is to make sure that Islamic parties unite, are ably led, and fill the vacuum of the Jakarta Charter. I wondered when I was listening to Greg, what his Indonesian colleagues on that panel might think and whether precisely the disunity and poor leadership and lack of specification of what the Islamic state might actually mean that characterizes these parties might not be considered a positive thing. If one were to organize the inert Islamic political mass into an effective force, could one live to regret the outcome of a policy that is so morally committed to democracy as an end in itself? Would that policy be insensitive to the collateral damage one can do by pursuing quite so vigorously such a red, white and blue agenda?

When you add to that the "Axis of Evil" I think the distinction between the moral and the empirical begins to fade away and then the possibility of analysis itself is cast in this serious question. If I haven't alienated anyone yet, let me keep going. I would like to talk about the utility of leverage and I would like to ask a question, the answer to which is not really clear to me. I just think it's an important question. Is Indonesia better off when the United States badly wants something from it? Something for it to do, or something for it to stop doing? Or is Indonesia better off when the United States has no such priority, no such pressure? Think of a spectrum between American indifference and American obsession. Is there perhaps a point, in which a relationship that is so fundamentally and so structurally asymmetric, which of course works against Indonesia, Indonesia can find some minimal leverage in American concern? In the interest that the United States has for Indonesia to do something or to stop doing something is it not conceivable therefore, that since September 11 there is an increasingly relentless American focus on what Indonesia "needs to do?" Perhaps this opens up a situation in which Indonesia acquires some modest leverage in which it becomes possible to say, "Well, if you want us to do this so badly, arrest Basyir and so on, then what are you going to be doing for us?" After all they saw the edifying spectacle of Mrs. Arroyo coming to Washington and going away with quite a bit, quite a bit more actually than Megawati went away with. Now they may look at what's happening in Basilan and the Sulawar archipelago and say, "Oh my God, that should never happen here in our archipelago."

Nevertheless, I want to approach this issue of leverage from a somewhat more creative point of view. The asymmetric character of the relationship is critical to my argument. Let's remember what the Indonesians did to the Dutch in the old IGGI. It was easy for Soeharto to do that because the relationship really wasn't all that asymmetric. Let's think of the difficulties that Prime Minister Howard is facing in Indonesia, I believe today, with regard to the refusal of Amien Rais to meet him and so forth. Now Australia is a next-door neighbor, and in that sense more proximate, at least, and I suppose more important perhaps even than Holland, but it's no United States. One can afford to have poor relations with

Australia in a way that becomes a little more problematic, unless you are a full-blown Sukarno, with the United States. I do want to emphasize the structural condition within which leverage has these multiple uses.

With regard to activism, again forgive these comparisons. Since communism is dead and has been consigned to the ashcan of history, all the more reason to resurrect its terminology. If Karl Marx asked the question, 'What is going on?' Then Lenin of course asked the question, 'What is to be done?' There is a sense in the emphasis in activism on results in present day American policy, a very Leninist character. Not just what is being done, but what have you, Indonesia, done? Not just the day before yesterday, but actually yesterday as well? I think we all know that – and there are people in the room who may wish to disabuse me of this since I have no security clearance and I'm therefore limited to the media – but I think it is factually the case that there was at some point a matrix, on paper, in which you have the names of particular countries marching down the page to the left and in which you had columns as to what these countries have done with regard to specific issues in the global war on terror. That is not surprising incidentally in light of what happened on September 11: it is entirely understandable. I'm still looking at the consequences of this incredibly activist focus on the need to wrap up this network, to make arrests, to search for and capture, or kill the individuals responsible for what happened on September 11 and who might be responsible.

Let's remember this is also a matter of prevention. People who were living in Jakarta in the last couple of years had an experience with vulnerability that was perhaps greater than I experienced out in California watching what happened in New York on television. So these are real emotions we are dealing with. The issue of prevention is crucial. By one account of 22 top al Qaeda leaders, 16 remain unaccounted for. My colleagues at Stanford, when we met in October, assured me (these are experts on chemical, biological, nuclear war, very technical people, engineers, people with science degrees) there was 100 percent certainty that within a matter of weeks there would be another major terrorist attack following the September 11 event. Now you know, if certain shoes had exploded one can imagine the averted events. So far, knock on wood, nothing major has occurred, but notice how that also animates American policy, because who is going to say next week, that yet another disaster occurred, and could've been prevented by the United States if it had an even more activist foreign policy that it presently pursues in terms of making sure that all those countries had done enough yesterday and would do even more today and the day after to track down these individuals.

This leads to the remarkable fourth point I want to make with regard to personality. I want you to imagine a spectrum with at one extreme, individuals who need to be captured, punished, or in the famous purposely ambiguous phrase, "either brought to justice or had justice brought to them," (implying the kind of use of violence in the war metaphor here) to the extreme opposite, in which one looks cosmically at the nature of Islamic society and asks the Bernard Lewis question: "What went wrong?" to quote the title of his latest overview of centuries of Islamic history. One looks at the sociology, one looks at tectonic shifts in the relations and sizes of different classes and so forth. It's a little bit comparable to what one does when you walk into a bad neighborhood here in the United States and either you are immediately driven to the worry that these kids may have been brought up poorly and that leads you to educational reform or whether you are primarily concerned to arrest the bastards who were creating the crime and causing the instability.

I think this shows up nicely in successive issues of *Newsweek* magazine which reflect this fluctuation along this spectrum. On the fourth of February, that is last week, we have Malaysia described as a good place to lie low. Notice the implication that terrorism is a matter of terrorists who are looking for a place to lie low and incidentally, what better place than Indonesia which has the virtues among other things, of being a lot larger than Somalia. Which is another reason for concern, American activist security-based concern with regard to Indonesia.

Here's the current issue of *Newsweek*: "The Bible and the Koran, Searching the Holy Books for Roots of Conflicts and Seeds of Reconciliation." Where's the appropriate point to settle down for policy purposes in this spectrum? Obviously it is easier to focus on the evil one, or the evil ones, on individuals and to focus on punishment and prevention as the appropriate response. A pretty dramatic example of this, highly relevant to Indonesia, is the current issue of the *Asian Wall Street Journal* in which the title is: "Indonesian Cleric Becomes the Focus of Terror Manhunt." And here's the first sentence: "Asian police and intelligence officials say they have put a face on the global threat posed by Southeast Asia's Islamic militants, a bearded, Indonesian cleric named Ridwan Isamudin," the famous, and still apparently missing, Hambali. And here we have a chart showing the web of terror. This is Southeas t Asia's web of terror, I'm quoting the *Wall Street Journal,* and in the center of the chart is yes, Hambali. And Indonesia is also well-represented in the periphery, in fact immediately beneath Hambali we have Fathur Rahman al-Ghozi, who studied at Al Mukmin, which is of course the school run by Abu Bakar Ba'asyir, pictured right next door to al-Ghozi. This kind of analysis drives you to individuals, personalities and essentially a law and order response in which American impatience, which is my next topic, is increasingly easy to understand.

Impatience with Indonesia: why can't you be more like the Singaporeans? If there could be terrorists planning attacks on American installations and personnel in a ship as tightly organized and run as Singapore, imagine what can be going on in Indonesia. Again, another driving source of alarm. I want to skip ahead for fear of exhausting the time. Military to military relations, the famous and not yet disappearing issue of mil-mil relations is a good illustration of some of the ambiguities that I've been dealing with. The quite clearly posed question of security versus human rights. I have tried hard today and failed to obtain a definitive answer to the question: Has the Bush administration in its latest budget submission specifically requested military assistance to Indonesia? One source tells me absolutely not. The *Asian Financial Review* tells me the opposite. It does occur to me that if I were in the Bush administration there might be certain advantages to including in that draft, proposed legislation, a specific reference to military assistance to Indonesia. Because then, if Congress throws is out, as they may well do, then at least I could say privately to the Indonesian government, "Well...I tried." On the other hand, that might be far too Machiavellian on my part since I simply lack information. I do, however, wish to say that September 11 quite clearly has created a situation in which authorization – blanket authorization, without specifying the name of the recipient country – global authorization for the campaign against terrorism has opened up an opportunity to make an end run around the Leahy Amendment. Maybe not a blatant end run in the sense of a U.S. government transfer of deadly equipment, you know, bombs and guns, perhaps not. But indirectly under the guise of training forces around the world to help us engage in this battle against terrorism, what might amount to something close to virtually the same thing. This is a fascinating realm, again with ambiguity. It is not coincidental in this context and I have to be fair about this. This is something I support and together with Bob Hefner during Congressional testimony emphasized the need to assist the Indonesian police. Again this is a way of trying to avoid the Scylla and Charybdis problem. That is to say the police is no longer the military. It is not KOPASSUS anyway, although the police in many respects is just as corrupt as the military. I would argue in Aceh perhaps has even more responsibility for some of the depredation that has occurred in that part of Indonesia. At least from an American point of view there is a bit of swaggering on what should be after all a civilian institution. It will be fascinating to watch this as it develops. There will be some effort to try and balance these two priorities rather than trying to elide them as in the opening rhetoric I mentioned in the beginning, as if human rights were the same thing as security and vice versa, which seems to me is quite naive.

A very brief comment with regard to Aceh. The Acehnese situation at the moment is extraordinarily interesting. I would argue that if you agree that the recent meeting in Geneva constitutes a modestly limited success in efforts to move towards a peaceful outcome in Aceh, then I think you should entertain the possibility that GAM, the Aceh Freedom Movement, came to the table in considerable part because of what happened on September 11. There are implications for the degrees of freedom within which they could maneuver vis-à-vis Jakarta in relation to the U.S. What I found intriguing is that General Zinni, whom we will recall from failed efforts to reconcile Palestine and Israel, was present at that two-day meeting that just ended in Geneva. I've been so negative in so many ways it would be helpful to end on a positive note, not that I'm exaggerating the importance of this encounter, but I do want to suggest that not all of the outcomes from September 11 in terms of American policy towards Indonesia are necessarily negative.

Michael Billington, Executive Intelligence Review: What do you think the impact would be of an Israeli movement in Palestine which now seems very possible or a U.S. campaign in Iraq which is being pushed in the administration and elsewhere? How would that impact the internal situation in Indonesia and the region?

Sukma: If the United States initiates a military campaign in Iraq I think it will have a very profound impact on domestic politics in many Muslim countries, not only Indonesia. In terms of Indonesia I think we are going to see a replay of what happened in the weeks after September 11. In that context it would be very difficult also for Megawati's government to deal with such an attack on Iraq. But in general we can also expect that the war on Iraq is basically necessary. And then governments and the Islamic organizations might be able to detach this issue from its religious contexts similar to what happened in 1990 during the Gulf War. There was also growing protest at the time of the war against Iraq, after the Iraqi invasion of Kuwait, that it was in fact war against Islam. Soeharto and a number of Muslim leaders at the time managed to detach the two aspects so the Gulf War was not basically conceived as a religious war. But that was easier because it involved Kuwait, another Muslim country. But the situation will be different and more difficult in the case of Iraq if indeed an attack is imminent.

Abdurrahman: I have read that if the United States is able to prove the al Qaeda connection then maybe we can understand the intentions of the Bush Administration. But if the United States invades Iraq I believe the opposition in Indonesia will try to find new issues to criticize Megawati. There are so many groups within radical Islam that would manipulate a United States invasion into Iraq for domestic political purposes.

Emmerson: An American attack on Iraq for American relations with Indonesia would be somewhere between disastrous and catastrophic. Having said that it seems to me what happens prior to that is critical. If the administration would like to incrementally ratchet up the pressure for Iraq to accept inspectors, it seems to me more people are likely to think of that as a legitimate issue, and there can be a prolonged preparation to see just how intransigent Baghdad seems to be. This strikes me as far more plausible than a sudden attack on Iraq. This could have different consequences. But there is a mountain of distrust that would have to be overcome not just in Indonesia but widely in the Muslim world, where just as the story about 4,000 Jews that did not show up for work at the World Trade Center on September 11 continues to circulate, so do we get a fairly vigorous blaming of the United States for the deaths of children in Iraq.

Woodward: I want to amplify Don's point. This rumor is spread all over the Muslim world like many of the others we have talked about. The number is 500,000 Iraqi children murdered by the United States; that's the way it comes across in Arabic, Persian, Turkish and Indonesian and that's the kind of mountain that would have to be overcome.

Oscar Rambas, Manado, North Sulawesi: I heard about the push to incorporate the Jakarta Charter in the Constitution [to formally establish Islamic Law to apply to all Muslims-ed]. If that happens, I'm afraid Manado is going to declare independence and no longer want to be part of Indonesia.

Sukma: On the issue why no military officials are being punished for the violation of human rights I think the answer is quite simple. If you look at the current government it is basically a coalition government in which Megawati only commanded 33 percent of the vote. Since the fall of Soeharto Indonesia's political system has become highly competitive in which all civilian forces are competing against each other. There lies the greatest problem and threat to the democratic transition where in a very highly competitive system civilian forces do not want to antagonize the military because they need the support of the military in order to compete with other civilian forces. You can see this all across the globe where democratic transitions are taking place – it is not only in Indonesia. This is the real problem and the greatest threat to democracy in Indonesia. No president will be able to address the question of military accountability, especially if the United States restores military-to-military relations. That will give even more credibility to the military to consolidate their power vis-à-vis the democratic forces in the country.

On the question of the Jakarta Charter I don't think there is anything to worry about. If you look at those who advocate this it is only a very small portion of the vote within the entire parliament. It is only PBB [Crescent and Star Party] and PPP [National Development Party] and even the PPP made a deal with Megawati that they would withdraw support if their chairman [Hamzah Haz] was elected vice president at the time. So if anyone wants to revive the Jakarta Charter it has to go through the parliament and that is almost impossible in my view. In fact big Muslim organizations like NU and Muhammadiyah have already publicly opposed attempts to revive the Jakarta Charter.

Donald Weatherbee: What Pak Rizal just said echoes what has been said in other sessions that the real problem in Indonesia is a crisis of governance. How do we get better governance? All of the indicators are that as we march towards 2004 Indonesia may just go over the cliff. Are we really and implicitly talking about a failed state?

Emmerson: The failure of a state lies in the eyes of the observer. If we compare Indonesia to admittedly spectacular examples of state failures I would certainly think that Indonesia is not there yet. Nor do I think this is a Greek tragedy that has only one horrific outcome. Having said that, one of the difficulties is time. Long-term solutions require time for implementation and to take your question and put it slightly differently how much time is there for these long-term responses? Today if I'm not mistaken a delegation from USAID has focused an increasing portion of its money, time and energies on governance and is going to Indonesia for a monthlong assessment of what needs to be done with regard to this particular issue. They are looking at ways the United States might assist the process of governance. If state failure does occur it will not occur for lack of American attention to the problem.

The problem is that the impatience of the United States for results is out of synch with the necessarily long term and structural character of the political reform that would be required. An example is the electoral issue which came up earlier. Should the United States nudge the Indonesians – through Indonesian graduates of American universities with degrees in political science – to move towards a district system? What is the relative benefit of allocating scarce resources to that sort of process of electoral or constitutional reform as opposed to perhaps different and more immediate efforts to address issues like corruption, the judiciary and so forth? Some of these issues unravel the more you look at them.

Barbara Harvey, retired Foreign Service: This is partly in response to Don Weatherbee's question whether Indonesia is a failed state. I think many of us who have been involved with Indonesia over the years do despair from time to time. At the same time we need to recognize that a transition from a long established authoritarian government like the Soeharto regime to a more open democratic one is going to be difficult and at least Indonesia now has options that it didn't have before.

In contrast to the situation in the 1960s, the first time I was in Indonesia when I thought that Indonesia was a failed state, there has been an increase in the number of educated people; the number of people active in the NGOs; people questioning what is going on in Indonesia themselves. There is now a better opportunity to come through this really difficult time.

Marc Hoffman: There are a couple of things I've noticed and I cannot figure out the relationship among them. Many of us heard Amien Rais at a USINDO gathering talking about Zionism. He seemed to be saying that Zionism was behind some of the disturbances in Indonesia. He drew a distinction between Judaism which he was compelled to respect because of his religion and Zionism but I frankly did not understand the distinction he was making. Another thing I noticed after the September 11 tragedy was that Ambassador Gelbard objected to something published in the papers by Dewi Fortuna Anwar saying the World Trade Center was attacked because it was a symbol of Jewish power in America. There are stories about Muslim leaders telling their congregations that they should be careful because they are under threat from this conspiracy. What are the implications of these misperceptions for American policy? What is happening in Indonesia?

Woodward: I have looked into the anti-Semitic rhetoric that one hears in Indonesia. I don't know exactly how the stories move around. This has been going on for at least 30 years. There is a story that Neil Armstrong heard the call to pray on the moon and became a Muslim but he could never say so because he would have lost his government. This story is known in every village and town from Morocco to Eastern Indonesia. There are a whole lot of strange rumors that float around. The anti-Semitic rhetoric is rooted in documentation of the origins and the protocol of the elders of Zionism. The Russian secret service published reports justifying pogroms against Jews and these have been translated into many languages. I was somewhat shocked to pick up a copy in an Indonesian bookstore with an introduction that said the Jewish bankers, the communists, the Chinese, and the CIA are all involved in this conspiracy to destroy Islam all over the world. I might add that as strange as these stories seem to us, if you float around rural America and ask people about Muslims, the stereotype is a guy riding a camel with a bomb in a suitcase and a Kalishnikov assault rifle in the other hand. In terms of the public diplomacy question I think these are exactly some of the issues we need to combat and say "Hey people, these rumors are not true."

6

GLOBAL ISLAM AND THE SECULAR MODERN WORLD

TOWARD GLOBAL CIVILIZATION OF LOVE AND TOLERANCE

In Islam, the Umma is more than a religious concept; it connotes social solidarity and cultural identification beyond ethnic and regional boundaries. In this way, the Umma (community of believers) serves as the most fundamental of what ªerif Mardin (1989) refers to as "Islamic idioms," that is, shared paradigmatic concepts that serve the ultimate function of reproducing social structures over time and space. Mardin develops the notion of the Islamic idiom as follows:

The Islamic 'idiom' is pervasive in the sense that covers all aspects of life and society and that it is shared equally by upper and lower classes...Daily life-strategies are framed by the use of the religious idiom, and the fund of Qur'anic symbols on which it is based has a widespread popular usage...it is because this idiom is shared that there appears something that we could name 'social legitimation' in Islamic societies, a legitimation that derives from the widespread use of this idiom (1989: 6-7).

In Islam's formative period, the Umma linked a trans-regional system of Muslim trade and pilgrimage networks. In the contemporary era, these networks are linked to developments in information and communication technologies, which have subsequently provided the structural opportunity spaces for Muslim social movements (MSMs) to mobilize via a revival of the Umma as a universal Islamic precept.

Outlining his "clash of civilizations" thesis, Samuel Huntington (1996) argues that the rise of MSMs is indicative of a deep culture cleavage between the West and Islam; "the underlying problem for the West is not Islamic fundamentalism. It is Islam, a different civilization whose people are convinced of the superiority of their culture and are obsessed with the inferiority of their power (216-18). Legitimizing Huntington's argument, the 20th century Pakistani ideologue Abul a'la-Mawdudi once said that as a result of Western intrusion, Muslims, "have turned away from God, towards man's exploitation by man and towards moral degeneration and cultural pollution" (1984: 77-78). Although justified by reciprocal acts of brutality, these two perspectives illustrate little more than a discursive by-pass, with one mirroring the other in enmity and incomprehension. On either "side," the clash argument is presented as both just and inevitable:

"This is the world's fight. This is civilization's fight. This is the fight of all who believe in progress and pluralism, tolerance and freedom." George W. Bush in method is the result of actors' ability to successfully harmonize the sacred components of Islam with the profane language European modernity. What emerged from this dialectic between the sacred and the profane was a specifically articulated Islamic discourse on modernity. Islam became more than a sacred belief system, it became a set of criteria for modern social and political engagement. I conclude this essay with a presentation of the Turkish-based, globally networked education movement of Fethullah Gülen. Typifying the civil/cosmopolitan form, I argue that the Gülen Movement is exemplary of a mature expression of Islamic modernity, a potential black box for "the clash thesis," and a progressive, personalized Muslim social movement rooted in Turkey's unique history of societal secularization and folk Islamic tradition.

TWO DISCOURSES ON MODERNITY

The main problem associated with much of the scholarship on MSMs is that authors assume modern world history to be characterized by Western modernization and a linear process of global modernization thereafter. In terms of modern MSMs, this view posits "Islam," a unique culture and civilization, as naturally unable to integrate with the culture and civilization of the modern West (Huntington 1997, Lewis 1993, Pipes 2002). MSMs are viewed as designing and plotting a cultural and ideological counter offensive in retaliation to a century of perceived Western intrusion and domination232. Exemplified by the current Danish "cartoon crisis," the magnetism of this view is hard to avoid. Europeans seem to view the influx of Muslim migrants as attacks on the moral fabric of Western society:

Many French people feel deeply uncomfortable about defiant, assertive Islam. France, after all, is home to Europe's biggest Muslim population (outside Turkey): some 5m, next to 3m in Germany and 1.5m in Britain. The country has about 1,600 mosques or prayer halls. Many young French Muslims find no difficulty in balancing private faith with French secularism. But an increasingly vocal minority, many of whom speak no Arabic and freely mix Nike trainers with the hijab, finds such compromise unacceptable (The Economist 2/5/2004). 232 What I am calling "civilizational literature," Olivier Roy (2004) calls "the culturist approach" to Muslim politics. Despite the difference of our terms, Roy and I are critiquing the same trend observable in much of the literature. I prefer "civilization" to "culture" because the former connotes an "end state" in human social development. According to classical "evolutionary theorists" (e.g., Spencer, Tylor, and Morgan), "civilization" (after savagery and barbarism) is the last stage of cultural development. The "clash of civilizations" is argued to be an immanent reality because of the current "end-state" (in the evolutionary schematic) characteristic of world cultures. Huntington's thesis rests on the notion that his "seven or eight civilizations" are no longer subject to processes of cultural evolution, hence the inevitability of a "clash."

The explanatory shortcoming of the "clash thesis" stems from its proponents' inability to conceptualize and analyze the mutual construction of world populations within the context of a single temporal event, modernity233. The Middle Eastern historian Reinhardt Schulze (2002) helps illuminate as follows: The major primary force of the Islamic world in the 20th century is not Islamic culture (or even 'Islam' itself), but the temporal context of modernism, which has deeply involved the political public in supranational world affairs...If this leads to a plausible and meaningful result, which corresponds to events, we may succeed in grasping the multilingual aspect of modernism and also providing the Islamic world with a place of its own in modern history. At the same time, we may realize that the European dialect of modernism is merely one of many cultural dialects of modernism (6-7). For Schulze, the European discourse on modernity expresses humanist philosophy, strict secularism, republican nationalism, industrial development, military institutionalism, modernized (Europeanized) education, and religious suppression in the public sphere. Alongside the European discourse, argues Schulze, was the development of its Islamic counterpart. Rather than staging an attack on modernity, however, formulators of the Islamic discourse sought to oppose the oppressive and exploitative version of modernity promulgated by European colonial regimes. Just as a Spanish speaker would likely refuse to learn mathematics if he were taught in Turkish, Muslims often refused to learn the European discourse on modernity as it was promulgated by self-designated "modern" elites. In this way, Muslim intellectuals struggled to cultivate a movement that could "transform" Muslim society by reframing traditional Islamic categories into a modern sociological existence. The writings and speeches of late 19th century and early 20th century Muslim intellectuals inspired the development of an entire lexicon of Islamic idioms to meet the challenges of economic, political, and social subordination in the Western dominated world system. In this way, "Islam [became] a channel through which persons who had failed to become integrated into the secular system [of Ottoman modernization policies] were engaged in their own project of boundary expansion, and search for freedom" (Mardin 1989: 83-4). How was such a lexicon developed? How did 19th and 20th century Muslim intellectuals manage to develop a specifically Muslim theory of the modern world? Answer: By creating a Muslim expression of modern temporality.

ISLAMICIZATION THE PROFANE OR THE PROFANATION OF ISLAM?

In his foundational study on The Elementary Forms of Religious Life, 19th century French social theorist Emile Durkheim argued that all societies share a foundation for religious thought. All societies separate their known and unknown realities into one of two domains of existence, the sacred and the profane. The sacred domain is that which is exceptional, extraordinary, "supernatural," divine. The profane is that which is simply not sacred: everyday practice versus prayer; regular days versus holidays; the natural versus the "supernatural;" the body versus the soul; etc. According to Durkheim, the sacred and the profane are necessary opposites, diametrically opposed social phenomena that must remain separate so as to sustain their meaning:

> The sacred and the profane have always and everywhere been conceived by the human mind as two distinct classes, as two worlds between which there is nothing in common...this is not equivalent [however] to that saying that a being can never pass from one of these worlds into the other: but the manner it does take place, puts into relief the essential duality of the two...In fact, it implies a veritable metamorphosis....The two classes cannot even approach each other and keep their own nature at the same time (Durkheim 1915: 54-55).

When the sacred and the profane merge, one necessarily subsumes the other. This creates either a wholly sacred, or a wholly profane social object. Durkheim uses the cross-cultural example of religious rites of passage during puberty, whereby the child, after having gone through the sacred rite of passage, ceases to be a profane youth and emerges as a sacred subject of his faith. What happens when lay Muslim scholars (non-Ulama) reframe sacred Islamic categories to merge with the profane institutions of European modernity? Is the result a profanation of Islam or an Islamicization of the profane?

Addressing this question, I am indebted to the work of Talal Asad (2003). As he aptly argues, in modern politics, secularism, the discursive and structural removal of the sacred from the profane in regard to civic and political organization, is somewhat of a pre-requisite. This is because modern political organization (i.e., bureaucratic regulated, territorially bound nation states) emerged out of the necessity to efficiently regulate accumulation in a capitalist world economy. Throughout modern history, incorporation into this system forced regions to rationalize their traditions so as to harmonize their societies with the dictates of modern regulation.

Asad argues that the European Enlightenment created a model for modern political organization by reconceptualizing the sacred as transcendent, "mythic," and personal. This gave rise to Deism as the philosophical model for modern belief. By positing God as a passive creator, the natural world (and subsequently the social and political world) emerged as non-sacred objects. As part of the profane world, nature could be questioned, analyzed, tested, and manipulated in the interests of human knowledge. In this way, argues Asad, "profanation" was a necessary prerequisite for political struggle and legal rationalization:

'Profanation' is a kind of forcible emancipation from error and despotism. Reason requires that false things be either proscribed and eliminated, or transcribed and re-sited as objects to be seen, heard, and touched by the properly educated senses. By successfully unmasking pretended power (profaning it) universal reason plays its own status as legitimate power...At the very moment of becoming secular, claims are transcendentalized, and they set in motion legal and moral disciplines to protect themselves (with violence where necessary) as universal. Although profanation appears to shift its gaze from the transcendental to the mundane, what is does it rearrange barriers between the illusory and the actual (Asad 2003: 35-6).

In Europe, when the sacred (Christianity) merged with the profane (the Enlightenment), the dialectical result was a profanation of European society. Deist philosophy largely removed spirituality from the public domain, thus relegating the Church's authority to the private sphere.

In the modern era, a similar merging of the sacred and the profane occurred in Muslim societies, albeit, with diverging results. Responding to the challenges of European colonialism and the eventual development of secular nationalist Muslim majority states, MSMs mobilized in an effort to combat the "profaning" of their life-worlds. In their effort to compete (politically, socially, and economically) in the modern world, early MSMs needed to legitimate modern social and political organization using the sacred language of Islam, thereby creating socially and politically applicable Islamic idioms: an Islamic discourse on modernity. Modern Muslim social movements are the observable synthesis from the dialectical tension between European and Islamic modernities.

As with all social phenomena, however, variation is a definitive feature of Muslim socio-political mobilization. Such variation is explained by 1), the ability of MSM theorists' to successfully articulate the necessities of European modernity with the language of Islam in order to meet the demands of the secular modern world, and 2) the structural/systemic conditions existing in a given social/political sphere that allow for the expression of an Islamically defined social and political agenda.

THE IDEAL-TYPE MUSLIM SOCIAL MOVEMENT

In an effort to distinguish varying forms of MSMs from one another, what follows is an "ideal-type analysis" of MSM ideology.234 Ideal types serve as variables by which one can measure the thought and action of real groups and real actors by way of variation from the ideal. I develop the ideal type ideology of 20th century MSMs by interrogating the texts of three prominent 20th century Muslim intellectuals, Sayyid Qutb (1906-1966), Sayyid Abul A'la Mawdudi (1903-1979), and Bediüzzaman Said Nursi (1873-1960). I develop the ideal type asking five questions of MSM ideology:

1. Epistemology-What are the sources of legitimate knowledge?
2. Ontology – What is the nature of reality? What is the movement's worldview? How is reality conceptualized?
3. Anthropology – What is the nature and function of identity?
4. Teleology – What is the purpose of the movement?
5. Methodology – What is the agreed upon method used to achieve the stated purpose?

Epistemology: For all pious Muslims, the source for legitimate knowledge is the collected canon of the Qu'ran, the Hadith, and the Sunna. There are four Sunni legal schools; that is, there are four classical interpretations of the Sunni Sharia (Islamic Law), the Maliki, the Hanafi, the Shafi'i, and the Hanbali235. In the 10th century, "the gates of ijtihad" (interpretive reasoning) were closed, and Muslims around the world restricted their incorporation of Sharia to one of the four traditions. Epistemologically, what distinguishes Sunni Islamists from classical Islam is the re-inauguration of ijtihad.

Ijtihad, argues John Voll (1983), is founded upon tajdid (renewal) and islah (reform). Throughout history the tradition of tajdid-islah was the foundation for claiming collective solidarity among the scores of ethnically, linguistically, and nationally diverse groups of Muslims: Tajdid-islah can be distinguished from other great forms of Islamic expression by the degree of willingness to accept or engage in great cultural synthesis in a conscious way. In great interactions of cultures and civilizations that have occurred throughout the history of Islam, tajdid-islah efforts have opposed synthesis that risked undermining the special Quranic foundation of Islamic society (Voll 1983: 41).

All MSMs are engaged in a modern process of Islamic tajdid-islah. In the modern era, however, calls for Islamic revival and reform emerged predominantly under the auspices of lay intellectuals, who transgressed the traditional primacy of the Ulama (Islamic scholars). Coffeehouses supplanted mosques as primary venues for intellectual discussion, new organizations emerged that focused on issues of unemployment, welfare, healthcare, recreation, and political emancipation. Such processes illustrate that MSM did not emerge as a rejection of European modernity, or even European culture. What 19th and 20th century Muslim intellectuals rejected was the medium of deliverance (i.e., European colonialism) and the perceived attack on Muslim epistemology.

In their effort to construct a rival modern ideology, Muslim intellectuals claimed religious/moral authority in the name of Islamic Law (Sharia). Despite their political (i.e., secular) motives, the new Muslim intellectual drew upon sacred Islamic idioms in an effort to make "profane" European political regulation a "sacred" rite of Islam. Esposito and Voll (2001) explain the significance of this historical development as follows:

The new style of Muslim intellectual...was committed to effective transformation of society but within the framework of ideologies and programs that could be identified as authentically

Islamic. In spirit, these new Muslim intellectuals were a continuation of the radical tajdid (renewal) tradition in Islam (20) 236.

Ontology: For all pious Muslims, Islam is believed to be the vehicle by which one can realize God's ultimate unity (Tawhid). According to the prolific Kurdish ideologue Said Nursi, "all existents demonstrate, through their continual decay and renewal, that they are the manifestations of the Sacred Names of an All-Powerful Maker, and the reflections of the lights of those Names...and also they are mirrors reflecting the grace of his perfection" (1995: 42). Despite the ultimate unity of creation, at a lower level, human reality is divided between Muslim reality and reality defined by ignorance of God's totality. According to the 20th century Egyptian hard-liner Sayyid Qutb, the state of ignorance typified by "the West" and its apologists is rationale for waging war (hab) against apostasy in the interests Umma purification. For Qutb, this state of ignorance is best understood as jahiliyyah, the hadith term for the state of human nature before God's revelation to the Prophet. Qutb explains how jahiliyyah permeated the Umma, how Muslim societies were corrupted, demoralized, and brutalized by the ignorance and the arrogance of Western colonialism and domination: We are surrounded by Jahiliyyah today, which is of the same nature as it was during the first period Islam, perhaps a little deeper. Our whole environment, people's beliefs and ideas, habits, and art, rules and laws – is Jahiliyyah, even to the extent that what we consider to be Islamic culture, Islamic sources, Islamic philosophy and Islamic thought are also constructs of Jahiliyyah (Qutb 1981: 20).

Ontology and epistemology converge in the realm of Islamic morality, the ultimate governor of human action. According to A'la Mawdudi, founder of the Pakistani Jama'at Islami (1941), "human life is governed not by physical laws, but by moral laws" (1984: 94). Recognizing the authority of moral laws requires Muslims to submit to the graduated hierarchy of iman (faith), Islam (surrender), Taqwa (godconsciousness), and Ihsan (godliness). The contemporary Turkish religious scholar M. Fethullah Gülen echoes Mawdudi stating that "morals are a set of noble principles that originate in high spirituality and govern human conduct. For this reason, people who neglect their spirituality, and are therefore lacking in spiritual values, cannot sustain conduct in accordance with these principles" (Pearls of Wisdom: 20). Reality is fashioned by morals that descend from the one-ness of God to the human world; Islam is the conduit by which humans are connected to the reality of Tawhid. 1978), Ismail al Faruqi (d.1986) in Palestine, Rashid Ghannoushi in Tunisia, and Hasan Turabi in the Sudan.

Anthropology: All MSM actors view Muslims as identified within the collective of the Umma. In the Umma, the individual is indistinguishable in the eyes of God: despite ethnicity or nation, the Muslim subject is first and foremost a Muslim. That said, MSM ideology views the modern nation state as an effective set of regulatory institutions in the modern world system. Regimes that are economically and politically subservient to the dictates of Western powers, however, or even worse, regimes that appear to emulate and/or promote Western values, are viewed as illegitimate and morally corrupt. The reversion to jahiliyyah and the prevalence of "materialism" (i.e., consumerism) is viewed as the cause for Muslims "turning away from God, towards man's exploitation by man and towards moral degeneration and cultural pollution" (Mawdudi 77-8). In order for such moral corruption to be routed, the Umma must be revitalized, and the Muslim individual must reverse the effects of modern Western domination by reinvigorating the primacy of the Umma as a social identity.

Teleology: The primary goal of the MSM ideology is focused on a revolution of leadership and the subsequent inauguration of a just society organized in accordance with Islamic morality. According to Mawdudi, "leadership that has rebelled against God and His guidance and is responsible for the suffering of mankind has to be replaced by a leadership that is God-conscious, righteous, and committed to following Divine guidance (1984: 71). In doing so, leaders must illustrate both "basic human" and "Islamic" moralities. "Basic human morality" develops when subjects achieve their goals through determination and stamina. "Islamic morality" develops by recognizing Tawhid. Only when an Islamic leader exhibits a high degree of both moralities will the Muslim populace follow in his footsteps and thus rise above their domination by unbelievers. Nursi elaborates as follows: O people of the faith! If you do not desire to fall into slavery and humiliation, come to your senses and take refuge against oppressors who would exploit your differences, in the citadel of the believers are naught else than brothers. Otherwise, you will be able neither to preserve your lives nor defend your rights...If you have any commitment to a collective life of social harmony and solidarity, then make the exalted principle of the believers are together like a well-founded building, one part of which supports the other your guiding principle in life! Then you will be delivered from humiliation in this world and wretchedness in the other [author's emphasis] (Nursi 1995: 69).

Methodology: The primary method for realizing a revolution in leadership and the construction of a moral society is the proper allocation of moral power through jihad (struggle). In order to overcome the restraints beset by jahiliyyah, the Muslim subject must struggle against that which attempts to strip him of his faith. This struggle is two-dimensional: 1) "greater" jihad within the self (nafs) toward the total and willful submission to the God, and 2) "lesser" jihad against the powers of jahiliyyah, against the onslaught of amorality, injustice, and ignorance. It is at this level that divergence emerges in the idealtype. On one side of the continuum, Mawdudi and Qutb argue that jahiliyyah represents everything that is wrong with modern society, a scourge on the potential for human perfection. For this reason, jahiliyyah must be confronted and corrected, with violence if necessary. Emphasis is placed on lesser jihad:

> The importance of securing power for the righteous is so fundamental that, neglecting this struggle, one has no means left to please God...[This] ultimate purpose of Islam...requires the good to possess collective organizational power; anyone who threatens to weaken that collectivity is guilty of a crime so serious that it cannot be expiated by the performance of Prayers not the profession of God's unity (Mawdudi 1984: 79).

On the other side of the continuum, emphasis is placed on greater jihad. As argued by Nursi, "fanaticism, being violent and unreasoning devotion, is incompatible with Islam. However, deep it is, a Muslim's devotion depends on knowledge and reasoning.

For the deeper and firmer a Muslim's belief in, and devotion to Islam...the further from fanaticism a Muslim is by virtue of Islam being the 'middle way' based on peace, balance, justice, and moderation" (Nursi 1995: 263). In this view, violence and intolerance are seen as alien to Islamic epistemology, and thus incompatible to the project of Islamic modernity. For all variations, however, the inability or unwillingness of the Muslim subject to wage jihad, however defined, is to negate his very being; it is to act in bad faith against the unity of the Umma under God.

According to MSM theory (summarized here via the writings of Qutb, Mawdudi, and Nursi), MSM ideology posits a moral and righteous subject of God, who, as a member of the larger Umma, is engaged in a jihad to usher in the institution of a moral society237. Since its official maturation in the form of the Egyptian Ikhwan Muslumin (Muslim Brotherhood), the relative success of a particular MSM has been dependent on its actors' ability to successfully harmonize its deviation from the ideal type with the secular apparatus of the modern nation-state. The result has been extreme fluctuation and diversity in strategy resulting in three distinguishable variations from the ideal: 1) Classical Modernist, 2) Global Jihadist, 3) Civil/Cosmopolitan.

CLASSICAL MODERNIST

According to the Turkish sociologist, Nilüfer Göle (1987), what happened throughout the postcolonial Muslim world was a successful campaign to commandeer the ideology of social development. Because Europe managed to successfully instill its dialect of modernism through the middle and upper classes and among the intellectual elites, populations throughout the Muslim world "lost their power as world history makers...This exclusion in turn results in the formation of societies with 'weak historicity,' that is with a weak capacity to generate modernity as a societal 'self-production' (Göle 1987: 12). What 20th century MSMs faced was a project to "re-Islamize" Muslim society, to "re-take" their capacity to make their own history. The teleology of the classical modernist, therefore, was to formulate an Islamic sensibility that embraced the temporal event of modernity while simultaneously rejecting European political and economic hegemony. The archetype classical modernist MSM was the Egyptian Ikwhan

Muslimin, a civic/political organization formed in 1928 under the leadership of Hassan al-Banna.

According to Banna, Islam distinguished itself from other global religions due to its "concern with not only worship but also social systems…when a Muslim community is ruled by laws other than its own, a clash is bound to erupt between it and the ruling power…" (Moussauli 1998: 111-112). In its early manifestation (1928 – 1936) the Ikhwan managed to cultivate a hybrid anthropology, a new nationalism based at once on religion (Umma), ethnicity (Arab), and nation (Egypt). In this way, Banna and the Ikhwan represented an alternative modernity, a rival ontology that proved to be a lasting threat to the objectives of the European modernity, as institutionalized by Atatürk's Turkey, Nasser's Egypt, and Pahlavi Iran (Al-Azmeh 1993, Lia 1999, Mitchell 1969, Sayyid 1997). After its first engagement in regional politics (the Palestinian Revolt of 1936-1937), the Egyptian Ikhwan embarked on an international redefinition of the Umma. This set the stage for the emergence of Sayyid Qutb, and a more politically specific program for MSM mobilization.

Global Jihadism

Global jihadism constitutes the most violent, widely publicized expression of MSM ideology. Providing the other side of the "clash of civilizations" perspective, global jihadists argue that Western media, education, lifestyle are degrading the Islamic character of Muslim society, leading Muslims astray (by influence and by force) from the Islam's moral fabric. Paying stricter attention to the ideal type, global jihadists understand Dar al-Hab (land of war) to be a global reality. As indicated by the term "global," this variation stresses the significance of the global Umma over and above all possible subject positions. Although international "pan-Islamic" movements are observable throughout modern history, global jihadism did not emerge in its mature form until the Soviet occupation of Afghanistan (1979-1989)238. At that time, Muslims from around the world came together to fight along side the Afghan mujahideen (s. mujahid: one who fights a jihad)239. The effective result of this experience was the development of a "global infrastructure of terror…that used Islamic symbols to tap into Islamic networks and communities" (Mamdami 2004: 130). Thus is the birth story of Osama Bin-Laden and Al-Qu'ida (the base), "a network of organizations and cells from across the Muslim world that hijacked Islam, indiscriminately slaughtering Muslims and non-Muslims alike" (Esposito 2003: x).

The teleological and methodological perspective of global jihadism legitimizes violent insurrection against other Muslims under the authority of kafir (apostasy). Such absolutism views apostasy as blasphemy, and subsequently positions apostates outside the sphere of the Umma. Once theoretically perceived as non-Muslims, so-called apostates are viewed as enemies of Islam. In the era of globalization, mass migration, and high-speed communication, the whole world is viewed as simultaneously entrenched in both the land of war and the land of Islam – "apostates" and "true Muslims" are culturally and politically interwoven. The immediate goals of global jihadism are to oversee the removal of US military instillations on the Arabian Peninsula, overthrow the Saudi royal 238 Pan-Islam refers to the failed political project of 19th century Islamic modernism. Pan-Islamists attempted to seize Muslim identity and use it in conjunction with Islamic nationalism so as to instigate a globally unified movement of Muslim states against the oppressive onslaught of European colonialism.

Islamic Modernism, in this sense, refers to the idea that modernity and Islam are not contradictory phenomena, but are mutually constructive. 19th century Islamic modernists argued that the Qu'ran commands scientific inquiry so as to fulfill humanity's requirement to understand the glory of God, which is represented in his creation of Earth. According to Fazlur Rahman (1990) modernists argued "the West had cultivated scientific studies that it had borrowed largely from Muslims and hence had prospered, even colonizing the Muslim countries themselves. Muslims, in learning science afresh from the developed West, would be both recovering their past and re-fulfilling the neglected commandments of the Qur'an" (50-51).

Civil/Cosmopolitan

What I call civil/cosmopolitan, others in the field call "liberal" or "moderate" expressions of MSM ideology (Baker 1997, 2003;

Kurzman 2001; Moussauli 1998). This variant focuses on "neglected traditions" of Islamic history and theology that "oppose theocracy, support democracy, guarantee rights of women and non-Muslims in Islamic countries, [and] defend freedom of thought and the belief in the potential for human progress" (Kurzman 2001: 4). Civil refers to the fact these movements tend to be focus their attention on civil society. They tend to organize under the dictates of existing political structures, and pose no explicit threat existing political and/or economic systems. They organize peacefully and in conjunction with existing laws. Cosmopolitan refers to the fact that these movements tend to advocate tolerance and dialogue with other social groups. Followers typically come from the middle class, they tend to promote liberal political values, they tend to possess high levels of education, and their goals tend to stress education, passivity, and a global outlook in regard to conflict resolution and human rights. In using the term civil/cosmopolitan, I wish to convey my interest less in the individual theories and/or arguments for "moderate" interpretations of MSM discourse, and more in the material realizations of this discourse in the form of political and social institutions.

In Egypt, Raymond William Baker (1997, 2003) argues that moderate tendencies are long standing trends in Muslim politics and are experiencing a contemporary revival. So-called "new Islamists," "urge the Islamic world to look both to the heritage and especially the experience of others to develop democratic political systems suitable for the global age" (Baker 2003: 171). Their agenda focuses on persuading Egyptian Muslim organizations to adhere to and promote traditional Islamic concepts of ijtihad (interpretive reasoning), shura (consultation), ijma (consensus), and Wassatteyya (Centrist mainstream) so as to generate just and worthy Islamic leadership that can forge an intellectually informed moderate fiqh (understanding of Islamic law) to embed into Egyptian political culture. Because they have no means to actualize this discourse; that is, because they have little capacity to mobilize Egyptian society (through education, media, etc.), and because they cannot gain access to political power, the "new Islamists" have had little impact on Egyptian society. This is primarily the result of their operating in a centralized, autocratic state that has little to no structural means for their free expression. Notwithstanding, the fact that the "new Islamists" exist at all is the result of recent Egyptian political reform, which has created the space for the potential actualization of their discourse.

By contrast, in the contemporary Turkish Republic, the experience of Ottoman modernization, staunch republicanism, and institutional secularization has given rise to variations of both classical modernist and civil/cosmopolitan forms of MSM organization.

I conclude this essay with a presentation of the civil/ cosmopolitan Fethullah Gülen Movement. Here I argue the following: 1) the mobilization and success of the Gülen Movement is the result of Turkish political and economic development in the 20th century, especially its liberal reforms in the 1980s and 1990s, and its drive toward ascension into the European Union. 2) The Gülen Movement is the world's most successful example of a civil/cosmopolitan MSM, a success that is measured both by its international diffusion and by its national and international recognition as a movement for world peace and interfaith dialogue.

The Civil/Cosmopolitanism of the Gülen Movement

According to political scientist Hakan Yavuz (2003a) "contemporary Islamic movements in Turkey seek to re-claim the Muslim self...Islamic movements produce, and are being produced by, new opportunity spaces for discussion where they can develop and experience novel lifestyles and identities" (7).

Such new spaces managed to thrive despite the Kemalist national project (1923-) of institutionalized "modernization from above." Incorporating strict interpretations of European modernity, the early Kemalist regime outlawed Muslim brotherhoods and religious groups, dissolved Sufi orders, and in 1924 terminated the thirteen century-old institution of the Sunni Caliphate. In 1926, Turkey replaced the Sharia (Islamic Law) with the Swiss civil code. In 1927, the Turkish written alphabet switched from Arabic to Roman characters, the fez and the turban became illegal, and in 1933 the state instituted female suffrage. The Kemalist goal was to disconnect Turkish society from its Ottoman past so as to construct a new connection between Turkish state and nation. Turkey's cultural and religious history was re-imagined in accordance with a new secular, modern, and republican "Turkish self."

This sociopolitical environment gave rise to Said Nursi and his followers, the Nurculuk (literally "Nursi-ites:" i.e., followers of Nursi). In the early 1980s liberal reforms under the Özal regime created opportunities for a popular revival of Nursi's teaching241. One such revival emerged in Ýzmir under the guidance of the religious educator M. Fethullah Gülen.

With modest beginnings in the 1960s, the GM emerged as a social force during the Özal period, whereupon it began to invest in the construction learning institutions across Anatolia. In the 1990s, political and economic development in Turkey provided the GM network with global routes to be explored.

The fall of the Soviet Union, the structural weakening of the Turkish state monopoly over information and capital flows, increased Turkish migration to Europe, and global developments in information and communication technologies all contributed to the transformation of the GM from a modest community of Nursi followers to an international civil/cosmopolitan Muslim social movement (Kuru 2005). Active in over 70 countries, the GM now manages an extensive education and media network that spans from Turkey to Central Asia, the Balkans, Southeast Asia, West Africa, Russia, Mongolia, China, Australia, Western Europe, and the United States.

The Özal regime emerged under the dictates of the 1982 constitution, which followed nearly three years of military rule in Turkey. The revival Nursi's teachings, and other public expressions of religion, were a product of the constitution's amended bill of rights, which covered social, economic, and political liberties of Turkish citizens. Among the more relevant were as follows: Article 5 – stipulates all individuals are equal before the law and possess "inherent fundamental rights and freedoms which are inviolable and inalienable."

Articles 28 and 67 stipulate that individuals have a right to privacy and to freedom of thought, and that the news media are free and not liable to censorship, without a court order, which can only be obtained "when national security or the 'indivisible integrity of the state' are threatened." (Library of Congress) Epistemologically, the GM reframes science and progress as Islamic principles. By conceptualizing the profane world (nature) as something sacred (proof of creation), the GM claims that advances in natural sciences prove nothing more than the reality of God's totality.

Indebted to the teachings of Said Nursi, Gülen argues, "religion, being a bountiful basin for science with its sources of knowledge, is an essential element, an important dynamic, a guide that has a clear method in matters that go beyond the horizons of knowledge" (2004: 142).

In this understanding, "science" and "Islam" should are viewed as two versions of the same story; one does not (cannot) discredit or falsify the other. GM epistemology posits that profane knowledge, previously monopolized by European categories, belongs in the realm of the sacred. Ontologically, Gülen asserts that the rise of the West ushered in an era whereby Muslims around the world forgot the divine inspiration behind human knowledge:

Since 'real' life is possible only through knowledge, those who neglect learning and teaching are considered 'dead' even though they are still alive...Science and knowledge should seek to uncover the nature of men and women and the mysteries of creation (Gülen, Pearls of Wisdom: 42-43).

Incorporating the Turkish term cehalet (jahilliyah: ignorance), Gülen adheres to the claim of the ideal type, arguing that humanity has strayed from the righteous path of Islamic morality by forgetting the primacy Qu'ranic revelation and Prophetic example:

When ignorance and unfed hearts and souls increase, materialism and carnality gradually subvert the desire for truth and annul any nobility of purpose...Wholly addicted to triviality and self-indulgence, they will deny any achievement to our ancestors and remain willfully ignorant of what real culture and civilization can make possible: a balance between spirituality and sanity, between virtue and happiness" (Gülen 2000: 194).

Anthropologically, Gülen contends that in the modern era humanity lacks ir°ad (moral guidance) (Agai 2003). Exemplified by the perfection of the Prophet Muhammad, moral guidance necessitates toleration, dialogue, and understanding. Tolerance and dialogue are central to the GM's conception of reality and its identity:

Among the many things we have lost, perhaps the first and most important is tolerance. From this world we understand embracing people regardless of difference of opinion, worldview, ideology, ethnicity, or belief. It also means putting up with matters we do not like by finding strength in a deep conscience, faith and a generous heart or by strength of our emotions (Gülen 2004: 46).

The union of tolerance, moderation, and dialogue is collectively referred to as ho°görü (literally "niceseeing;" compassion). Adhering to ho°görü, and actively promoting its qualities in both thought and practice, drives every aspect of the GM's international activities. For Gülen, the "ideal human," "carries a prophet-like heart in their exchanges with people.

They love and embrace everyone; they turn a blind-eye to the faults of others, while at the same time they are able to question the smallest faults of their own…they know how to live peacefully even with the most irritable of souls" (2004: 98). Teleologically, the GM struggles to cultivate an "ethical foundation" from which enlightened, ideal humans can thrive in the secular modern world. Such individuals, argues Gülen, will serve as leaders in the era of the "global village." Contradicting Samuel Huntington's assertion that "Muslims have problems living at peace with their neighbors242," Gülen defines the movement's project as follows:

In a world becoming more and more globalized, we are trying to get to know those who will be our future neighbor… one of the most important factors here is to eliminate factors that separate people…such as discrimination based on color, race, belief, and ethnicity…Education can uproot these evils…We are trying our best to do this (Gülen: In Ünal and Williams eds. 2000: 329-331).

Although operating in an explicitly secular modern world system, and seemingly engaged in a variety of secular projects, the GM's mission is understood by its followers to be a spiritual quest. This is because, for Gülen, the sacred is not comparable to profane understandings of human life. Illustrating a unique confidence relative to other modern MSMs, Gülen explains his rationale as follows: If we want to analyze religion, democracy, or any other system or philosophy accurately, we should focus on humanity and human life.

From this perspective, religion in general, Islam in particular, cannot be compared on the same basis with democracy or any other political, social, or economic system. Religion focuses primarily on the immutable aspects of life and existence, whereas political, social, and economic systems or ideologies concern only certain social aspects of our worldly [i.e., secular] life (Gülen 2004: 219).

Because the "truth" is understood through Islam, "worldly life" poses no threat to the reality, identity, or purposes of the movement.

Methodologically, the GM strives to fulfill its sacred mission in variety of ways. In 1994, followers of Gülen started the Turkish Writers and Journalists Foundation, a non-profit organization that organizes national and international conferences on the attributes and benefits of interfaith dialogue.

Followers of Gülen manage an expansive media network and are active in the construction of clinics, research institutes, and cultural foundations around the world. 243 Much of these institutions' success is due to the GM policy of working in accordance with its host country's national laws regarding education, religion, and social organizing, which can be seen as a deliberate articulation to adapt to diverse local contexts.

The primary methodological focus of the GM lies in the construction and operation of its nearly 700 schools worldwide. In the schools, Gülen argues, the GM does its part as a frontline advocate for global toleraton, dialogue, and peace:

Our efforts and enterprises are for humanity's sake. In a world becoming more and more globalized, we are trying to get to know those who will be our future neighbor...As regards international relations and humanity, one of the most important factors here is to eliminate factors that separate people, such as egoism, self-interest, and discrimination based on color, race, belief, and ethnicity...Education can uproot these evils. Education is the most effective and common tongue for relations with others. We are trying our best to do this; we have no other intention (In Ünal and Williams 2000: 329-331).

GM teachers work to educate adolescents and teenagers in mathematics and in the natural and physical sciences. Özdalga (2003) elaborates on how the GM manages to Islamicize the profane at the micro-level of the individual. Because "science," which by definition is a secular human endeavor, is viewed within the GM as a religious category, many teachers in the GM view their work in education as equivalent to prayer; "the teaching profession, thus conceptualized, is based on a combination of intellectual considerations (learning and teaching) and religious considerations (the ethics of giving)".

In this way, Gülen educators seem to be acting out a form of "piety through work," similar to the Protestant ethic observed by Max Weber. Exemplifying the civil/cosmopolitan form, GM teachers act in accordance with Gülen's teachings, treating faith as a matter of personal religiosity. Civic engagement is viewed as an external expression of that religiosity in the form of dedication, diligence, trustworthiness, and respect:

Who knows, maybe in the near future, thanks to these volunteers who devote themselves to letting others live...people will regret having fought each other over nothing, an atmosphere of peace that was not previously established in the marketplaces...nobody's blood will be shed and the weak will not cry... (Gülen 2004: 214).

The GM illustrates an almost effortless ability to articulate its ideology with modern science and rationality.

The GM is illustrative of the fact that, "a majority of Turks do not perceive a contradiction between Islam and their attachment to Kemalist symbols, viewing both as integral to national identity" (Zubaida 1996: 10). The sociological result of this dialectic is a "Turkish-Islamic synthesis," a strong identity uniting Turkish-ness with Muslim-ness into one subject position, a merging of the Turkish (European) and the Islamic modernities. In this way, the

GM represents a "vernacularization of modernity...[an] internal secularization of Islam in terms of rationalization, nationalization...[an] accommodation of faith to the overriding exigencies of reason and evidence" (Yafuz 2003a: 5). The mobilization and success of the GM supports the assertion that when existing economic structures inhibit social mobility, and when existing political structures inhibit the free expression of an MSM agenda, a reversion to intolerance, enmity, and violent insurrection is probable. When existing political systems allow for some degree of free expression, which is observable in Turkey's continual efforts to democratically reform its political structure; and when existing economic structures work in favor of a developing middle class, which is observable in Turkey's continual efforts to liberalize its economy-tolerance, passivity, and rationality will likely prevail.

CONCLUSION

The "Islamicization of the profane" begins with the manipulation of Islamic idioms to meet the demands of modern society. As a metaphor for Muslim identity beyond ethnicity or nation, the Umma is the primary Islamic idiom upon which the MSM contruct their collective agenda.

The reformation of Islamic idioms to meet the demands of European modernity allows Muslim subjects to imagine themselves as oppressed by modern jahilliyyah, that is, by the structural realities of authoritarian governance, unemployment, sectarian conflict, poverty, etc. This allows Muslim intellectuals the space to theorize about generations of colonial onslaught and to devise a methodological paradigm to draw upon in their struggle to overcome social domination.

Where MSMs illustrate the greatest degree of diversity is at the level of methodology. The methods used to achieve their stated purpose, be it the structural development of an alternative civil society (classic modernist), violent insurrection and/or terrorism (global jihadism), or the development of an "Islamically defined ethical self" (civil/cosmopolitan), is dependent upon the conditions present in a given society that allow (or discourage) the expression of Islamically defined social change.

In contemporary Turkey, a society rooted in over 250 years of structural modernization and secularization, Islam evolved along a unique path. Although suppressed by the early Kemalist regime and its processes of republican secularization, the folk traditions of Anatolian Sufism survived. Among the most significant of these survivals emerged in the form of Said Nursi and the Nurculuk. Over the course of the late 20th century, continual processes of political and economic liberalization created the spaces for these survivals to adapt. The Movement of Fethullah Gülen emerged as the most successful purveyor Turkey's brand of Islamic modernity, a civil/cosmopolitan MSM that seeks to realize peace through education, tolerance, and interfaith dialogue. It is my contention that the potential significance of such a movement's success should be of crucial interest to international policy analysts, social theorists, and religious scholars alike. In a world consumed with religious and political extremism, the potential global impact of the Gülen Movement is nothing short of fascinating.

7

ISLAM AND TRADITIONAL SEXUAL ETHICS

For Muslims, the institution of marriage based on mutuality of natural interest and cordiality between spouses represents a sublime manifestation of the Divine Will and Purpose. This is discernible in the Quranic verse cited below:

> *And one of His signs is that He created mates for you, that you may find rest in them, and He envisaged between you love and compassion... (Quran, 30:21)*

According to Islamic tradition *(sunnah)*, marriage has been deemed to be an essential requirement. Celibacy has been regarded as a malevolent condition fraught with evils.

The Islamic approach concerning marriage and morals differs from what is known about some of the traditional moralizations of a negative kind. Surprisingly enough, certain traditional moralists regarded sexuality as something basically wicked. They viewed sexual intercourse; even with ones legal spouse, as impure, evil, undesirable, destructive, and as if it were characteristic of the guilty and fallen.

Still more surprising is the generalized view harboured in the West that the traditional world commonly believed in the superstition that ascribed an evil connotation to everything pertaining to sex. The famous Western philosopher, Bertrand Russell, is no exception in this regard. In his book: *Marriage and Morals,* he generalizes that:

> "... *anti-sexual elements, however, existed side by side with the others from a very early time, and in the end, where ever*

Christianity and Buddhism prevailed, these elements won a complete victory over their opposites. Westermarck gives many instances of what he calls 'the curious notion that there is something impure and sinful in marriage, as in sexual relations generally.

In the most diverse parts of the world, quite remote from any Christian or Buddhist influence, there have been orders of priests and priestesses vowed to celibacy. Among the Jews the sect of the Essenes considered all sexual intercourse impure. This view seems to have gained ground in antiquity.

... There was indeed a generalized tendency towards ascetism in the Roman empire. Epicureanism nearly died out and stoicism replaced it among cultivated Greeks and Romans.... The neo-Platonists were almost as ascetic as the Christians. From Persia the doctrine that matter is evil spread to the West, and brought with it the belief that all sexual intercourse is impure. This is, though not in an extreme form, the view of the Church..."

Negative sexual attitudes continued through the centuries to affect masses of credulous people, in an adverse and also frightening manner of repugnance towards sex. The high incidence of psychosomatic disorders and spiritual ailments is largely and uniquely attributed by some psychoanalysts to a widespread prevalence of deeply ingrained negative sexuality.

What could have been the causative factors in the misconceptions about sexuality? What could be the reasons for men to deny themselves the natural satisfaction and the psychosomatic well being associated with healthy and desirable sex? Why should people lead their lives, so as to virtually condemn an essentially wholesome part of their lives? These are some of the complex questions for which thinking men have yet to provide meaningful and convincing answers. Yet, we all know that there could be many different reasons for, and causes of, aversion to human sexuality.

Apparently, the reasons include prejudicial thinking about sexual desire and intercourse. The prejudice was carried to the extreme among the Christians, in organizing their churches and the clergy.

The celibacy of Jesus Christ inspired them to the effect that married status for saints and preachers was considered tantamount to pollution of their chastity and piety. Accordingly, Popes are always chosen from among unmarried priests. In fact, all the members of the Catholic clergy are bound by their oaths of celibacy towards remaining virtuous.

Bertrand Russell says:

> *"Two or three beautiful descriptions of this institution (marriage) have been culled out of the immense mass of the patristic writings; but in general, it would be difficult to conceive anything more coarse or repulsive than the manner in which they regarded it.... The object of the ascetic was to attract men to a life of virginity, and as a necessary consequence, marriage was treated as an inferior state.... To 'cut down by the axe of Virginity the wood of Marriage' was in the energetic language of St. Jerome, the end of the saint"*

Church approves marriage for purpose of human procreation. The need for propagation of human species is not construed as something adequate to lift the stigma of impurity from any sexual act. Another reason for conceding marriage is to eliminate fornication between men and women. Again to quote Bertrand Russell:

> *"Christianity, and more particularly St. Paul, introduced an entirely novel view of marriage that it existed not primarily for the procreation of children, but to prevent the sin of fornication"*

The Catholic church regards marriage as sacrosanct and binding until death intervenes. Accordingly, dissolution of marriage, or divorce, is not permitted. The prohibition of annulment of marriage or divorce may have something to do with a possible desire to atone for the original sin, resulting in the expulsion of Adam and Eve in an unmarried state.

Irrational attitudes towards women prevailed among some of the ancient peoples. These included a notion that a woman was not a complete human being; for, her situation as a creature might well lie somewhere between a human being and an animal. Also, she was devoid of an articulate spirit, so that she could never make it to Heaven! Similar other superstitions were rampant in the past. Fortunately, however, the aforementioned beliefs and notions were not universally carried to the extreme. Any natural limits of women, as identified and evaluated in the past, were not encroached upon. Any impact of traditional ways of thinking did not go beyond cultivation of a sense of pride by men and inculcation of a sense of inferiority among women through generations.

Apparently, the belief in the inherent wickedness of sexual desire and intercourse made men and women absolutely and equally distressed in spiritual terms. Moreover, it caused a rather demoralizing conflict between the natural instinct's urge and the religious or sectarian belief about wickedness of carnal desire and sexual intercourse.

Spiritual ailments and unhappiness arising from the aforementioned conflict included disharmony between genuine natural desires and socially induced aversion towards their fulfillment. The problem assumed extraordinary proportions, in as much as it became the subject of intensive investigations by psychologists and psychoanalysts.

In the above context, the revolutionary logic of Islam can be of extraordinary interest. Islam gives no slightest indication to the effect that sexual desire is evil in itself, or that it is necessarily fraught with evil consequences. On the contrary, the Islamic endeavour in this regard is aimed at regulating human sexuality in a most humane manner.

In the perspective of Islam, human sexual relations are limited only by the genuine interests of the present society, or the posterity. In this connection, the Islamic approach follows well known guidelines, leading neither to any sense of sexual deprivation and frustration, nor to any repressed or inhibited sexual desire. It is a pity that scholars, like Bertrand Russell, who has evaluated the Christian and Buddhist morals, have refrained from specifically commenting on Islamic ethics.

In his book: *Marriage and Morals,* Bertrand Russell mentions in passing about Islam. For example, he says:

> *"Great religious leaders, with the exception of Mohammad- and Confucius, if he can be called religious-have in general been very indifferent to social and political considerations, and have sought*

rather to perfect the soul by meditation, discipline and self-denial."

Nonetheless, it is true that from the Islamic point of view sexual desire is not only compatible with human intellectuality or spirituality, but is evidenced as part of the nature and temperament of the prophets. According to one tradition *(hadith)*, love and affection for women were characteristic of the moral conduct of the prophets.

There are several other traditions and narrations indicating prophetic regard for women. According to some, the Prophet of Islam and the pious Imams too have all explicitly demonstrated their love and regard for their wives and the womenfolk. At the same time, they have strongly disapproved of any human inclination towards celibacy or monasticism.

One of the companions of the Holy Prophet, Osman bin Madaoon, devoted himself to Allah's worship to such an extent that he kept fast practically everyday, as well as regular nightly vigils in prayers. His wife brought the matter to the attention of the Prophet, who reacted with visible annoyance and proceeded at once to where his companion was and said:

"O Othman! Know that Allah has not deputed me to encourage any monastic life. My Shariah laws are meant for enhancing and facilitating human accomplishment of their natural lives. Personally, I offer my prayers, keep fast and maintain my conjugal relations. Accordingly, to follow me in Islam means conforming to the traditions laid down by me, which include the requirement that men and women should marry and live together harmoniously"

The Islamic position as explained above makes it clear that human sexuality in itself neither represents any inborn wickedness, nor it invariably signifies evil consequences. Furthermore, it clarifies that wickedness has been traditionally ascribed to human sexuality in the process of evolving religious morality in the Western world. Now, the Western world has taken a 180-degree turn in reversing its extreme traditional morals.

At present, the Western world believes in respecting and freeing sexual desires and involvements through lifting of traditional moral restraints. In fact, many Westerners now favour sexual permissiveness. They contend that whatever morality has been inherited by them carries no more than a religious connotation. They claim that today's new morals are based on not only philosphical, but scientific reasons.

Unfortunately, the negative sexuality traditionally and recently evolved in the West has penetrated the moral fabric of our society, too.

This is despite all the erstwhile difficulty of international communication. Now with the improved means of communication and regular international contacts, the modernistic Western speculations are virtually flooding our society, as will be explained later on herein.

SEXUAL ETHICS AS CONCEIVED BY MODERN THINKERS

Sexual morals constitute an integral part of behavioural ethics applicable to human beings. Included in sexual ethics are some of the various social norms, personal habits and behavioural patterns, which are associated directly with the sexual instinct. Some aspects of the sexual ethics and practices are specified below:

> *Female modesty, male sense of honour concerning female members of a household, female chastity, a wife's faithfulness to her husband; female inclination to cover her private parts, or her aversion to exposing any bodily nakedness in public; prohibition of adultery, interdiction of any visual or physical intimacy with women other than one's legal wife or wives; prohibition of incest, or marriage between persons too closely related; avoidance of sexual intercourse with menstruating women; debarring pornography or obscenity; and treating celibacy as either too saintly or undesirable.*

Sexual instinct is by its very nature quite extraordinary. Also, it is powerful in its manifestation. Accordingly, sexual morals are part of the most important of all ethics.

In his book entitled: *Our Oriental Heritage, Will* Durant highlighted the fact that marrying and settling down was always considered to be one of the very important moral duties of human beings. He said that the natural human capability for procreation involved difficulties, not only at the time of marriage, but before and after that, as well.

The difficulties could be aggravated by the intensity and vehemence A the sexual instinct, as well as its aversion to moral and legal constraints. Further, it might even lead to deviation from its natural course. All these and more, as mentioned by Will Durant, meant extreme confusion and organisational disorders, if and when a society could not provide necessary and effective safeguards.

Any scientific and philosophical discussion of sexual morals need first consider their origins and evolution. For instance, it is necessary to know how modesty and chastity of women have come to be safeguarded. The fact that men traditionally protect their women, as part of their own sense of honour, could be due to identifiable or specific reasons.

The male aptitude for possessiveness and protection of women may not necessarily be attributed to any inborn jealousy of men. For, human jealousy has universally been considered a negative emotion. Has an exception been made in favour of jealousy so as to safeguard husband-wife relationship? If so, why? If there are other reasons for men protecting the honour of their women, as if it were a question of their own honour, how can these be explained?

Likewise,the desires and social norms favouring clothing or covering of female body, curbing sexual promiscuity, prohibiting marriage between persons too closely related and similar other moral and legal restraints need be explained. Their examination can be in terms of whether or not they have their roots in the human nature, physiological and psychological.

Then, one may as well ask as to whether or not sexual morals are linked to the natural requirements of gregarious living Or, is it part of their inborn tendencies, feelings and concerns towards an appropriate human survival in the natural process. Or, is there any possibility that hisiorical causes, other than natural, have gradually affected and influenced human conscientiousness and behaviour? If the source of human morality has been entirely rooted in nature, it is hard to explain how not only the ancient savages, but today's isolated primitive tribes, living in the manner of their ancestors, were and are quite unlike the civilized people.

The origins and raison d'etre of sexual morality may be diverse. So can be the historical conditions of social evolution, with reference to human sexual ethics in particular. Nevertheless, the question relevant to us now is as to whether or not the traditional morals are valid in the modern conditions towards achieving overall human progress.

Specifically, we must ask ourselves whether or not we must now safeguard the traditional sexual ethics or replace them by instituting new morals.

Will Durant does not trace human sexual morality to any origins in the mother nature. He attributes moral evolution to reasons arising from historical experience, even some occasionally unhappy or cruel happenings in the past. He favours retaining the substance of traditional morals, while allowing continued evolution of the forms, in order to selectively practise the best without shortcomings.

Referring to morals concerning female virginity, modesty and bashfulness, Will Durant observes to the effect that traditional values and customs evidence a natural process of moral selection, involving trials and errors through centuries. According to him, virginity and modesty are relative qualities linked with conditions of marriage and traceable to even a past situation requiring purchase of, or bargaining for, wives.

Will Durant recognizes that the moral and social requirements of female chastity and modesty are of basic importance to any society, even if these qualities are sometimes capable of giving rise to psychosomatic and nervous disorders. Moreover, the relevant social regulations are essential for Promoting a harmonious continuity in sexual relations in the context of marriage and family living.

Freud and his followers subscribed to a different view of sexual morals. They sought to dispense with the traditional sexual morality, or to replace them with something altogether new. In the opinion of Freud and his followers, morals were based on limitations and prohibitions concerning human sexuality. They claimed that the limitations and prohibitions caused many human afflictions and gave rise to emotional disturbances, including subconscious fears and obsessions.

Basically similar arguments have been put forward by Bertrand Russell. He defends in his own way the position that nothing should be regarded as taboo. His views concerning marriage and morals are independent of any moral considerations, such as those of chastity, rectitude, modesty, any male sense of honour encompassing the female (which he suggests is actually jealousy) and similar others.

The proposed liberation of human sexuality from traditional moral restraints is tantamount to claiming that nothing ugly, bad or disgraceful can come out of it. The impression conveyed is one of relying on nothing but the human intellect and its rationalizations. The proposal concedes no more restraint on sex than any natural limitation of food intake!

Elsewhere, Bertrand Russell tried to answer a question as to whether or not he had any advice to give those who wanted to follow a correct and sensible path in matters of sex. His reply was to the effect that, after all, one should examine the question of sexual morality in the same analytical manner as in the case of any other problem. If, as a result of adequate examination, it was found that others would come to no harm from one's pursuing a certain manner of sexual conduct, we would have no reasons to condemn any such individual rationalization and practice.

Bertrand Russell replied in the negative to a second question as to whether or not, in his-opinion, any violation of female chastity could be viewed as an exception to his contention that actions causing no harm or loss to others should not be condemned. He explained that loss of virginity could be due to an act between two individuals. However, If it was construed as an act of violation of the chastity of a virgin, there should be evidence to the same effect before it could be condemned as rape.

For the time being, we may refrain from a detailed examination of the question as to whether or not human traits like modesty, or sexual chastity, are rooted in the mother nature. For, the question is very broad in scope. One can hardly give a completely scientific answer. However, whatever has been indicated thereon, so far, can neither be assumptive, nor approximate. For., it is recognized that those who base their opinions on assumptions often lack consensus:

For instance, human inclinations like sexual modesty are viewed differently by Freud, Will Durant and Bertrand Russell. The nature and content of their difference need not be detailed herein. Suffice it to mention that these writers seem to base their views on the assumption that human qualities like female modesty are not inborn or in any way specific to human nature. If so, their understanding of human characteristics shows what appears to be disinclination to seek a correct justification, or a microscopic approach.

Be that as it may, we can indeed make two assumptions regarding sex habits and inclinations. Firstly, we may assume that sex-oriented behavioural qualities have no connection whatever with the innate nature of human beings. Secondly, we may suppose that the "habits" are inculcated as part of other human practices and norms, under some kind of a social contract, designed to harmonize individual and social interests, as well as towards assuring peace and well being of mankind.

Let us now ask ourselves as to whether or not logic and reasoning demand intrinsic values and safeguards for assuring complete psychological harmony and maximizing human well being and peace. We may further ask ourselves as to whether or not any elimination of moral and social restraints and limits will be conducive towards achieving complete psychosomatic harmony of individuals and enhancing social welfare.

Then, we may well realize that logic and reasoning deem it advisable for us to oppose every customary practice and superstitious habit, which implicitly treats human sexuality as unclean and pernicious. At the same time, we are likely to consider it necessary that we should refrain from promoting any unrestrained sexual freedom which causes widespread excesses, transgressions and agonies.

The supporters of the proposed new sexual liberty base their arguments on three premises,

(1) Freedom should be ensured for every individual, as it does not interfere with that of others;

(2) All inborn sexual desires and aptitudes should be freely nurtured and brought to fulfilment without any inhibition or restraint, since their curbing or frustration leads to disorders of the ego; and

(3) Any natural desire subsides when it is fulfilled, and it becomes insistent and excessive when it is subjected to any negative moral restraint or ill conceived prohibition.

The sexual liberationists argue that emotional instability arises from discriminating among the natural instincts and desires, so that only part of these are satisfied while the others remain frustrated. So, they say, equal nurturing and development of all human inclinations is necessary for personal and societal well being.

Furthermore, they suggest that, for avoiding constant preoccupation with sex, the only correct way is to lift all moral restraints and social prohibitions. They claim that liberation of the natural process of sexual fulfilment will also preempt mischief, malice and vengeance characteristic of a situation involving moral restrictions.

The foregoing arguments constitute the basis on which the new sexual morality is proposed. God-willing, we should be able to render these arguments untenable, through an adequate investigation and a thorough evaluation of the three basic premises mentioned above.

PROPOSED NEW SEXUAL FREEDOM

A critical analysis of the basic principles of the proposed new sexual freedom has been indicated in the preceding chapter. In this chapter, we concentrate on examination of the salient features of the proposed new sexual liberation, specially on its reformatory content in relation to conventional morality. This will be conducive to a detailed analysis, which is not likely to be thorough otherwise.

That there are people W11 are already convinced about the reformatory content of the proposed new sexual conduct is to be recognised. At the same time, it is worthwhile-even necessary-that social problems, including those of sexual morality, are discussed from various angles. For, the question of sexual ethics has received the attention of famous thinkers of our age. Above all, it is notable that the proposed new, approach to human sexuality has tended to be readily accepted by young people, without evidencing any skepticism. Views of well-known personalities of our modern times are apparently taken to be infallible.

In our considered opinion, it is necessary that the esteemed readers are made aware of all the implications of even any rudimentary assimilation on the part of our impressionable young people of the novel ideas from the West, including some with innocuous labels, such as *freedom*, and *equality*. This is because we must know in which direction we are applying our minds, to what purpose and towards what end. If whatever we think and do is believed to be correct without verification, does it necessarily enable mankind to continue progressing?

Or else, does the Western intellectual and cultural penetration of our society represent too ill-informed and too illconceived a propaganda strategy that, if allowed to spread, is bound to lead mankind towards self-destruction?

The above questions are intended to be discussed herein, in a necessarily brief manner. A more elaborate discussion of the relevant issues will be found in the author's book: *The Rights of Women in Islam*.

With regard to the modernistic reform of the traditional sexual morals, the speculative reformers claim that the very basis of the latter no longer exists, or is in the process of vanishing. Since the reasons, the causative factors and the original conditions have changed, or are changing, they say that we have no longer any justification to continue practising the old morality, the severity of which has occasionally been evidenced.

Furthermore, they point out that, aside from the changed or changing conditions, there have been in the historical past events involving the old morality in an ignorant and cruel manner. They believe that the past experiences were inconsistent with the concepts of freedom, justice and human dignity. So, even for the sake of humanity and justice, they appeal that we must oppose all moral restraints on sex. Opponents of the traditional sexual morals say that the old concepts gave rise to the following:

(1) Male sense of possession of his female,
(2) Male jealousy,
(3) Male concern for establishing his paternity of a child,
(4) Asceticism and monasticism based on the assumed sinfulness and wickedness of human sexual relations,
(5) Female sense of impurity arising from her menstruating nature,
(6) Male abstinence from sexual relations with a menstruating female,
(7) Severe punishments at the hands of men undergone by women throughout recorded history; and
(8) Causing women to remain economically dependent on men.

They claim that the above state of affairs is attributable to the conventional sexual morality, indicative of the cruel and superstitious individual and social restraints applied under primitive conditions. They seek to replace the old values by modernistic permissiveness. For one thing, they point out, modern wives are not to be treated as chattels.

In the same vein, they proclaim that today contraceptives preempt any need to ensure paternity of a child in a forcible manner such as implicit in the old moral prescription of the female chastity!

The supporters of the proposed new sexual freedom further affirm that old ascetic and monastic orders and beliefs are dying out. Knowledge and sanitary means of personal hygiene are said to have freed women from harbouring any sense of pollution while menstruating. They are convinced that the days when men could manage to be cruel and oppressive are gone for ever.

They conclude that enslaving or illtreatment of women and making them utterly dependent on men are now things of the past. For, women are regaining socioeconomic freedom. Moreover, modern governments are gradually taking upon themselves major socioeconomic responsibilities of a husband and father, including mothercare and childcare. On the other hand, human jealousy is on the decline with the spread of modern sexual attitudes and behavioural norms. Accordingly, they suggest that we should no longer cling to the old moral system.

The foregoing criticism of old morality is offered by sexual liberationists as the basis of their proposed new morals. Of course, this is to be expected of those who oppose conventional morals.

Now, let us examine the reformatory content of the proposed new morals. At the: outset, we recognize the fact that their intended casting away of the traditional moral constraints on human sexuality constitutes the axis around which the proposed new morals revolve. Accordingly, the very first thing that is likely to receive their attention is what they consider to be a need to ensure freedom of individual action towards fulfilling one's sexuality, or towards bringing about conditions of free sexual love.

In pursuit of sexual liberty, they affirm the unrestrained joys of not only premarital but post marital experimentation with one's sexuality. They point out that, through the least expensive and rather safe means of contraception, sexual enjoyment can be diversified without necessarily involving any risk of pregnancy, legitimate or otherwise. Thus, they claim that any spouse can safely pursue his or her love affair to her heart's content, by taking lovers or becoming a love object without necessarily undermining their marriage. Moreover, they imply that not only illegitimate pregnancies can be avoided, but a wife can chose to have a legitimate child, without any moral concern about her extramarital affairs.

Any *communism* in sexual matters is obviously undesirable. Also, it is impracticable if the genetic need to ensure paternity of a child is to be ensured. Even those who propose the new sexual freedom seek to retain legitimacy of a child, or to safeguard the paternity as something not to be eliminated. After all, a father's blood relationship with his son and the latter's filial obligation and affinity towards the former are always recognizable. This is the philosophy behind selection of a particular spouse and one's marital undertaking to voluntarily confine sexual relations to her or him. In fact, conventional morality highlights no other, or greater, need than for rendering sexual relations in marriage specific to the couples themselves. Bertrand Russell's proposed new morals are cited below:

> *"... Contraceptives have made parenthood voluntary and no longer a result of sexual intercourse. For various economic reasons... it seems likely that the father will have less importance in regard to the education and maintenance of children in the future than he has had in the past. There will therefore be no very cogent reason why a woman should choose as the father of her child the man whom she prefers as a lover or companion. It may become quite easily possible for women in the future, without any serious sacrifice of happiness, to select the fathers of their children, by eugenic considerations, while allowing their private feelings free sway as regards ordinary sexual companionship. For men it would be still easier to select the mothers of their children for their desirability as parents. Those who hold. as I do, that sexual behaviour concerns the community solely in so far as children are involved, must draw from this premise a twofold conclusion as regards the morality of the future. On the one hand that love apart from children should be free, but on the other hand, that the procreation of children should be a matter far more regulated by moral considerations than it is at present."*

Bertrand Russell elaborates further as follows:

> *"When science becomes able to pronounce on this question (of eugenics) with more certainty than is possible at present, the moral sense of the community may come to be more exacting from an eugenic point of view. The men with the best heredity may come to be eagerly sought after as fathers, while other men, though they may be acceptable as lovers, may find themselves rejected when they aim at paternity...."*

Bertrand Russell's statements and proposals sometimes evidence a moral angle, too. For instance, he believes that traditional morality has been designed to cope with the strong and potentially troublesome human emotions, such as jealousy, which he advises men and women to consciously overcome. He says, in effect, as follows:

> *"According to the moral system that I propose, it is only right that couples should value mutual faithfulness. Alternatively,*

> *however, I, recommend that they overcome jealousy. A sober way of living is not possible without self- control. So, it is better to discipline the potentially strong and troublesome emotion of jealousy, and not to allow it to prevent or impair the growth of the feelings of love and affection. Any shortcoming of conventional morality does not lie in its justification of self-control, but in the manner of exercising it.*

In other words, what Russell indicates is that he recommends the same self control as prescribed by the ancient moralists. However, he envisages self-control, not in any conventional terms of ensuring self -respect and rectitude, but in completely overcoming jealousy. He contends that the ancients sought to unduly limit human sexuality.

In contrast, he advocates jealousy-free attainment of human sexuality. Conventional morality, providing for personal honour as well as vindication of individual modesty and self-respect, is considered by him to be outmoded. Instead, it seems as if he would like to see husbands who are least jealous of their wives' intimacy with other men and who are even grateful for the social permissiveness that allows extramarital relations with third persons.

At the same time, Russell says to the effect that children ought to be born to married couples only. He would like to ensure this through adoption of different contraceptive means of sterilizing any premarital, extramarital or post marital sexual relations. Furthermore, he recommends that:

> *"It is also by no means impossible that the jealousy of husbands, by a new convention, adapt itself to the new situation, and arise only when wives propose to choose some other man as the father of their children. In the East, men have always tolerated liberties on the part of eunuchs which most European husbands would resent. They have tolerated them because they introduce no doubt as to paternity. The same kind of toleration might easily be extended to liberties accompanied by the use of contraceptives..'*

The foregoing typifies a kind of reform of the extant social ethics, which in all probability would entail a never-ending process. No doubt, it will mean radical changes in the other ethics, too, including legal safeguards concerning the female modesty, incest, pornography, homosexuality, abortion, sexual intercourse during menstruation and similar others. Some of these, like protection of female modesty and banning pornography are sometimes upheld. Other questions like homo-sexuality have been occasionally treated outside the purview of sexual ethics, and in a clinical manner, so that medical reasons, and not necessarily moral restraints, can prevent any deviant behaviour!

The modernistic sexual ethics described above require to be thoroughly examined before any ready acceptance. In the present context, only its basic elements will be discussed and evaluated. Then, the philosophy underlying Islamic morals, which are quite distinctive from the Western-traditional as well as modern-morality, will be explained. This will highlight the Islamic position to the effect that:

> *"The only school of thought still capable of guiding humanity, through the distressingly unwholesome effects and untoward consequences of Western speculations concerning the dynamic philosophy of human living and sociological evolution, is that of Islam. It is high time that West- oriented societies, with all their scientific and industrial advantages, realize their continuing need to turn Eastward in the process of their assimilating a salutary philosophy of life, as they have indeed done in their past epochs."*

A CRITICAL EXAMINATION OF THE THEORETICAL BASIS OF THE PROPOSED NEW SEXUAL FREEDOM

In the preceding chapter, the salient features of the proposed new sexual morality have been discussed. Now, it is intended to evaluate its basic principles. These are restated below:

(1) Personal liberty of every individual should be invariably respected and protected, provided it does not conflict with that of others. In other words, an individual's liberty is limited by no other consideration than the liberty of another individual.

(2) Human wellbeing lies in their individual nurturing and fulfillment of their inborn aptitudes and desires. If these natural inclinations are interfered with, it will lead to

egotism and personality disturbances arising from sexual frustration in particular. And, the natural instincts and desires are bound to go awry, if these are not fulfilled or satisfied.

(3) Limitations and restraints on the natural instincts and desires of human beings tend to intensify the cravings and inflame the passions. Their uninhibited fulfillment signifies contentment, enabling a person to overcome any excessive preoccupation with a natural urge, such as the sexual one.

The three principles above respectively concern human philosophy, training and psychology. They are put forward as justification for what the new moralists consider it to be the correct way, i.e. dispensing with the conventional morals, restraints and limitations, in order to ensure individual liberty, to promote, and not to frustrate, sexual gratification.

First, let us examine the above principles on the basis of statements and views of the supporters of the proposed new moral system. For, none of them seem to have fully identified the principles underlying their contributions to the proposed new morality.

The principle of individual liberty is actually basic to the sociological realization of human rights. However, those who seek to promote the new concepts of morality evidently-and wrongly-assume that personalized sexual freedom has no social implications. This is because of their obvious assumption that when individuals are free to pursue their sexual interests, they are expected to observe no more than privacy, so as not to adversely affect the rights of other persons.

At the same time, they recommend safeguards in the interest of society, even to the limited extent of assuring paternity and care of children. According to their proposed new safeguards, a wife is to bear her husband's child only. Otherwise, she is free to pursue her sexual motivations, using contraceptives, which not only avoid pregnancy, but enable her to ignore the time-honoured moral restraints of chastity and faithfulness, if she so desires.

In the above context, two implications concerning individual freedom require detailed examination. The *first* one arises from the modernistic contention that personal liberty cannot be limited, except by that of other individuals and the need to respect theirs. The *second* implication refers to the claim that sexual relations requiring the assurance of paternity and filial affinity of a possible child do not involve any further connection with society, public life and social prerogatives.

With regard to individual liberty, let us consider the philosophy behind the same. The essential thing in any individual management of personal freedom, and in one's entitlement to its protection, is his or her qualitative need for gradually evolving a harmonious and respectable manner of progressing one's individual life, towards enhancing the higher faculties. Due emphasis on the aforesaid need is noticeably missing in several Western interpretations or applications of the concept of personal freedom. In any case, individual freedom should not lead to any sexual permissiveness, enabling one to pander to lusty impulses and self centered desires. For, any misconception of personal freedom cannot be encouraged, or respected, by those who can (or ought to) realize its dire consequences.

That personal liberty of any individual, born free with the innate desires and self will, should be cherished as long as he or she respects the entitlements of other persons, can be rather very misleading. For, aside from the need to avoid any self expository interpersonal conflicts, it is necessary for any society to recognize that the larger and higher interests of a person himself or herself ought to conscientiously limit his or her individual freedom. Any continuing neglect of the aforementioned moral requirement can further aggravate the harm already done to the very basic concept of morality and the wrong done to the understanding of personal freedom in its own name!

Bertrand Russell was once asked as to whether or not he would consider himself bound to any particular system of morality. He replied in the affirmative and proceeded to explain his answer by giving a hypothetical example of how individual morality can be viewed in the social context. The scenario he mentioned was more or less as follows:

> *"Supposing Mr. X wants to do something which is useful to himself, but harmful to his neighbours. Then he carries out his*

> *intention, inconveniencing his neighbours. The latter decide among themselves to the effect: 'We cannot do something that he cannot take undue advantage of. A situation like this is rather suggestive of a criminal implication..."*

Bertrand Russell emphasized reasoning and intellectual judgment in the above case. Then he pointed out that morality did signify the need to harmonize the private and public aspects of individual behaviour.

From a practical viewpoint, the aforesaid case of new morality hardly suggests any Platonic utopia. Russell's interpretation of morality evidences no precedence of any inexorable values of life over the intrinsically or potentially baneful things. There is no trace in his suggestions of anything that makes human beings subject themselves and their material interests to any higher intellectual or spiritual considerations.

On the contrary, morals indicative of comprehensive meaning and significance are termed by him as 'taboos'. The only thing he considers to be sacred or inviolable is accomplishing one's personal inclinations and desires without inhibition. The only restraint on any particular manifestation of individual freewill approved by him is its compatibility with that of other persons. Even so, he leaves unanswered the question as to what congenial power or faculty should be instrumental in keeping personal freedom within limits of reason, sanity and decency, and to render it harmonious with that of others. Nevertheless, Bertrand Russell's scenario mentioned above is useful in attempting a possible reply to the question of individuals limiting each other's personal liberty. Accordingly, the scenario can be adapted as follows:

> *"Mr. X's neighbours can restrain or stop him from harming their interest, while serving his own. He is convinced that his neighbours in their own interest will mutually agree to prevent him. Accordingly, he is reconciled to the fact of his helplessness to do anything without coordinating his own interest with that of his neighbours."*

The foregoing is illustrative of the sterility of Bertrand Russell's moral philosophy, based —as it is on the crucial stipulation that an individual can (or ought to) serve his own interest and, at the same time, safeguard the rights and interests of the general public. This is so, considering that no norms of individual and group behaviour can be identical.

Evidently, certain hypothetical assumptions underlie the new morality proposed by Russell. For one thing, he implies that individuals and groups in a society can always manage to employ their benign powers envisaged under the proposed new morality. Secondly, he assumes that interpersonal and group unity and consensus are always readily forthcoming against individual transgressors. Then, he takes it for granted that an individual, who stands alone and weak, can nevertheless always decide to initiate any action against something of interest to a majority.

However, individual and collective powers of thinking and action can vary. People adversely affected by an individual transgression are seldom prepared to achieve unanimity and unity. Furthermore, one does not always decide to act against any majority interest, specially without confidence in one's own strength.

The ethics proposed by Bertrand Russell may be cogent enough to be recommended to any weak members of a society. For, the weak may be readily cowed down by sheer force of the strong and influential whose rights they may dutifully respect. However, when it comes to, actually preventing any transgression by the strong and powerful-, against the weak, the proposed ethics will probably fail to take effect.

For, the strong may well gang up against the weak. They may stifle any rare protest, or overwhelm any sign of resistance, from among the weak. What is worse, the strong can always say that their behavioural philosophy is not against the new ethics as recommended! In actual practice, they can even deem it unnecessary to harmonize their personal interests with those of the others.

Accordingly, Russell's moral philosophy may be construed as one of the most effective means of perpetuating the dictatorial concept of *might is right*. No doubt, Bertrand Russell devoted his active life towards advocating the cause of freedom, while defending the rights of the weak. Yet, ironically enough, his moral philosophy tended to consolidate vested interests and dictatorial tendencies in a society. This type of contradiction is often discernible in Western philosophizing, so that it would appear that what is preached is intended to be different from what is practised.

The second implication concerns marriage and family living, in that their private and public (or social) aspects are to be determined. No doubt, individual happiness and mutual enjoyment of life are sought by persons intending to marry. Now, two questions arise as to how best to serve and enhance a couple's interest towards achieving and maintaining a happily married life. Firstly, one may ask as to whether or not any enjoyment of life is best accomplished within the privacy of a family itself? Alternatively, should any pursuit of sex oriented happiness be extended beyond the privacy of family living to public gatherings, including places of work, social encounters, downtown entertainment areas and the milieu outside a family, where people usually seek to accomplish sensuous or sensual pleasures?

Islam has recommended that a couple's mutual enjoyment be confined to the privacy of their family living, so that they remain fully oriented towards each other. Islam has determined that any sex-oriented pursuit of happiness and enjoyment in public is to be avoided. Accordingly, any vicarious satisfactions derived from a sexually permissive society, including female exhibitionism in public are not allowed in Islam.

Western societies, which seem to fascinate some among us in more or less a blind manner, evidently favour the alternative proposition in the second question above. They have shifted the focus of attention to sex from the privacy of family living to its vicarious satisfaction in public. They do pay dearly for this moral lapse. Some of their thinkers express concern about deteriorating individual and societal morality in a sex-obsessed milieu. They are also stunned when they find how some communist societies have successfully taken sex off the public arena, saving the youth in the process.

Life's enjoyment cannot be equated with lustful or sensual living.

Individual happiness does not lie in maximizing the pleasures of eating, sleeping and sex. On the other hand, one may suppose that human propensity to enjoy sex-like pleasures, and conversely suffer dissatisfaction, can be as instinctively limited as that of animals.

However, this assumption can be wrong, since human seeking of physiological contentment is susceptible to be carried beyond married life and family living to the society at large.

However, persons of opposite sex whose souls, rather than bodies, have attracted each other can indeed be sincere in their mutual affection, after they agree to become husband and wife. Their marital happiness can extend beyond' the passionate youth to mutually cherished companionship towards even ripe old age.

Likewise, it is conceivable that a man used to the most intimate and satisfying relationship with his legitimate and faithful wife can indeed discriminate against any animal-like pleasures of the body, such as obtainable from a prostitute: Accordingly, one would not like to deflect in the least from what is most desirable and wholesome to what is sensuously pleasurable and conveniently transient.

Clearly, it is very essential that activities involving human sexuality are limited to couples, who are married, and to the privacy of their family living. For this purpose, it is necessary to safeguard the functional integrity and mutual compatibility of a family and its social milieu.

Marriage and family living are very significant functional aspects of a society. They are responsible institutional aspects for the benefit of the posterity. Family upbringing of children determines the quality of successive generations. In this context, individual and mutual capabilities of husbands and wives, towards appropriately raising children, is a crucial factor. At the same time, a father's concern for his offspring is bound to be conducive to a positive upbringing of the latter.

Human congeniality, in both individual and social contexts, is best developed in a harmonious family atmosphere. A child's exuberant spirit and natural temperament is substantially conditioned and trained by the parents.

When appealing to the good sense and common interest of two persons, we invoke their affinity with the community they may belong to, or the possibility of their regarding each other like two brothers. For that matter, we may even emphasize the brotherhood of mankind. The mutual devotion and faithfulness of pious *mumineen* is compared in the Holy Qur'an with the sincere regards that brothers have for each other.

Brotherhood among human beings does not come merely from any blood relationship or racial affinity. When we speak of brotherhood of man, what we signify is that the congeniality of two brothers in a family can well be reflected among individuals in a society. If brotherliness and affection which can be imbibed in a family are eliminated, it is doubtful if people can really show genuine consideration for each other.

They say that in Europe there is considerable sense of justice, but fellow-feeling is very limited. Even real brothers, as well as fathers and sons, evidence very little affection for each other. This is quite in contrast to the general run of people and families in the East.

Why, it is so? The answer revolves around the fact that human love and sympathy are qualities which are attributable to a wholesome upbringing of children by really affectionate and united families. Evidently, families in Europe no longer are able effectively to cherish these qualities. The solidarity between husbands and wives, often noticeable in the East, is frequently missing in the West. A significant reason can be the fact that Westerners have come to believe in sex without love or inhibition. Sexual experimentation and diversification do not allow any specific interpersonal love to develop. They tend to be indiscriminate in seeking sexual enjoyment.

BASIC NEED FOR HUMANE CONDITIONING OF NATURAL INSTINCTS AND DESIRES

The need to refine and condition the raw natural instincts and desires of individuals in a benign manner is a basic one. Harmonious personal growth is conducive to wholesome interaction with fellowmen, which in turn leads to a salutary impact on the humanity at large. An appropriate conditioning and training of an individual's natural potentialities brings about spiritual rewards, too. These include a spiritually balanced personal outlook and intellectual composure, necessary for any sound and beneficial endeavour. Psychosomatically balanced persons are emotionally stable and competent to achieve social harmony and peace.

On the other hand, any unduly inhibited or imbalanced growth of an individual personality is quite undesirable. So are any adverse external influences or pressures and strains of a negative kind. For, negatively conditioned people become susceptible to causing excesses, untold miseries and cruelties not only to themselves, but to others.

The traditional non-Islamic moralists regarded sex and love as if these were manifestations of an obnoxious evil to be shunned. In contrast, the modernistic societies tended to consider free love as not only desirable but respectable. No doubt, the free love concept began to receive every preferential treatment and encouragement for its worldwide growth.

With regard to Islamic morals, these can be properly understood with reference to the following points:

(a) Islamic morals and their compatibility with the objective requirements of natural growth of sexuality as part of inborn human instincts and potentialities;

(b) Suppression of human concupiscence;

(c) Modernistic sexual permissiveness as a major cause of sexual or sex-oriented aberrations or deviations of human behaviour, preventing harmonious growth of the natural instincts and potentialities of an individual;

(d) Democratic attitudes towards sexual behaviour;

(e) Sexual morality, as compared to general ethical conduct in the economic and political fields;

(f) Love and the forlorn condition in which it remains a longing; and

(g) Love and harmonious growth of human personality.

To begin with, the fact that natural human instincts should be nurtured, and not suppressed, is to be recognized. At the same time, it is necessary to conceptualize beyond any simplistic determination in terms of good and bad.

The Islamic approach takes into consideration the overall need for promoting a salubrious growth of human personality as an a priori requirement, based on deductive logic. The premises recognized in Islam include the factual position that every constituent part of the human body has a specific purpose or function. The biological purposes and functions are sustained by a person's will o nurture the same, even beyond the instinctive motivations. Accordingly, human volition, intellectual capabilities and similar other aspects of spiritual nature must be enhanced, too.

We could well imagine a situation where no traditional evolution of morality is allowed. This would mean that the inborn human potentialities are either harmoniously cultivated or prevented from such development. In any case, it stands to reason that human faculty to discern things and to comprehend the natural order of things, would have induced the necessary process of harmonization.

A hundred years ago, scholars and social scientists recognized the need for a psychosomatically balanced development of human personality. Societies of the time lacked a correct overall human perspective. There was a markedly deficient realization of the moral traditions. Negativating tendencies affected all-round human development.

In fact, there has never been any doubt about promoting an all round growth of human personality. This is implicit in the very word training, which has always been used to indicate human development.

Any correct and effective approach to training of human beings must aim at overcoming tendencies leading to disturbances of personality and morbid conditions of disorder and indiscipline, affecting the body, the mind and the spirit. A naturally harmonious and spiritually balanced human growth should include the training of the sex instinct in particular. In the above context, Islam offers the most appropriate guidance. This position is intended to be clarified and established in the discussion that follows.

At the outset, we must stipulate that any preconceived or ill conceived notion concerning Islamic ethics must be avoided.

For instance, some people appear to harbour the notion that Islamic morality inhibits, rather than promotes, any free growth of human faculties. They wrongly believe that the Islamic explanations carry no intrinsic significance in the matter of refining and improving the natural human instincts.

Actually, the Holy Qur'an is replete with instances of emphasis on human refinement, such as when it asserts that a conscientiously righteous person is one who has been able to refine, discipline and purify his natural instincts and desires.

This quotation further implies that human conscience is liable to pollution. At the same time, it suggests that human beings can improve their individual conscientiousness by overcoming any polluted state affecting the same. Above all, the Holy Qur'an considers pollution-free conscience to be indispensable for attaining righteousness and happiness.

There can be no denying the intrinsic meaning and significance of the moral values taught by the Glorious Qur'an. The aforementioned teaching and its explanation pinpoints a conscientious approach to the problem of human refinement. No school of thought or moral procedure rules out human susceptibility to pollution of the conscience or psyche and the consequent need to purifying and ameliorating the undesirable condition. Human psyche is vulnerable to prurient desires, moral aberrations and psychpathological disorders, just as the human body or organs are liable to disease.

An individual can feel within himself or herself the specific nature and extent of any physiological or psychological or spiritual ailments of his or her own. An individual does this to an extent far more real and complete with regard to himself or herself, than in respect of other persons, or for that matter, even in the case of any environmental pollutions. Thus, it is possible and necessary to ensure righteousness and rectitude on an individual basis, through a psychosomatically and spiritually harmonious personality development. The Holy Qur'an makes this point thoroughly clear.

There is another Qur'anic description of the raw, natural self of an untrained person: According to this description, a person's untamed or inappropriately trained self is referred to as a *commander* of evil (thoughts and deeds). Does it mean that a non disciplined *self* can be wicked by nature, according to the Qur'an?

The reply to the abovementioned question cannot be positive. this is because, theoretically speaking, a human being, if born malignant, cannot be expected to be amenable to any training that seeks to metamorphosize him into becoming naturally benign. On the contrary, the very existence of naturally malignant beings deserves to be treated as undesirable, since they are potentially harmful. They ought to be prevented from growing and assuming menacing proportions. Their malignant impact would require to be curbed even by occasionally eliminating them!.

So, the correct answer is that there is no wickedness built into the very nature of a human being. Only, in particular situations, and in specific circumstances, an individual becomes vulnerable to wickedness and nurturing it, developing a malignant disposition in the process.

Any negative representation of man's basic nature as a source of evil and wickedness is not implied in the Quranic philosophy, as already indicated above.

Then, one may as well ask two more questions. Firstly, what can be the particular circumstances or specific causes, which lead human beings toward becoming wicked and corrupt? Secondly, how can the depraved and corrupt be rendered harmless and brought back to the righteous path of sanity and moderation?

Answers to the above questions require a comprehensive and positive understanding of the relevant Qur anic teachings. For, they lie beyond any wrong and narrow minded interpretations, such as arising from any literally isolated or absolute or negative understanding of the Qur'anic description of human self as *commander* of evil. Actually, according to the Holy Our'an. the self can be not only a commander of evil, but a conscientious reprover. Elsewhere, the Qur'an, refers to the self also as an abode of human peace and excellence.

The Quranic descriptions of *self* indicate that human nature can have different stages of growth and manifestation. At one stage, it can be prone to mischief and wickedness. Where anything undesirable is already perpetrated, it can also ruefully blame itself. Above all, it is capable of attaining the most desirable stage of human excellence and composure, beyond vulnerability to anything bad or wicked.

Islam does not presuppose any inherent wickedness of human nature. So, it is at variance with the speculative philosophies and systems of human training evolved in India, or those enunciated by some ancient cynical philosophers. Furthermore, it differs from the teachings of Manes, of ancient Persia. The Islamic approach is distinctive from that evolved in Christianity, as well. Islamic code of moral conduct does not evidently subscribe to any denial, or suppression, of human instincts, nor does it prescribe anything reminiscent of penal servitude in overcoming carnal desires.

The ancients might not have clearly realized that under specific circumstances or in certain situations or at some stage of personal disciplining, human nature could get awry and become vulnerable to wickedness or evil that is capable of assuming dangerous proportions. However, in modern times, when a scientifically investigated basis of human personality development has been arrived at, there can be no longer any doubt about the need to discipline one's own *self.*

The Holy Quran significantly reveals and pinpoints various aspects of human personality development. Identification of the negative tendencies of human nature is meant for emphasizing the positive aspects that can lead to an excellent flowering of human personality.

Even where the *self* has been described as *commander of evil* the contextual inference is to the effect that human *self* is capable of inviting evil. This distinction is important, in that human beings are made aware of their predominantly raw instinctiveness which, unless refined and trained, is naturally forceful enough to overwhelm any humanely cultivated qualities conducive to spiritual enhancement. This seems to be an aspect yet to be fully identified by modern psychologists.

Nevertheless, it is widely accepted today that emotional disorders can occasionally lead to mental illness. This can happen in some mysterious and arbitrary manner, in which the faculty of conscious perception is not involved. Consequently, the mind functions in an aberrant manner, so as to carry out the dictates or impulses of emotional origin.

The positive and negative factors in human personality development are further examined later on herein, in the context of modernistic sexual permissiveness. Meanwhile, an explanation of the meaning and connotation of suppressing carnality is desirable.

With regard to suppressing human concupiscence, Islam does not envisage it in any way. This is true for other instincts, too. Then, what is meant by suppression of carnal desire? Does it mean elimination of causes leading to it?

In the Islamic context, it signifies effective and moderate coping with the human concupiscence. This is emphasized also in many scholarly explanations of Islamic morality. Islam teaches human beings to overcome the natural predisposition of the bodily sensuality to rule over any sensibility of the mind. In other words, an individual must not be led by his natural instincts, but manage the same in a wholesome manner. As mentioned earlier, Islam does not preach any ascetic suppression of concupiscence or natural desires.

To elaborate on the above point, it may be noted that, when a person is commanded by his instincts, he or she evidences a disorderly manifestation of human personality, a disruptive and overwhelming influence capable of affecting human conscience. Not allowing instincts to sway one's conscience necessarily implies pacifying and quenching the natural outpourings of carnal desire, or offsetting the palpability to temptation, emotional disorders or even sexual promiscuity.

Ofcourse, eliminating temptation means taming the animal-like instincts. This is possible when temptation is avoided in a natural and harmonious manner. This necessitates overcoming tendencies leading to social evils and psychological ills. Thus, eliminating temptation does not require casting out the external forces, human or otherwise, which may be causing it.

On the contrary, what is required is to eliminate the internal causes and tendencies. This is necessary to avoid malignant development of the libido. Vulnerability to any undesirable external influences is also overcome in the process. A wholesome development of human instincts is a process requiring either a salutary compliance or a moral inhibition of their negative upsurge depending on their nature and content.

Incidentally, it is notable that the phrase: *killing the carnal desire,* does not occur in any specific teaching of Islam. Any reference to it is only by way of explaining the need for a salubrious growth of personality.

Towards satisfying natural instincts and desires, any one-sided approach entails shortcomings, which are not often removable subsequently Since the last century, sex-oriented psychological research achievements concentrated on proving that suppression of the natural instincts and desires was fraught with many adverse consequences to individuals. The microscopic investigations and findings proved to be valuable in themselves.

For one thing, traditional thinking to the effect that the more the baser instincts are suppressed the greater the scope for enhancing the higher faculties (such as the intellectual) has become valid. There is growing realization that extraordinary and far-reaching consequences, affecting individuals and their society both, underlie suppressed or unsatisfied instincts and desires, which are often hidden from the conscious mind.

The question of satisfying carnal instincts and spontaneous desires could well be left to one's own judgment. For, only human intellect can prevent any untoward instinctive development. One can purposefully manage one's own natural promptings and ensure that they are not negativated or harmed or frustrated in an unwholesome manner.

Many nervous and mental disorders affecting individuals, and even society as a whole, have been traced by psychologists and psychiatrists to personal feelings of deprivation, specially with regard to the sexual instinct. They have proved that emotional deprivations give rise to psychological complexes. The psychological afflictions can assume even dangerous proportions, resulting in sadism, morbid insolence, extreme jealousy, becoming a recluse or a cynic and similar others.

These findings concerning human instincts and desires represent some of the psychologically significant discoveries and successes achieved by mankind.

An increasingly popular awareness of and interest in the nature and content of the human senses may lead to further research and findings. The discoveries are likely to be of a kind that conforms to the needs of technological and industrial progress. These may be conducive to better identification and greater employment of the natural, specially inorganic, forces. However, psychological and spiritual aspects of problems may not receive popular attention. Thus, their awareness may be confined to learned men and the wise.

Psychosomatic integrity in human personality development has been emphasized since the beginning of recorded history. Islam, too, has significantly pinpointed its need. Traditional moralists, as well as behavioural scientists, have always tried to reflect the cumulative knowledge and wisdom evolved in the past in one way or the other. Nevertheless, the fact remains that the psychosomatic approach has been scientifically established only during the last one hundred years or so.

Now, let us see how best the principle of psychosomatic wellbeing can be practised. Evidently, it cannot be used as easily as penicillin. It is an abstraction that requires a certain ability to comprehend. Moreover, it is suggestive of the intricacy and diversity of psychological and other problems, which often have been investigate-d in, a microscopic perspective. At the same time, obscuring considerations of morality and underrating personal character development have come to be the order of the day, which apparently suits many ease-loving and hard-pressed people of modern societies.

Worst still, the genuine need for promoting a wholesome fulfilment of natural instincts and desires, of a harmless kind, has been misinterpreted or misapplied in actual practice. Thus, an unrestrained gratification of human sexuality has come to be prescribed, ostensibly for avoiding their undesirable frustration. Consequently, the psychological complexes and tensions have tended to increase rather than decrease.

Statistics often indicate a virulent growth of psychological diseases, mental disorders, suicides, crimes of passion, anxiety, mental anguish, or restlessness, hopelessness, pessimism, jealousy, malice, or malevolence and similar other psychosomatic manifestations of unwholesome human personality development. The inhumane development of an ever-increasing number of individuals has been explained to be arising from the modernistic permissiveness with regard to natural instincts and desires, including uninhibited or unrestrained sex.

For centuries there has been widespread and insistent opposition to any permissiveness towards lust and sensuality. This was mainly in order to avoid the baneful effects of human sensuality or deviation, on individual morality, spirituality and activities, as well as on the peace and integrity of society. All this has been sought to be reversed in a sudden and arbitrary manner by the protagonists of a modernistic permissive society.

The reversal was sought, as if eschewing lust and subjecting oneself to chastity, rectitude, endurance, moral and social restrictions or limits, is capable of disturbing a person's spiritual wellbeing and his own society's peacefulness. Above all, the reversal was sought as if morality and avoidance of lust or sensuality are actually irrelevant to any benign personal conduct, or a positive development of human personality.

The volte face has come about as if there has always been a great and insistent demand for lifting the moral restraints or limits. The social change was sought as if it were really necessary to absolve people of their moral scruples, duties arid obligations and thus liberating them from an.assumed malevolence.

The reformist motivation seemed to be geared to some imaginary need to let people enjoy themselves to their hearts' content, irrespective of any moral compunction or conscious commitment to chastity and rectitude. All these are supposed to be conducive towards peacefully maintaining whatever social order has come to prevail, while purporting to free the people from psychological disorders!

Evidently, the seductive concept of freeplay of natural instincts and desires has been offered as a reformatory safeguard against moral and social constraints, as if these have a corrupting impact! Furthermore, the concept has readily appealed to many young and single persons, including a substantial number in our own country.

From what we have noticed, the supporters of a permissive kind of society have a peculiar way of thinking. They seem to believe that nothing is better for an individual than placing himself or herself at the disposal of the sweet dictates of the heart, while allowing the latter to be dominated even by lust.

At the same time, they apparently rationalize that the actions resulting from their way of thinking can be construed as both human and moralistic to the point of their being accepted as potential experts in sophisticated social behaviour. They apparently suggest that their thinking augurs them well, even if it represents a subject of ridicule to others. Furthermore, they profess to seek both self-gratification and service to their kind. They mean to ensure satiation of every bodily urge and to cope with any spiritual need, as well.

In other words, they seem to equate good or normal conduct with sensuality. Their imagination is not totally dissimilar to the metaphorical use of *love* by some mystics, in the manner of Sufis. They apparently sought communion with whatever images of female beauty and love they could visualize, even in Divine terms!!

Consequently, the modernistic freeplay with the natural instincts and desires failed to replace psychosomatic illnesses or neurotic disorders by any spiritual contentment. Human afflictions continued to spread, bringing one misfortune after another in an increasingly pernicious manner. No wonder, some promoters of uninhibited sexual development, such as Freud, were sensible enough to retract from their original claims, or subsequently modify or clarify the same.

They reiterated the position that there was no easy way out of the traditionally evolved social norms and constraints. They clarified to the effect that human sexual concupiscence is not a programmable quantity, or a self-contained input, for any complete or instant satisfaction. They also referred to the need for sublimating it, so as to channel human energies directly towards intellectual enhancement in solving problems of educational, scientific, cultural, socioeconomic and technological significance.

New morals of the kind advocated by Bertrand Russell, are supposed to be conducive to a positive development of human personality. At the same time, it is alleged that traditional morals inhibit human development. The fact that, in the wake of the new morals, human afflictions and distress have become aggravated disproves the abovementioned claims, so that they deserve to be subjected to the same allegations as they make against traditional morals.

Today, social scientists are microscopically endeavouring to cope with particular manifestations, as well as specific difficulties, found in their societies. In the present social conditions, young persons are consciously avoiding marriage. Pregnancy and upbringing of children are becoming somewhat abhorrent to many women, who seem to be less interested in even housekeeping.

Marriages are in evidence more in the traditional societies and conservative families than in the modern ones. On the other hand, neurotic conflicts in persons of both sexes are on the increase evidencing unusual psychosomatic and spiritual ailments.

Some among the social scientists opine that the traditional social values have been fundamentally overtaken and superseded by the manpower requirements of the modern industrial revolution. Actually, however, morals, traditional or otherwise, ought to remain the same in their intrinsic values and connotations. They are not affected by any changing patterns of human living from an agricultural setting to an industrial one.

Changes in any familiar patterns of human living and social interaction are only construed to be fundamental in some revolutionary intellectual way! The seemingly revolutionary thinking is attributable to some individuals with whom must lie the grave responsibility for any consequent misfortunes befalling humanity.

Even Bertrand Russell speaks of the pitfalls involved in speculative thinking, including his own. For instance, he favours an unrestrained gratification of the sexual instinct on one hand, and concedes the necessity of adhering to a time-tested system of its self-regulation, on the other. However, it is not intended, at this stage, to elaborate further on the pros and cons of modernistic thinking concerning human sexuality.

In reality, any appropriate compliance with the natural instincts, instead of suppressing them, does not mean the same thing as liberating sexuality by denouncing the age old moral restraints and constraints. The natural instincts and desires are not incompatible with chastity and virtue. In fact, they are adequately satisfied only within a chaste and virtuous regulatory framework, which avoids the evils of promiscuous behaviour, enforced celibacy or self-denial and the resultant emotional disturbances.

In other words, appropriate nurturing of human instincts means nothing different from overcoming lust and baser inclinations. The basic distinction between human beings and animals is that the former are capable of two kinds of desires: one is a genuinely natural urge and the other is a pseudo-desire.

Genuine desires conform to the naturally essential requirements, such as the desires for food, survival, self-protection, the sexual drive, the inclination for aggression or domination and similar others. Everyone of tire genuinely natural desires have a specific function, which they serve with a definite purpose. Aside from the fact that they are limited to their specific functions and purposes, all these are individually capable of forming a basis for a pseudo-desire, such as the well-known false appetite.

Most natural desires are amenable to complete satisfaction. Satisfying the others, including the sexual drive, involves psychological complications. For, the mind and the human spirit is at times capable of sustaining bodily desires beyond the natural limits of physiological satisfaction. Some intellectually sustained cravings never reach a saturation point!

Accordingly, it is quite misleading to suggest an uninhibited gratification of carnal desires, by prescribing freedom from moral restraints and curbs on the natural instincts. Those who prescribe it fail to distinguish between the qualities of human beings and animals. They ignore the fact that there can be no end to human desire or craving.

Human beings are prone to seize every opportunity towards self -satisfaction. They unceasingly avail every occasion to advance their own interests. This is equally true in matters of acquiring wealth, economics, politics and government, as well as in seeking to dominate others or to intensify sexuality.

To suggest that relieving the sex urge is like attending to one's call of nature, such as urination or defecation, is quite misleading, too. Any question of evacuating from one's self his or her own moral scruples or conditions, in the process of obtaining instant sexual relief, does not arise. Conversely, safeguarding one's morality cannot mean the same as accumulating urine. For, unlike moral continence, retention of urine is bound to cause bodily comfort and disease.

For a better appreciation of the above point, let us assume that a person finds, along the avenues and streets he frequents, several clean, well-kept and even cost-free public urinals. Yet, one could not use them to his or her heart's content to an extent beyond what one's bladder permits! Accordingly, these nice urinals could not (or should not) unduly attract a person (to urinate).

Some modernistic people assume that all human inclinations, irrespective of whether or not these concern sex, aggression, domination or mammon worship, should be freely allowed to be satisfied. This is supposed to be capable of eliminating human deprivation, frustration or dissatisfaction, in the process of satisfying one's desires. Their reasoning is based on a false assumption. For, as pointed out earlier, complete gratification of all human desires is not possible.

Human capacity to seek gratification of the natural and acquired desires is not instinctively limited, as in the case of animals. Had this not been the case, there would have been no need for any human regulation of not only the sexual intercourse, but socioeconomic and political interactions, as well. Even moral restraints would have been unnecessary where natural constraints made it impossible for anyone to seek excessive satisfaction,.or indulge in excesses. The very limitation of natural capacity (to commit any excesses) would have served the purpose, as in the case of animals.

However, ethical limits and procedural regulations are necessary for promoting just practices and fair transactions in the socioeconomic and political fields.

Likewise, limitation on, and regulation of, sexual behaviour and the related activities, consistent with the needs of chastity and rectitude, should also be acceptable to everyone.

LOVE, SEXUAL DISCIPLINE AND CHASTITY

That principles of human liberty and democracy should govern morals, too, is both right and correct, as in the case of politics. The intrinsic meaning is that human beings should cope with their inborn instincts and natural desires, in the same way as a just and democratic government does in respect of the masses of people.

Islam treats questions concerning sexual behaviour on the same ethical basis as is commonly recognized today in the regulation of political and economic activites. For, individuals are prone to making genuine and willful mistakes in ordering their sexual lives on the basis of their own moral judgment. They may, through misconception, or wantonly, ignore the need for maintaining a democratic concern for morality, in coping with their individual problems, arising in circumstances evidencing lack of any personal restraint and overall chaos.

In principle, any societal regulation of political and economic activities ought to recognize the relevant human instincts and tendencies. For, the aggression instinct and tendency to dominate others can be instrumental in politics. Economic activities may be prompted by a desire to accumulate wealth. Likewise, sexual aptitude can lead to indulgence in lustful activities. However, it is not known why the supporters of the proposed new sexual freedom deem a laissez *faire policy* fit for sexual affairs only, while they seemingly accept the controllability of political and economic activities.

One of the important aspects of sexual ethics concerns the emotion of love. Since the ancient times, the essence of love has been given special attention in philosophy. Ibn Sina (in the Islamic millenium) brought out a treatise on love. Human love has been commonly acknowledged as a wholesome reality, in terms of its all embracing and sublime nature. In literature, specially the poetic, love has not only been eulogised, with a sense of pride (to the extent of proclaiming the superiority of the heart over the mind), but contrasted with lust's debasingly animal-like nature.

Mostly in our literature we find that love has been extolled not only in terms of its Divine connotation, but even in its down-to-earth human emotional context. In either case, there has been no confusion of love with any kind of lust.

Incontrast, there have been others, who chose to equate love with a sort of libido, or any persistent metabolic intensity of the sexual instinct. Evidently, they tended to assume that love is rather incapable of sublimation even in Divine terms. They treat love as if it has neither any spiritual origin, nor it is (or ought to be) humane in quality, nor it can be humanitarian in purpose.

Those who treat love as both Divine and human differentiate between the animal-like manifestation and the humane accomplishment of love. The others make no such distinction, so that love and lust become synonymous.

Today, a third category of thinkers has become evident. They believe that all kinds of love are sexually prompted, but gradually the carnal motivation assumes a spiritual or contemplative aspect under specific conditions. To them, love is primarily sexual, with only occasional platonic manifestations. However, this dual or two-fold quality of love is affirmed by them only in terms of its expression, objective and effects. There is no duality in so far as the origin and causation of love are concerned.

With regard to the last category of thinkers mentioned above, it is not a matter of surprise that they believe in a material basis of human spirituality They see no unsurmountable difficulty in the mutual transformation of the material and spiritual aspects of human behaviour. In fact, one of them claims that every spiritual affair has a natural basis and every natural thing has a spiritual extension.

Be that as it may, we need not discuss the above in any great psychological and philosophical depth. We can thus avoid going into the pros and cons of the many ancient and current interpretations of any basis of love. For the time being, it should be enough to suggest that love, in effect, can bring about creativity of the human intellect and spirit, as well as induce artistic and cultural refinements of sociological importance.

The above suggestion is valid, irrespective of whether or not love originates in the sexual instinct, and then becomes capable of expressing itself in physical and also spiritual terms, in an interchangeable manner. Any sublime effect of love is far different from its alleged instinctiveness, or simple animal-like concupiscenee, which seeks no more than its physiological gratification.

Love does evidence itself as lust in some circumstances. When lust overtakes human beings, the latter become self-centred, regarding love as a mere tool or means of self gratification. However, when human beings evidence love as a genuine affection, they are no longer self-centred. On the contrary, their love signifies the most desirable spirit of self-sacrifice.

In other words, individuals in genuine love are capable of overcoming their self-centred motivations for the sake of each other.

World literature is replete with love's many-splendoured qualities, including those of a catalyst, teacher and inspirer. From Persian literature, we may quote a verse from Sadi, as follows:

Whoever falls in love beyond himself,

yields to love but his own self,

Whoever loved not, evolved not manfulness,

Silver unmelted gives not brightfulness.

Another famous Iranian poet, Hafiz, refers to a nightingale's love of roses and muses as follows:-

By rose's grace, nightingales do their singing

All those songs and lyrics so pleasing

Beyond what their beaks do improvising!

No doubt, love has been eulogised in many ways, both in the East and West. Yet, there has come to be a difference between the Eastern and Western conceptualization of love. To many Westerners, love can be worthwhile as long as it embodies the sweetness mutuallv attainable by lovers. Individuals of opposite sex in the West prefer the desirability and enjoyability of living together, in mutual love and comfort, to the constant annoyance and boredom of living as singles. They aim at maximizing enjoyment of life.

In the East, love is regarded as something inexorably desirable in itself. For, it lends an overall perspective to the human personality, while ennobling and inspiring the spirit. No wonder, love has been described as a catalyst, purifier and in similar other ways. Evidently, in all these and other attributes, one can hardly discern any implicit suggestion to the effect that love is no more than an introduction to the sweet union that usually follows it, or to mere feelings of enjoying living together in body and spirit.

Even to some impressionable Easterners, love between prospective spouses may signify something preliminary to their subsequent pleasures of union and living together only. However, even their preliminary experience of being loved by each other can (or ought to) progressively enhance their humaneness. This is not like its becoming something merely conducive to any anticipation of enjoyments from conjugal relations or cohabitation.

In either case, if love is construed as a real introduction to union of man and woman, in terms of becoming one in body and spirit, this is all the more conducive to the wholesomeness of human achievement.

In short, in love, as in several other matters, Westerners and Easterners differ in their intellectual. approach. A typical Westerner is often unable to nurture love within any abstract framework that goes beyond any mechanical process of coping with problems of routine living. Eventually, he comes round to distinguishing love from lust, and also to believing in empathy and spiritual harmony, which it is capable of breeding.

Otherwise, love comes to him as a handy natural talent, leading to marriage or cohabitation, according to the social requirements of living. On the other hand, a typical Easterner seeks to cherish love beyond the requirements of routine living.

Had love been sexual in origin, quality and effect, probably it would not have necessitated separate treatment in sexual ethics.

Whatever was. discussed earlier concerning the pros and cons of sexual ethics would have been rather sufficient. However, love's origin or, at any rate, its psychological quality and social effects can be quite safely construed as independent of the sexual instinct.

Accordingly, morals concerning nurturing of human inclination to love can be treated in a manner distinguishable from that of the sexual instinct. Gratifying the sexual instinct is not the only concomitant of love. For, sexual gratification is not enough to sustain love, which needs psychological contentment, too. Moreover, any denial of love can possibly lead to afflictions, which cannot be remedied by any animal-like gratification of the sexual instinct, assuming that the former is derived from the latter.

Bertrand Russell endorses the need for profound love as follows:

> *Those who have never known the deep intimacy and the intense companionship of happy mutual love have missed the best thing that life has to give; unconsciously, if not consciously, they feel this and the resulting disappointment inclines them towards envy, oppression and cruelty.*

Sometimes, it is claimed that religion is love's enemy. The usual reasoning behind the claim is based on a situation, where a religion fails to distinguish between love and lust. Thus, the wickedness of lust is ascribed to love, as well. The allegation is not true in the case of Islam.

Yet, it can be relevant to Christianity. Islam does not treat sexual passion as wicked in itself, not to speak of considering its direct or indirect association with love as something bad or undesirable.

Deeply sincere and mutual love between spouses is highly respected in Islam. Islamic teachings commend realization of love on a sound and lasting basis.

In the general context of religion versus love, there is one point that is often overlooked. This concerns the tendency for mutual opposition between human intellect and love. Some moralists have wrongly overlooked this in indiscriminately excluding love from morality. They only regarded love as blind and capable of overruling the intellect. They believed that love is not amenable to reason, inferring wrongly that it is also least susceptible to conventional and legal, or moral, disciplining. In other words, they saw nothing but anarchic exuberance and rebelliousness in love.

Accordingly, religions or social systems, which based their morality on intellectual considerations alone, were not conducive to any salutary treatment of love. They treated love as something beyond the scope of any recommendation or advice. This is notwithstanding the fact that what is deserving of advice in matters of love can well concern one's modality of response to any casual manifestation of love in extenuating circumstances over which one is supposed to have no control. This is in order to maximize the sublime and beneficial effects of love, while remaining immune to its harmful consequences, if any.

In the above context, the main question that arises concerns the mutually inclusive relationship of love and chastity. One may ask whether or not love can, in its most positive sense, flourish in any permissive social environments. Or, is it simply a question of whether or not love's meaningfulness is invariably linked with any social preference for chastity, envisaging a certain prosaic status for women?

In his book: *The Pleasures of Philosophy, Will* Durant acknowledged that love was generally agreed to be the most fascinating thing in the course of human life. At the same time, he noted with surprise that very rarely attention was focused on the origin and growth of love, in the relevant multilingual, poetic and philosophical works of most sensational poets and writers on the subject of love.

Will Durant further pointed out that the analytical part of literary and scientific material concerning love was extremely limited. Typical coverage ranged from the ordinary reproduction of protozoa to the self-sacrificing spirit of Dante, or the poetic ecstacies of Petrarch among similar others. In all these efforts, any thorough investigation of the astonishing factuality, the natural origin, the factors in wholesome evolutionary growth and similar other aspects of love were found by him to be missing.

Earlier herein, we have identified three distinct schools of ancient arid. modern thought concerning the origin and purpose of love, so as to deduce its unique or two-sided interaction with the sexual instinct. We have noted that love, as conceived in the West and the East both, is distinct from lust.

Also, it is universally recognised as praiseworthy and respectable, although the relevant conceptualizations differ, as already explained. What remains to be examined now is mainly the question of love in relation to chastity, specially in order to specify the areas and conditions in which they can flourish.

With regard to love and chastity, the relevant social regulations can be either explicit or implicit in moral terms. Where these are explicitly regulated, women may be assigned an elevated position in society, so that they are ordinarily not approachable by men. In the other situation, where love and chastity are implicitly promoted; but not regulated, women's position is subject to the utter tedium of placing themselves at the disposal and protection of their men. One may wonder as to which one of these two sets of conditions are apt to enhance love and chastity.

Incidentally, it is notable that the so called open or permissive societies are *ipso facto* incapable of promoting conditions for any deep and intense love relationships. Their conditions lead to waywardness and wantonness, in the process of seeking transient affairs, if not while indulging in momentary and lustful pleasures. No wonder, women's position in these so called free environments continues to be rather prosaic, while both men and women remain liable to miss heartfelt and genuine mutual love and responsiveness.

Permissive social environments further sensuality and licentiousness. They are not conducive to beneficial love held in esteem by philosophers and sociologists, in terms of its intensely evolved, deeply responsive and unselfish effects. Given appropriate social conditions, love can indeed enable personalities mellowed by it to concentrate individual energies for good purposes, render their perceptions clear and keen, induce empathy towards the beloved, as well as promote genius-like originality and excellence of thoughts and achievements.

Genuine love's wholesome qualities have been commended not only by the ancients, but the modern writers, including some who favoured the proposed new sexual freedom. In his magnum opus: History of Civilization, Will Durant mentioned about both male homosexual connotation of the traditional Greek depiction of love in their ballads and the heterosexual love episodes of the Thousand and One Night fame, dating back to centuries earlier than those of the Middle Ages. He indicated that interest in the oriental stories of natural love grew to an extent more than that in the routine. exhortations of the Church towards promoting chastity and virtue.

Furthermore, Will Durant regarded a literary compilation, such as the Thousand and One Night, as a possible source of inspiration for the subsequent lyrical compositions abroad. He referred to one usually sarcastic contemporary Western writer's extraordinary remark to the effect that love meant the same to human carnality as life signified to human spirituality.

Indeed, as observed by Will Durant, many began to wonder how the abstraction of human sensuality into the most sensible love can be explained. People became curious about the intellectual and similar other factors that transform an animal-like instinctive hunger, such as evidenced at times by human concupiscence, into serene and tender love. The curiosity revolved around the point as to how the carnal passion might become the spiritual compassion.

Will Durant further probed into any introspective sublimation of carnal desires and the consequent platonic imaginings about a beloved in various intellectual contexts. He raised a question as to whether or not the aforesaid sublimation was the conspicuous outcome of the growth of civilization, involving progressively late marriages!

He apparently believed that an answer to the question he posed might lie in a human tendency. He pointed out that whatever one sought and did not find could become dear and extraordinarily valuable. Thus, appreciation of beauty could vary with the intensity of desire. And, desire would tend to intensify when inhibited and to diminish when satisfied.

Will Durant referred to William James contention that female modesty was riot instinctive, but inculcated by successive generations of women, out of fear that any behaviour to the contrary would attract undesirable interest or contempt of others. He pointed out that shameless women could not be of any sustained interest to men. Only women who refrained from any exuberant gaiety and who abstained from either inviting or conceding male attention were best oriented to attracting men.

According to Will Durant, any exposure of the intimate parts of the human body, from their normal state of concealment, might not evoke more than casual interest on the part of viewers. In any case, it would seldom lead to any instant arousal of carnal desire. For, even young men would prefer modesty in young women. In doing so, they might not necessarily comprehend that the delicateness of female reserve could be indicative of a high degree of tactful reaction, as well as tenderness.

Furthermore, modesty in women might be capable of endearing them to men and awakening mutual love, in anticipation of any subsequent consummation. Thus, men could be prompted to enhance their capabilities and resolution towards significant achievements, by drawing on their otherwise dormant life-oriented energies.

At the same time, Will Durant mentioned the fact that modern young women would seem to be only too willing to discard conventional morality, as if it were some old clothes that went out of fashion. He observed that these women could be audacious not only in displaying themselves, but in their sartorial tastes. Consequently, diminished masculine imaginability concerning female appeal was specified by him to be the only adverse effect of the radical change in the women's outlook and behaviour. He opined that, had it not been for men's residual imaginability, perhaps there would have remained no visualization of female beauty.

As for Bertrand Russell's romantic love, we may quote his own words as follows:

"The essential of romantic love is that it regards the beloved object as very difficult to possess and as very precious.... The

belief in the immense value of the lady is a psychological effect of the difficulty of obtaining her, and 1 think it may be laid down that when a man has no difficulty in obtaining a woman, his feeling towards her does not take the form of romantic love."

Then, Bertrand Russell says:

"From the point of view of the arts, it is certainly regrettable when women are too accessible; what is most to be desired is that they should be difficult but not impossible of access.... In a state of complete freedom, on the other hand, a man capable of great love poetry is likely to have so much success through his charm that he will seldom have need of his best imaginative efforts in order to achieve a conquest."

Furthermore, he mentions in another context as follows:-

"Among modern emancipated people, love in the serious sense with which we are concerned is suffering a new danger. When people no longer feel any moral barrier against sexual intercourse on every occasion when even a trivial impulse inclines to it, they get into the habit of dissociating sex from serious emotion and from feelings of affection; they may even come to associate it with feelings of hatred."

CONCLUDING REMARKS

Strange that Bertrand Russell deemed it fit to emphasize the need for love in the serious sense almost in a moralist vein! His proposed new sexual freedom has not been fully clarified. For, he adjudged chastity and virtue to be dispensable for all sexual purposes. He construed marriage to be in no way obstructive to free sexual love. He implicitly recommended free sexual relations even with persons other than legal spouses, provided legitimacy of *conception is* ensured. In short, he approved of all kinds of *non-violent* and harmless sexual relations. All these he advocated seemingly because he found no reason to uphold *conventional sexual* morality, except for comparing and coordinating one's. private and public interests.

With his extreme thinking, as indicated above, Bertrand Russell could not have been expected to project any correct image of morals, which would seek to regulate human sexuality, in order to nurture it on the basis of tender feelings of love and affection. In any case, it is very clear that Bertrand Russell and others like him have sought to introduce a kind of communal sexuality. Societies where free sexual love prevails can hardly promote any genuine love.

At any rate, in the permissive societies, *love* would not come to mean the same as interpreted by philosophers of old. We may recall that love has been represented as the zenith of one's life and of one's enthusiasm for living a teacher, trainer, inspirer and a catalyst. In fact, people who spend their entire lives without the benefit of love remain unfortunate enough not to deserve to be human.

In the above context, two essential points are notable. The first one concerns the position that love, from the points of view of quality and purpose, is distinct from animal concupiscence and sexual lust. Moreover, it belongs to the realm of spirituality, which aspect is incompatible with the principles of materialism. Yet, it is accept able for one who ponders over spiritual matters even in what would appear to be a materialistic perspective. This much is admitted by Bertrand Russell himself when he says that "love is something far more than desire for sexual intercourse"

Furthermore, Bertrand Russell recognizes love and (ironically enough) sexual morality when he says:

> *Love has its own proper ideals and its own intrinsic moral standards. These are obscure both in Christian teaching and in the indiscriminate revolt against all sexual morality which has sprung up among considerable sections of the young generations.*

The second point elaborates on the spiritual aspect of love. Spirituality of love is evidenced in two stages. At the outset, it is indicated by a state of love in which emotional restiveness and *intensity* develops in the absence of the beloved. Subsequently, it manifests itself in sustained agitation of individual spirit. This leads to intellectual concentration and to prevalence of chastity and virtue in the spirit of the lover, so that occasionally geniuses are produced. In either case, human spirit undergoes great changes.

However the aforementioned great transformations of human spirit are possible only in a situation where lovers remain separated and/or their love remains unrequited. No sublime achievements are likely in a situation where lovers do not miss each other. At any rate, in the latter case, even passionate love may not reach the very height of its intensity of which it is intrinsically capable, towards achieving the significant qualities noted by philosophers.

A person becomes capable of manifesting great love from within himself or herself. Then, the spirit becomes agitated and seeks rest in the person or in the image of the beloved.

The image may be construed even beyond its real counterpart Thus, eventually, the former assumes greater significance to its accustomed lover than that of the real person of the distant beloved.

Where lovers remain united, mutual affection and kindness, as well as sincerity and repose, may be evidenced by them. A soundly endeavouring married couple will take the vicissitudes of life in their stride. Their combined abilities to do so can well be enhanced by their spiritual or intellectual compatibility, too. At the same time, they should be able to keep up their moral integrity, if their society is corrupt and polluted. In other words, They should not be tempted by any prospects of free sexual love offered by their society.

Spouses who are able to continually uphold chastity and virtue do so primarily by confining their sexual enjoyments to their conjugal rights. Then in old age when sexual passions subside, they can keep up their mutual affection through carefully nurtured and established chaste and virtuous companionship. Couples bound by sexual interests alone cannot be expected to evolve a well-integrated family living pattern and a lasting companionship.

A wife's entitlement to alimony and to practically sharing her husband's wealth represent the most significant economic and financial provisions instituted for marriage and family living. These are in consideration of the exclusiveness of the spouses' conjugal relationship.

The genuine interaction between a couple, which is anticipated in marriage and family living, is envisaged in terms of their individual and collective endeavours as well as in the broader context of appropriately maintaining their social environment.

Mutual affection and sincerity, as well as humane compassion and tenderness, are highly desirable attributes in married couples, in the context of their mutual and social interactions. These are often in evidence in societies governed by Islamic moral and legal checks and balances. In the others, such as those in the West, these qualities are seldom noticeable.

In the case of separated lovers, the afflicted individual spirits are likely to become all the more sensitive and piognant. They soar and delve, as well as keep attracting and getting attracted. In the other case of united lovers, who evidence mutually affectionate enjoyment and deep sincerity, their marital union itself will be capable of producing significant attainments. One may be rather skeptical about the former.

However, with regard to the latter, one is more likely to agree.

The Divine creation of the female counterpart of man emphasized their companionship and mutual affection. This is made clear in the Glorious Qur'an, as follows: The above passage contains two keywords, which are indicative of the Divine intention in creating the human pair. These keywords are: (meaning cordiality of love and graciousness). Their significance is very clear that God not merely created woman as mate for man, but indicated also that the pairing had envisaged inculcation of the abovementioned humane qualities.

Needless to add that the above humane qualities are indeed far different from those of human sensuality, or libido, as interpreted by some modernistic societies.

Mowlavi (Rumi as popularly known in the West) reflected the above point in his stanza mentioned below:-

The World owes to God its loveliness,

That which He forms retains its exquisiteness,

Since He made it as Man's abode,

How Adam's love for Eve can erode?

That is how it is with Mankind

Humane love is ordained not for animal-kind

For, pure love and compassion are to Mankind

What aggravation and lust are to animal-kind.

According to Will Durant, love attains perfection when it is sustained through old age. Then, it will provide cushioning effect during the loneliness of senility and approaching death. His view confirms the fact that love extends far beyond libido, in that anyone relying on the latter does so in vain and rather superficially on the basis of the sexual instinct alone.

In fact, Will Durant believed that the spirit of love could survive beyond the last trace of human physiological fitness. In senility, loving hearts retain their fresh spiritual excellence. while emotional needs of the body are perfectly fulfilled on a continuing basis.

To sum up, love assumes significance when its intrinsically humane qualities are nurtured and evidenced. Any separation of lovers accentuates, rather than falsifies, this position Full blossoming of love is attained with chastity and rectitude on the part of lovers.

Genuine love is unlikely to flourish in sexually and secularly permissive societies. They do not provide the necessary conditions for promoting the same, even in any romantic or poetic contexts. An average married couple in modernistic societies lacks an overall perspective, such as that of Islam, so that they remain unable to attain a deeply unifying and sincere love relationship.

8

PRESENT STATUS OF ISLAM

The last two hundred years have seen enormous challenges to all religions. Intellectually, Darwin, Freud, Marx, Nietzsche and the development of modern scientific ways of thinking have transformed the way we see the world and man and woman's place in it. Critical study of religious texts has implied that these are human creations rather than divine revelations. Politically, two of the major ideologies which dominated the twentieth century, Fascism and Communism, were anti-religious. Technologically, patterns of life have changed dramatically in the more affluent parts of the world.

Religion, as we have suggested, has to some extent, especially in the West, been pushed to the margins of life, although the secular society of which many people spoke so confidently in the sixties and seventies is now more questionable. Secularism is a word used to cover several phenomena. It implies the autonomy of daily life. It excludes the interference of religious authorities in government and in political and economic life. Thus in the USA, there is a clear separation of church and state. Likewise, India, constitutionally — if not in practice — is a secular state in the sense that no religion is meant to be given favored treatment. A secular society may also mean one in which individual citizens do not have any moral pattern of behavior imposed upon them by the state. For example in many Western countries homosexual acts, which were until quite recently illegal and punishable by law, are now considered a private matter for consenting individuals. In the same way, in many countries, abortion, with certain restrictions, is no longer illegal. Secularism may also describe a change of mood by which people no longer seek to explain life by reference to religious beliefs. They will look for a natural rather than a divine cause of illness or disaster. Some sociologists of religion suggest that in the West religion should be regarded as a private or even a 'leisure time' activity. This, of course, is not a view that a committed Christian would accept and is even more alien to the devout Muslim, who, if he or she has been brought up to think of Britain or America as 'Christian' countries, is puzzled by what seems to him or her their moral decadence, especially in terms of permissive sexuality and drug-taking.

In addition to these challenges, which all religions have had to face, much of the Islamic world has had to cope with Western imperialism and the political, economic and military dominance of the super-powers, and now particularly of the USA. Many of the challenges to religion mentioned above were cradled in Western society, so they can seem to Muslims a Western threat.

It is hard to generalize about two centuries and large areas of the world. Individual Muslim countries are each different. The responses of religious people to change can, however, usually be classified in terms of those who seek to maintain the tradition, those who claim to be returning to the pure faith, reformers who allow for alterations to practice, but no substantive change and those, often labeled modernists by their critics, who draw on outside sources in their reinterpretation of a faith. Different writers use rather varying labels for these four categories.

The Cambridge scholar Akbar Ahmed includes amongst those who maintain the tradition, scholars such as Ali Shariati and Ali Ashraf, as well as Ismail Faruqi and Hossein Nasr, both of whom I had the privilege of getting to know through the World Congress of Faiths. These writers concentrate on the larger message of Islam and avoid narrower sectarian quarrels. Often, their scholarship has been inaccessible to and rather remote from ordinary Muslims.

The term modernist is used by Akbar Ahmed of creative thinkers in the nineteenth and twentieth centuries, such as Sir Sayyed Ahmed Khan, who established the Muhammadan Anglo-Oriental College at Aligarh, which was consciously modeled on Oxbridge, and which I once briefly visited. Another modernist, who I take him as an example, was Sir Muhammad Iqbal (1876-

1938). One of the best known Muslim exponents of Renewal, he wished to create a synthesis of Muslim and Western thought.

Iqbal tried to reinterpret Islam in the light of the Sufi heritage and Western philosophy, especially the creative evolution of Bergson. The key feature of Iqbal's thought was the notion of reality as pure duration, with God and human beings interrelating dynamically in the universe. He believed that the marriage of intellect and love could transform human beings into a higher level of being. Iqbal's constant theme was 'Arise, and create a new world'. His poetry in Urdu and Persian inspired Indian Muslims in the first half of the twentieth century to shape and improve their condition of life and was a factor behind the creation of Pakistan.

In his *Reconstruction of Religious Thought in Islam* (1928), Iqbal gave a more systematic elaboration of his Islamic vision, arguing for a return to independent judgement, *ijtihad,* and the establishment of a legislative institution for the reformation of Islamic law. One Indian Muslim professor of philosophy drawing attention to the word 'reconstruction' rather than 're-interpretation' said that Iqbal 'while he seems to be elaborating the meaning of a verse of the Qur'an, is really using it as a peg to hang his own ideas on.'

Wilfred Cantwell Smith, who taught in Pakistan and later became Professor of the History of Comparative Religion at Harvard, wrote, in a book published in the middle of the last century, 'Today if Islam would function in this radically new world in which we find ourselves, it must be refashioned to give dynamic initiative and vision to man facing a life of opportunity and to give him creative love towards the community of his fellow men. Such a refashioning was a service rendered to Islam chiefly by the outstanding Muslim poet and thinker of the century, Muhammad Iqbal.' Cantwell Smith's comment, which he might well have revised later in his life, is interesting for the assumption, common at the time that he wrote it, that liberal re-interpretation must be the way forward for religion in the modern world. As a long standing member of the Modern Church People's Union, I sympathize with this, but it is not the dominant mood in Islam today, although Iqbal's influence is not forgotten.

The term modernist is also used by Akbar Ahmed of some contemporary writers, but in a different sense to that in which we have been using it. The common feature, he says, 'is the general belief that religion as a force or guide is no longer valid in our age.' He mentions writers such as Tariq Ali, Salman Rushdie, who have been influenced by Marxism and, on the right, Shahid Burki and Rana Kabbani, although the latter has moved closer to the traditionalists. Writers on both flanks, he says, echo ideas and concepts from outside the Islamic tradition.

Far more common than modernists are those who are concerned to reform abuse or corruption, but who in no way wish to question the message of Islam. Reform, of course, can be quite superficial but it can be far reaching. I take too examples: Maulana Wahiduddin Kahn, who is a member of the Indian Muslim minority, and Farid Esack, who is a from South Africa, where again Muslims are in a minority.

Maulana Wahiduddin Kahn 'stands out as a voice in the wilderness', said Dr Yoginder Sikand, in a paper I heard recently at a conference at the Punjabi University in Patiala. Kahn called for an understanding of Islam that is both rooted in the original sources of Islam, while at the same time willing wholeheartedly, although critically, to engage with modernity, responding positively to serious concerns such as questions of peace, inter-religious dialogue and political activism.'

Maulana Wahiduddin Kahn was born in what is now Uttar Pradesh in 1925. At first he joined the Jama'at-i-Islami Hind, which was founded by Abul 'Ala Maududi. Kahn was searching for a socially engaged spirituality, but he came to see that the agenda of the Jama'at, which was working for the establishment of an Islamic state in India was impractical. He moved for a time to the Tablighi Jama'at, but by 1975 he had cut his links with it because of its hostility to the creative application of Islamic law to the challenges of changing social conditions. In 1976 Khan set up his own research center in New Delhi. He believed that a new understanding of Islam was necessary to appeal to modern educated Indians.

Khan accepts that Muslims in India are and are likely to remain a minority. They need to seek a solution to their problems by internal reform rather than by conflict with the state or the dominant Hindu majority. He takes seriously the issue of pluralism and inter-community relations and stresses the need to build bridges with people of other faiths. He quotes from the Qur'an the saying 'Unto you your religion and unto me mine.' (109, 6). Islam enjoins Muslims to live with others as brothers in spirit. Khan argues that the Muslims of India today find themselves in a position similar to that of the Prophet and his followers in Mecca, when the nascent community was small and relatively powerless. Just as the Prophet at that time concentrated on peaceful preaching so Muslims in India today should do the same. They should also concern themselves with the problems and issues of the whole country instead of just thinking about their own communal interests.

Khan suggests that the traditional distinction between the 'house of Islam' or lands ruled by Muslims, *dar-ul islam,* and lands ruled by non-Muslims, traditionally known as *dar-ul harb* or 'the house of war' needs to be rethought.

The term 'house of war' only applied to those lands where Muslims were persecuted for their faith and had to resort to violence in self-defense. There should be a third category, which he calls the 'house of invitation' or *dar-ul da'wah,* to refer to lands under non-Muslim control but where Muslims are welcome and have full civil rights. Here the Muslim responsibility is to address non-Muslims with the message of Islam but not to seek confrontation. A similar view was expressed when a delegation from the World Muslim League visited Oxford in March 2002. In answer to a question Dr Abdullah of the League said that the distinction between the 'house of war' and the 'house of Islam' was a historical concept which does not apply today. He stressed that Muslims in Britain should see themselves as good British citizens.

Maulana Wahiduddin Khan also insists that non-Muslims should not be spoken of a *kafirs.* To do so is 'to violate God's injunctions.' The term *kafir* should only be applied to someone who knowingly rejects or conceals the truth.

Khan has not created a 'movement' and he has been attacked for collusion with the 'enemies of Islam.'

Reference has already been made to Dr Farid Esack's book *On being A Muslim.* This and another book, *Qur'an, Liberation and Pluralism.*, are both written in the context of the struggle in South Africa against apartheid — a struggle with which many Muslims, including Esack, identified. This struggle led Farid Esack to reflect on key Qur'anic passages used in the context of oppression to rethink the role of Islam in a plural society. He shows how traditional interpretations of the Qur'an were used to legitimize an unjust order, but that these same texts, if interpreted within a contemporary socio-historical context, support active solidarity with people of other religions in the struggle for change. In describing the objectives of his book, Esack puts first the wish 'to show that it is possible to live in faithfulness to both the Qur'an and to one's present context alongside people of other faiths, working with them to establish a more humane society.' Towards the end of the book, he refers to a Call of Islam publication *Women Arise! The Qur'an Liberates You,* which says that 'we must unleash a debate on the question of women so that equality and freedom become achievable.' But the document hastens to add that 'this debate need not depart from the pages of the Qur'an at all for within these pages there is sufficient evidence to suggest that Muslim women can and must play a full role in our society.'

The key difference, which is not always easy to make in practice, between those I label Reformers and those who seek Renewal is that those who are Reformers do not question Islam's authoritative sources, but are willing to debate how these have been interpreted. Those who speak of Renewal seek to marry the teachings of Islam with philosophical ideas drawn from external sources. There are other examples of reformers who could be mentioned, such as Chandra Muzaffar, from Malaysia, who is President of the International Movement for a Just World and whose spiritual commitment has led him to participate actively in politics. Most reformers are also involved in inter-faith activity. Where, the application of faith to the search for peace and social justice is a high priority, it is natural to look for allies among people of other faiths who share this passion.

Others who share this social passion blame the West for many of the ills and are less interested in interfaith dialogue. Akbar

Ahmed uses the term radical to group together thinkers, such as Shabbir Akhtar, Parvez Manzoor, Ziauddin Sardar and Kalim Siddiqui, known for his leadership of the British Muslim Parliament, who all reject the possibility of a *modus vivendi* with the West. In this they are similar to those who seek a return to the pure faith, who are sometimes called reactionaries and sometimes labeled radicals, although I am by no means suggesting that they would support violent opposition.

Reactionaries are those who recognize the challenges of the modern world to Islam and seek to resist them. They may welcome technological advance and scientific discovery, but reject many of the assumptions of secular society. I think it is necessary to repeat the distinction I made in the chapter on the Qur'an between reactionaries and traditionalists — using the word in a very different sense than when I referred above to Seyyed Hossein Nasr and other scholars. Traditionalists live much as their parents did and continue to practice the religion in which they were brought up without much awareness of the challenges to it posed by modern society. Reactionaries consciously reject and resist those challenges. For a very small minority, that resistance may be expressed by violence.

As an example, I take the Wahhabiya movement, partly because of its influence. Muhammad ibn Abd al-Wahhab (1703-87) initiated an ultra-conservative puritanical movement, which adhered to Hanbalite law in the Arabian peninsula during the eighteenth century. The movement rejected centuries of legal interpretation as well as the mysticism of the Sufis. Al-Wahhab found a champion in the tribal leader Muhammad ibn Sa'ud and the Saudis became the main supporters of the movement. In 1801, the Wahhabis slaughtered two thousand ordinary citizens in the streets of Qarbala, so violence is nothing new to this movement.

Another influential figure was al-Afghani (1838-97), who was born in Iran but who spent his formative years in Afghanistan. He aimed to rally the Muslim world to realize its power as an international community and by raising its political and intellectual standards to combat Western colonialism. Freedom from foreign rule was he hoped to be followed by the establishment of a pan-Islamic state and the union of all Muslims under a caliph. He regarded the Arabic language as of primary importance in promoting Muslim unity. His programme, he believed, would lead to improvements in the living standards of all Muslims. He affirmed the transcendental truth of Islam in his *The Refutation of the Materialists*. Towards the end of his life, he was hunted down by the Iranian authorities, but although three of his colleagues were hanged, he himself died of cancer.

In the early part of the twentieth century, the Muslim struggle against the West turned into a mass movement. In 1928 an Egyptian called al-Banna (1906-49) founded the Muslim Brotherhood, al-Ikhwan al-Muslimun, which rapidly gained support across the Middle East. Banna, who like many other radicals was a middle class intellectual, was in sympathy with the ideas of Afghani and deplored the disunity and moral laxity of Egyptian society, which he blamed on British occupation. One day, he wrote, six laborers from a British camp came to see him and said:

'We are weary of this life of humiliation and restriction. Lo, we see that Arabs and the Muslims have no status and no dignity. They are not more than mere hirelings belonging to the foreigners. We possess nothing but this blood... and these souls... and these few coins... We are unable to perceive the road to action as you perceive it, or to know the path to the service of the fatherland, the religion and the nation as you know it. All that we desire now is to present you with all we possess, to be acquitted by God of the responsibility, and for you to be responsible before Him for us and for what we must do.'

So the Muslim Brotherhood was born. By 1949, it had 2,000 branches and some half million members. Banna told his followers in 1943, 'You are not a benevolent society, nor a political party, nor a local organization having limited purposes. Rather, you are a new soul in the heart of the nation to give it life by means of the Qur'an.'

Banna's aim was to free Egypt from British control and to establish an Islamic state, eliminating such Western influences as night-clubs, casinos and pornography. After the Second World War, al-Banna took up the cause of the Palestinians, but his activities were restricted by the Egyptian government. At the end of 1948, many members of the Muslim Brotherhood were arrested. Soon afterwards a young member of the movement shot and killed the prime minister of Egypt, Nuqrashi Pasha and seven weeks later Hasan al-Banna was himself assassinated by secret servant agents.

The Brotherhood never fully recovered from the death of its founder, although the writings of Sayyid Qutb, who was executed in 1966, had considerable influence. His widely read *Malim fi al-Tariq* argued that social systems were of two types. Either there was a Nizam Islami — a true Islamic order — or a Nizam Jahli, that is the rule of pre-Islamic ignorance. As Egypt did not belong to the first category, it belonged to the second and therefore it was the duty of true Muslims to wage jihad against ignorant and despotic governments. In passing it is worth emphasizing that radical Muslims are often as critical of many Muslim governments, which they consider in the pay of the West, as they are of Western powers themselves. Members of the Muslim described Egypt's defeat in the Six-Day War 'as a sign of God's punishment for leaving the path of Islam.' They too were responsible for the assassination of President Sadat, whom they accused of treachery against Islam and the Palestinian people by his agreement to the Camp David Accord.

The most spectacular victories for militant Islam have been the Iranian revolution in 1979 and the capture of Kabul by the Taliban in 1979. The Shah of Iran and his father had tried to westernize their country. Traditional Muslim style of dress were banned and western education promoted. Opponents ran foul of the much feared secret police. When Muslim clergy protested, the Shah dismissed them as 'black reactionaries'. He expelled the most vociferous protester, Ayatollah Khomeini (1902-89), a leader of the Twelve Shi'ite Muslims, who in exile became more dangerous and eventually succeeded in overthrowing the Shah in 1979. As leader of the revolution, he purged Iran of Western influences. His *fatwa* or ban against Salman Rushdie's *The Satanic Verses* was widely accepted in the Muslim world.

The Taliban was originally a military group, formed in response to the invasion of Afghanistan by the Soviet Union. As part of the Cold War against the Soviet Union both America and Britain trained Taliban fighters in guerrilla warfare and supplied arms and money. When they gained power, the Taliban showed themselves even more rigorous than Ayatollah Khomeini in imposing a version of Islamic law, which most Muslims regard as crude and distorted.

Recent years have also seen a revival of the original militant movement founded by al-Wahhab with a network of organizations, under various names. These groups have been involved in prolonged struggles in Algeria, where the Islamic party won a general election but were denied power and where there have been atrocities on both sides Militants are said to be responsible for the deaths of seventy tourists at Luxor in 1997 and to be linked with armed groups in Kashmir. The most notorious group is, of course, al-Qaida, led by Osama bin-Laden, which the USA accuses of responsibility for the twin tower tragedy on September 11th, 2001.

It must be emphasized that the great majority of Muslims want nothing to do with violence and most have condemned the terrorist attacks on America. Even so, it is important to hear what some of these militants are saying so as to see how the world is seen through the eyes of the most alienated Muslims. Terror draws its sustenance from disaffection which is caused by the hopelessness of those who feel victimized by poverty and injustice.

Ayatollah Khomaini was a long standing critic of the Shah of Persia's regime, but during his exile, he broadened his opposition to attack the institution of monarchy itself and to call not just for adherence to Islamic law, but for the establishment of an Islamic state. In about 1969 he gave a series of lectures to his students, which were published as a book entitled *Velayat-e Faqih.* It is a blueprint for the reorganization of society. It is a handbook for revolution. There are four main themes. First the book condemns the institution of monarchy as alien to Islam, abhorrent to the Prophet and the source of all Iran's misfortunes over 2,500 years. Secondly, it presents the Islamic state, which is based on the Qur'an and modeled after the Islamic community governed by the Prophet in the seventh century, as a practical form of government realizable in the lifetime of the present generation and not as some distant ideal. Thirdly, and this is particular to the Shi'ite tradition, the claim of the clerical class, as heirs of the Prophet, to the leadership of the community is forcefully asserted.

Justice and an expertise in Islamic law are essential for those who rule. 'The real governors', he says, 'are the Islamic jurists themselves.' Although leadership is vested collectively in the religious leadership (*ulama*), it can be vested in a single leader. Fourthly, *Velayat-e Faqih* calls on all believers to work actively for the overthrow of the non-Islamic state. 'We have no choice', Khomaini wrote, 'but to shun wickedness, and to overthrow governors who are traitorous, wicked, cruel and tyrannical.' He urged revolution, but not violence.

The statements of Osama bin-Laden are more directly political in tone. In a 'World Islamic Front Statement' entitled 'Jihad Against Jews and Crusaders', he argues that the United States of America has created a state of war against the Muslim world and in particular the people of the Arabian Peninsula. He speaks of the occupation of the Arabian Peninsula, which contains Islam's most holy places, arguing that it is being used by the Americans as a staging post for continuing aggression against the Iraqi people, of whom he claims more than one million have been killed. Further he complains of the 'occupation of Jerusalem and the murder of Muslims there' — Israel, being seen as an American puppet state. These American actions, in his view, amount to a 'clear declaration of war on God, his messenger, and Muslims.' Further because 'the *ulema* have throughout Islamic history unanimously agreed that the *jihad* is an individual duty if the enemy destroys Muslim countries', Osama bin-Laden, therefore, declared that it is a duty for every Muslim who can to kill Americans and their allies and he quotes from the Qur'an (2, 193 and 4,75) to justify this call.

This is an extreme position, which I in no way seek to justify, but if there is to be an alternative to violent reaction to violence, then at least we need to hear the complaint of those who sympathize with Osama bin-Laden's attack on America and the West. Two years ago, not for the first time, I visited a Palestinian Refugee camp. In the bitterness and despair of those we talked to I felt more than ever their deep sense of injustice and of a wasted life. The causes of the situation are complex and neighboring Arab nations have been almost as much responsible as Israeli governments. The human tragedy is overwhelming as also is the suffering of many families in Iraq, because of sanctions imposed by the USA and Britain (although nominally by the UN). One could add to the political complaints, the failure of Western powers to protect the Bosnian Muslims or to curb the ruthless Russian suppression of Chechnyan rebels. Terrorism is not to be condoned and I deplore all violence, but in every age victims of ruthless regimes have been driven to armed resistance. One person's terrorist is another person's freedom-fighter.

There is also a sense amongst some Muslims that Western concern for human rights is selective and that the world economic system operates largely to the benefit of the West and certain Arab rulers who are in league with them. To some eyes globalization is seen as bed-fellow of modernism.

I do not want to pursue the political analysis, but it is impossible to separate political and religious issues in the present situation. What is felt by many Muslims as injustice, contributes to oppositional attitudes and the rejection of all that the West stands for. Raficq Abdullah, a Muslim lawyer who lives in London, writes that for millions of Muslims who live in poverty and who feel profoundly marginalized, modernity has nothing to offer them. It embodies 'the virulent return of *jahilliyah* or ungodliness which now infests the whole world including Muslim societies... It is justified by man-made laws which transgress God's legislative authority as enshrined in the religious law or *Shariah*. This comprehensive failure to abide by the only sovereign law which is God's exclusive attribute and prerogative is the cause of moral decay and spiritual bankruptcy. A true Muslim's only shield against this seemingly intractable threat to his or her identity is a reversion to the authentic experience of Islam as it was practiced during the lives of the Prophet and the rightly-guided Caliphs.' Raficq Abdullah is at pains to make clear that Islam is not a monolithic entity, but adds that the rejection of modernity and the 'West' is shared by both Sunni and Shi'a Islamists. As Raficq Abdullah makes clear, he does not share these views, and accuses those who take this position of committing 'epistemological legerdemain by projecting their deeply nostalgic version of events of the founding moment of Islam as ahistorical categories, as givens which it would be sacrilegious, indeed blasphemous, to place under critical scrutiny'.

Raficq uses the term Islamists. I have tried to avoid the term 'fundamentalist', which as I have already explained is misleading and 'extremist', which may be an excuse for not listening to the call for justice of those who feel marginalized. As Raficq Abdullah points out the way in which some in the West speak of all Muslims as if they were terrorists is as bad as the way some Muslims see all Westerners as enemies of the true faith. As Edward Said has observed, 'the real battle is not a clash of civilizations, but a clash of definitions.'

The struggle should not be the West against the world of Islam, rather a struggle is going on for the soul of Islam. Professor Khalid Duran, of the Foreign Policy Research Institute in Philadelphia, writing well before the tragic events of September 11th, made a distinction between *Muslims* and *Islamists.*' He compares the distinction to that in Germany between *evangelisch* and *evangelikal* (Protestant and Protestant fundamentalist). Similarly before the fall of the Berlin Wall both regimes in Germany claimed they were democratic. Two titles which sound almost the same may have sharply different meanings. One Muslim explained the difference by saying that 'Muslims say "God is most great", whereas Islamists say "Islam is most great", although that is rather too simple.

Most of the Muslims I know and the ones whom we are likely to meet in dialogue are Muslims — in the sense I am using it. They are also usually heirs to the Enlightenment so share many of the assumptions of the modern paradigm. Even so, we need to try to understand something of the appeal of the Islamists.

As we have seen, the origins of the Islamic Movement lie with the Wahhabi movement that emerged in Central Arabia in the eighteenth and nineteenth century. Its aim was to revive the Muslim society of seventh century Medina in its 'pristine purity'. A similar vision inspired Hasan al-Banna who founded the Muslim Brotherhood Party. He wanted to return to original Islam 'cleansed of all later accretions such as theology, philosophy and mysticism. Compare this to the motto of Z. A. Bhutto's Pakistan People's Party 'Our religion is Islam, our political system is democracy, our economic orientation is socialism' — a slogan that was anathema to Islamists. There is a real ideological struggle in many Muslim countries reflecting radically different understandings of the Muslim religion.

In part, the Islamists, as we have seen, reject centuries of legal scholarship and the mystical tradition. They are fundamentalist in the sense that scriptural statements are not seen in their historical context and are treated as absolute-whereas any revealed statement ought to be open to interpretation. This points to the very different assumptions of those who are and are not heirs to the Enlightenment. In his book on Judaism, Hans Küng speaks of paradigm shifts and suggests that you can have periods when people of the same faith are living in different paradigm times, which means that they have few shared assumptions about life and the world. Islamists reject 'modernism', partly because their view of life starts from different basic assumptions.

The struggle within Islam is primarily a matter for Muslims, but sympathetic friends need to be aware of the struggle that is taking place, and to be supportive of those Muslims who are willing to take the risk of dialogue. They can help to make known the views of the latter group, thereby resisting the stereotyping of Muslims which will make prophecies of a clash of civilizations self-fulfilling. This is also a time when more than ever Christians need to seek dialogue with those Muslims who are willing to take part in it.

It is also vital to help Muslims in Europe and America feel that they are accepted as full citizens and that they have a stake and share in our society. One of the dangers in some urban areas of Britain is that young Muslims not only feel alienated from 'white English society' but are also increasingly alienated from the mosques and the leaders of the Muslim community. In 2001, I was invited to the Awards for Excellence ceremony organized by the *Muslim News* and also to the opening of a new Muslim center near Paddington Station by Prince Charles. It made me more aware how many Muslims are making a rich contribution to British life at all levels of our society. But many others, like a young Muslim woman at a check-out in Cowley or a Rhodes scholar at one of the colleges in Oxford have told me that they feel marginalized and have experienced discrimination and racial abuse. The search for a genuinely multi-cultural and multi-religious society is more important than ever and the work of the various interfaith organization needs to be strongly supported.

On the international scene, governments, *all* governments have to address the root causes of poverty and injustice — and this includes tackling trade discrimination, the arms trade as well as seeking solutions for long-standing areas of tension in the Middle East and in Kashmir and Sudan. People of faith have constantly to call upon the leaders of the nations to live up to their responsibilities. The tragic events of September 11th could be a wake-up call to seek for the new world order that some of us talked about and hoped for with the start of a new millennium.

ISLAM AND MODERN AGE

Every religion prescribes its own prayer system, Islam also does. Every religion has its own unique system and it is this uniqueness which is precious. Islam prescribes its prayer system without challenging prayer systems of other religions as it recognises the uniqueness of prayer systems of other religions. It puts it succinctly as under: "And everyone has direction to which he turns (himself), so vie with one another in good works." (2:148).

Thus it is clear that everyone has ones own way of worshipping and one should not denounce each others way of worship. According to Imam Raghib the word 'wijhat' is more comprehensive. It means not only direction but also entire 'shari`ah'. Thus according to Raghib what Qur'an states in the above verse is that each religion has its own 'shari`ah' which has its own uniqueness.

There are different words used by the Qur'an for worship, the most frequent being 'ibadah'. The word 'ibadah' is also used in senses more than one. It is derived from the word 'ubudiyyah' which means to express ones humility and humbleness. But the word ' ibadah' carries in it even greater sense of humility; it, in fact, carries the utter sense of humility. Thus the first requirement of worship in Islam is to feel utterly humble before the Greatest Being and Most Powerful Allah.

Human beings are created by All Mighty Allah and to worship Him they must develop within themselves the utter sense of humility. Thus the Islamic concept of worship implies humility. Thus by implication it also becomes an essential part of Islamic ethic. Thus arrogance is unethical. No wonder than that Qur'an repeatedly denounces arrogance and calls it 'istikbar'. Its opposite is both ' istid`af' (to be weak) and ' ubudiyyat'.

Pharaoh (Fir'aun) has been described in the Qur'an as 'mustakbir' (having arrogance of power) as also the Satan.

The direct implication is that those who are arrogant are like Pharaoh or Satan. The true servant of Allah has a sense of utter humility and believes that only Allah is the Greatest-'Allahu Akbar.'

This is very basic formula of Islamic worship. Anyone who is arrogant and has a feeling of powerful cannot be true worshipper of Allah. A true worshipper of Allah is one who has no trace of arrogance, of 'ananiyyah' or egotism. This has another important implication. It negates the very concept of one being ruler over the other and thus creates democratic ethos and human dignity.

Elsewhere also the Qur'an lays emphasis on dignity of entire humanity-children of Adam when it says: " And surely, We have honoured the children of Adam, and We carry them in the land and the sea, and We provide them with good things, and We have made them to excel highly most of those whom We have created." (17:70)

Thus once we accept Allah as the Greatest by implication all human beings are His humble servant without any distinction of caste, colour, creed or race and all are equal before Him and no one is superior to the other. The Qur'an clearly sates that " O mankind, surely We have created you from a male and a female, and made your tribes and families that you may know each other. Surely the noblest of you with Allah is the most pious (God-conscious) of you." (49:13).

It will be seen that it is very important statement of the Qur'an and is quite fundamental to the concept of worship in Islam. All human beings are equal in the sight of Allah and distinction of tribes, families etc. are only to know each other and not to take pride-leading to arrogance in ones belonging to one nation or the other, or one tribe or family or other.

The real distinction could be only of piety, honesty and integrity of character and most honoured in the eyes of Allah is one who is most pious. Any Muslim who feels superior to the other on the basis of tribe or family or nation or colour cannot be true worshipper of Allah as this air of superiority leads to arrogance which is quite contrary to the very concept of ' ibadah' and ' ubudiyyah'. One who worships Allah must intrinsically subscribe to the concept of equality of all human beings. There is no place in Islam of low or high status at all.

This is further symbolised by the congregational prayer in Islam. All have to stand in one line in Islamic congregational prayer. A true worshipper of Allah would show equal respect to all human beings irrespective of their origin, their identity and their status. Any worshiper who apparently stands in one line but carries the feeling of superiority over others in his heart, cannot be construed as true and free worshipper. Such a person is not bondsman of Allah but of his vain desire. He who is bondsman of his own desire cannot be a free person and can never claim to enjoy the pleasure of a free man's worship. Thus a false sense of superiority is the very negation of true worship. A free man's worship is based on passionate belief in freedom and dignity of all human beings as Allah alone is creator of all and He alone is real object of worship.

Thus a passionate belief in one God also assumes great significance in Islamic tradition. Because only such belief in oneness of God leads to the negation of worshipping lesser beings. It can lead to worship of human being by another human being and thus deifying some among us or deifying some other objects. This would also lead to superiority of some over others negating the concept of equal dignity for all children of Adam as stated in the Qur'an.

The Sufis, the mystics of Islam, base their concept of 'wahdat al-wujud' (unity of Being) on this concept of 'tawhid' (unity of Godhood) and it is this concept of unity of Being which demolishes all distinctions. The concept of Absolute Being is possible only if we believe in the concept of absolute unity of humankind. And sufis made no such distinctions. Distinctions invariably lead to a sense of superiority and hence go against the concept of worship of a True Being. In Islam an act of worship is a means, not a goal. The goal is a true moral and ethical conduct. The Qur'an says "Surely prayer keeps (one) away from indecency and evil; and certainly the remembrance of Allah is the greatest (act)." (29:45) Many treat prayer 'salah' as a goal, not a means as stated in the above Qur'anic verse. A real worshipper would never indulge in any indecent act ('fahsha)' or would never go near an evil.

The important question is what is evil? The word used for evil here is 'munkar' i.e. anything which is rejected by the society as harmful. Anything which is harmful to human society must be rejected and must be desisted from. There are some evils which are absolute in nature and must be avoided irrespective of time and place. Injustice and falsehood are such evils. The greatest evil thus is being untruthful.

One of the names of Allah is 'Haq' i.e.truth. Thus truthfulness becomes the important element of Allah\rquote s worship. Anyone who deviates from the path of truth cannot claim to be worshipper of Allah. A true worshipper of Allah will never compromise on the question of truth. He will gladly sacrifice his own interests to uphold the cause of truth. Those who sacrifice everything including their own lives deserve to be true worshiper of Allah. A true worshiper would not entertain falsehood in any form. A true worshiper's tongue will speak nothing but truth. He will never utter anything which is not truth. One has to be fearless to be truthful. Only one who fears Allah and no one else can speak truth and avoid falsehood.

Also, Allah is Just and one who worships Allah cannot be but just. Justice is part of worship and one who works tirelessly for establishing justice in the society is real worshiper of Allah. The path of truth and justice is paved with difficulties and sacrifices and a true worshiper does not mind in the least to face these difficulties and make sacrifices for the cause of justice and truth. To court martyrdom for the cause of truth and justice is the highest form of worship one can think of. Thus the Qur'an describes true worshiper as follows: "The patient and the truthful, and the obedient, and those who spend and those who ask Divine protection in the morning times." (3:16). Truth requires inexhaustible degree of patience and hence the above verse refers to the quality of patience along with truthfulness. Allah has been described as 'Rabb al-`Alamin' in the Qur'an i.e. Sustainer of the universe. 'Rabb', according to Imam Raghib, is one who takes a thing from one stage of perfection to another stage until it reaches the final stage of perfection. Allah is 'Rabb' in this sense and any of His worshiper has to work tirelessly for achieving this objective. He or she will do nothing which will obstruct this path of perfection. This also includes the protection of environment and ecological balance. For the perfection of our world its ecological balance is very vital. The greed for consumption leads to destruction of ecological balance. Thus a worshiper can not be insensitive to the destruction of environment.

The quality of 'rububiyyat' (sustaining) will be incomplete without mercy and compassion. Thus in the very first chapter of the Qur'an Allah is described as 'Rabb, Merciful and Compassionate'. Only one who is merciful and compassionate can take this universe from one stage of perfection to another stage until it reaches the ultimate stage of perfection. And one who engages oneself in this work on human plane has to have qualities of mercy and compassion for all i.e. for entire humanity on one hand, and, for all the creation of Allah, on the other. A person who is compassionate will not wantonly destroy anything and would show feeling of loving care for all creatures. Thus a worshiper has to be compassionate and merciful towards all.

The Qur'an also makes it clear that the act of prayer is not merely a ritual to be performed. It is an act which transforms ones inner being and makes him or her a perfect person. Perfection of inner being is very important aspect of act of worship. Thus Qur'an describes the act of worship as under: " It is not righteousness that you turn your faces towards the East and West, but righteous is one who believes in Allah, and the Last Day, and the angels and the Book and the prophets, and gives away wealth out of love for Him to the near of kin and the orphans and the needy and the wayfarer and to those who ask and to set slaves free and keeps up prayer and pays the poor rate; and the performers of their promise when they make a promi se, and the patient in distress and affliction and in the time of conflict; and these are they who keep their duty.\rdblquote (2:177)

This is very seminal verse which describes the basic features of worship. Thus worship is not a mere physical act of bowing and prostrating; it is much more than that. The Islamic concept of ' ibadah' is as much social as spiritual. Thus among ' ibadat' are included 'fasting, zakat' and 'Hajj'. These have their own significance. Fasting ('saum') again is not mere an act of going hungry from sunrise to sun set. It is to learn to control ones desires and make ones soul pure by removing all impurities. Controlling ones desires (what the Qur'an calls 'nafs ammarah') is very important element of fasting.

It amounts in fact to developing a spirit of renunciation in the midst of having and developing sensitivity towards others suffering. To be sensitive is very important element of ' ibadah'. And fasting is meant to sensitize the people. Only a sensitive soul can stand up and fight against untruth and injustice. Thus the real significance of fasting is to develop sensitivity towards misery and suffering and devote oneself to eradication of all forms of suffering and misery.

Thus in the above verse (2:177) describing the act of true worship emphasis is laid on spending ones wealth out of love for Him for the near of kin and the orphans and the needy and the wayfarer and to those who ask and to set slaves free. In those days of slavery Islam talked of dignity of all human beings and repeatedly laid emphasis on setting the slaves free. Here in the above verse setting slaves free has been described as an act of worship.

Slaves suffer intensely and slavery deprives human beings of their human dignity and hence setting slaves free is an important ingredient of act of worship. A believer or a worshiper would not tolerate any act of indignity to any human being. Thus he has to be passionately committed to human freedom and dignity and has to work to abolish all forms of human unfreedom, slavery being the most abominable for of human indignity.

The above verse also emphasises the need for spending for the poor, the orphans, the widows and the wayfarers. This is precisely what the payment of zakat (poor rate) is meant for. Thus the Qur'an says: " Zakat (charity) is only for the poor and the needy, and those employed to administer it, and those whose hearts are made to incline (to truth), and (to free) the captives, and those in debt, and in the way of Allah and for the wayfarer-an ordinance from Allah." (9:60).

Thus it will be seen that zakat is basically meant for the weaker sections of society so that their sufferings could be minimised. Zakat is also required to be spent on paying off the debts of indebted. It is poor who are indebted. The poor are generally indebted and they must be freed of it if their sufferings are to be eliminated. Again, it is for this reason that the Qur'an prohibits interest.

It is the poor who have to pay high rates of interest for fulfilling their basic needs. Those who charge high rates of interest on consumption loans are real blood suckers and they can never qualify for worship. On the other hand, Qur'an warns them to be prepared for war with Allah if they do not waive off interest on such loans. In fact war against interest is war against poverty and suffering.

Thus it will be seen that establishing social justice is as important part of act of worship as an act of praying. It also has a macro dimension. Entire third world is poor and indebted today. It is the rich countries of the West who exploit the people of the third world and put burden of indebtedness on them. There is need for setting up funds on the line of zakat to waive off debts of third world countries and interest thereon. This would greatly relieve the third world of its suffering and for the West it will be an act of worship. But all of us know that Western countries are not going to oblige the third world. This socio-economic dimension should not be lost sight of.

The Qur'an is so sensitive to various dimensions of suffering that it specially mentions the problem of wayfarers also. In those days the wayfarers had to face number of difficult problems while traveling. No basic facilities were available on the long and arduous course of journey. The Qur'an thus required a part of the zakat fund be spent on alleviating the sufferings of these wayfarers. It indicates the degree of sensitivity Qur'an desires to create in us. It is, therefore, highly necessary that a worshiper be hyper sensitive to others sufferings in every form. He should work tirelessly for the welfare of an entire humanity.

Hajj is also included in the act of Islamic worship. It is desirable that Muslims should go, if he has means, for 'Hajj' once in life time. What is its significance as an act of worship? What is its social dimension? As pointed out earlier Islam teaches equality of all human beings irrespective of tribe, nation or family. When one meets other human being one should meet him/her on plane of equality. Hajj provides this opportunity to a Muslim. Muslims from all over the world congregate for Hajj in Mecca. They belong to different nations, different tribes, different races and colours. Also they are made to wear a simple 'un-sewn' white cloth to further emphasise their equality before God. This huge congregation of human beings from all over globe without any distinction of nation or tribe, caste or colour is recognition of equality of all human beings and it is a practical lesson in ordering a world free of ethnic, national or racial distinctions.

This is a great act of worship and the greatest service of humanity, provided it is taken in that spirit. Ka'ba is a house of Allah and all those who come there are equal before Him in every respect. If the hajj is taken in its real spirit it can lead to creating of a world free of all ethnic and racial tensions.

Thus it will be seen that an act of worship is not merely a ritual as it has come to be widely practiced. A real act of worship is much more than mere physical act of bowing and prostrating, or fasting mechanically as a ritual or performing hajj by merely going to Mecca. These acts of worship have other dimensions, which are very important in reordering and refashioning our world, a world without suffering, a world without discrimination, a world without inequalities and without bondage. Such a world can be created only with a passionate commitment to dignity and freedom of humanity. It is this passionate commitment with humility before Allah which can constitute a real act of a free man's worship which has spiritual as well as social dimension.

The great philosophers of Islam like al-Farabi, Averros and Avicina rose to the height of their fame after the Abbasid power began to decline. Of course, the encyclopedic work like Ikhwanus Safa (The Brethren of Purity) was written and compiled during the heydays of the Abbasids. There is a great deal of controversy as to who compiled the work which could be described as most modern of its time for its liberalism, openness and sweep. The Isma'ilis claim that the work was compiled by their Imam Husain al-Mastur to effectively reply to the Abbasids through their own weapon.

However, others feel that there was a society in Basra which met secretly and discussed the most burning religious and philosophical questions of the time and written records of these were maintained and these records were later on compiled under the title Ikhwanus Safa. Whatever the truth, the fact is that this encyclopedic work was very comprehensive and it runs into 52 volumes, each volume devoted to some subject or the other. It adopted the then most modern approach to the problems and discussed everything in the light of reason and proved their contentions, even of faith, by use of intellect and not blind belief.

It will be interesting to quote here from some philosophical and theological works to show how philosophical and theological controversies were debated in the light of reason. Even most orthodox theological propositions were examined in the light of reason. I quote passages from Al-Ghazali's Al-Munqidh min al-Dalal (i.e. That Which Delivers from Error) to show the nature of debates. It should be borne in mind that al-Ghazali was an orthodox theologian and opposed to philosophical reasoning.

He wrote a book Tahafut al-Falasifa (i.e. Bewilderment of Philosophers). Ibn Rushd, a great philosopher and the contemporary of Ghazali replied by writing Tahafut, Tahafut al-Falasifa (i.e. Stupefication of the Bewilderment of Philosophers).

Thus al-Ghazali says in one of his passages in his Munqidh min al-Dalal: "In this and similar cases of sense-perception the sense as judge forms his judgments, but another judge, the intellect, shows him repeatedly to be wrong; and charge of falsity cannot be rebutted.

> *"To this I said: 'My reliance on sense-perception also has been destroyed. Perhaps only those intellectual truths which are first principles (or derived from first principles) are to be relied upon, such as the assertion that ten are more than three, that the same thing cannot be both affirmed and denied at one time, that one thing is not both generated in time and eternal, nor both existent and non-existent, nor both necessary and impossible.';"*

Further Ghazali continues: "Sense-perception replied: 'Do you not expect that your reliance on intellectual truth will fare like your reliance on sense-perception? You used to trust in me, then along came the intellect-judge and proved me wrong; if it were not for the intellect-judge you would have continued to regard me as true. Perhaps behind intellectual apprehension there is another judge who, if he manifests himself, will show the falsity of intellect in its judging, just as, when intellect manifested itself, it showed the falsity of sense in its judging. The fact that such a supra-intellectual apprehension has not manifested itself is no proof that it is impossible.' "

QUALITY OF ARGUMENTS

Ghazali then gives the example of dream: "My ego hesitated a little about the reply to that, and sense-perception heightened the difficulty by referring to dreams. 'Do you not see', it said, 'how when you are asleep, you believe things and imagine circumstances, holding them to be stable and enduring, and, so long as you are in that dream-condition, have no doubts about them? And is it not the case that when you awake you know that all you have imagined and believed is unfounded and ineffectual? Why then are you confident that all your waking beliefs, whether from sense or intellect, are genuine? They are true in respect of your present state; but it is possible that a state will come upon you whose relation to your waking consciousness is analogous to the relation of the latter to dreaming.' "

The argument goes on. The question is not which point of view was right or wrong; the more important question is the quality of arguments, their objectivity and methodology which was quite modern. So the theological and philosophical debates were intellectually rich and based on certain agreed methodology which could be construed as quite modern from the norms of those days.

Another parameter of modernity, though not insisted upon by Bernard Lewis, but by some other Western scholars, is gender justice and human rights. If we go by the Islamic ideals and not the practice in Muslim societies, Islam stood for gender justice. The Qur'anic pronouncements in this respect were quite revolutionary from the standards of those days. What is most important is that Islam accepted the woman as a legal entity with definite rights in terms of marriage, divorce, inheritance, maintenance, property and so on.

But the conservative 'Ulama, under the influence of their own societies, interpreted, in many cases through inventions of a Hadith (Prophet's sayings), the Qur'anic verses in such a manner as to rob her of the very rights granted to her, in many cases in the most unambiguous terms, by the Divine Book. No other legal system by then had granted her legal individuality, not even the Roman law, which was the most advanced law in the pre-Islamic world.

However, the time was not ripe to practice gender justice as we understand today, much less gender equality. Whatever was given to women was taken away by the Muslim society through the backdoor. In that sense too, Islam was a modern religion which, at least theoretically, brought about radical change in the status of women. There is, therefore, an urgent need to rethink women's rights related issues in the Muslim world. It is ironical that the Muslim world is charged today with oppressing their women and denying them justice.

As for democracy, the Qur'an requires the Holy Prophet to consult people in secular matters, or matters relating to the community (see verses 3:159 and 42:38). This approach could have produced a democratic culture and the early companions of the Prophet did practice it for a limited period of time. However, soon such efforts were sabotaged by some power-hungry people who converted Islamic democracy into dynastic rule. And the tryst with democracy ended there and Muslim society has not known democracy and democratic values ever since.

Feudalism and authoritarianism which were totally alien to the Islamic spirit came to be legitimised and most oppressive and exploitative regimes came into existence in the Islamic history. The early democratic spirit was never re-discovered. it is only in our time that some Islamic countries have ushered in democracies to varying degrees. But, it must be admitted that most of the Muslim countries are ruled by monarchs or military dictators. Thus we have to face the odium that Islam is against modernity.

ISLAMIC WORLD AND MODERNITY

The response of Islamic countries to the concept of modernity as it obtains today varies from country to country. One thing in common, again with one or two honourable exceptions, is that all of these countries have accepted domination of the West, particularly the USA.

Some of them even consider this domination as the ultimate in modernity although their societies continue to be utterly feudalistic in values. Neither do they have democracy nor any trace of gender justice. However, most of these countries vie one with the other in buying latest weaponry from the West. This also is considered by them as a symbol of modernity.

In Saudi Arabia, Saudis are governed by a highly authoritarian monarchy with no trace of democracy or gender justice. In this so-called Islamic regime women enjoy no independence worth the name. Though they are allowed to work in establishments run only by women, they are not free to work anywhere else. They are not allowed to go out alone without being accompanied by a mehram i.e. a man within the prohibited degree of marriage.

No independent thinking in the fields of religion, philosophy and other social sciences is permitted. In every field there are pre-established official dogmas to which all Saudi citizens have to conform. There is no respect for human rights as there is no democracy. So all parameters of modernity are absent.

Yet one finds a superficial aura of modernity. The Saudi cities are concrete jungles including the holy cities of Mecca and Madina. There is so much blind imitation of the West in designing buildings that no trace of Islamic heritage has been left. There is no Islamic ambiance even outside the holiest mosque of the Islamic world to which millions of pilgrims flock every year i.e. K'aba. Just outside the holiest mosque of the Islamic world there are huge concrete buildings. Mecca appears to be like any other Western city. No attempt has been made to preserve its Islamic heritage, not even in architecture. Could this be construed modernity? If it is, it is very superficial.

There is no re-thinking of Islamic issues, no freedom of thought, no critical evaluation of Saudi practices but only blind imitation of the West in its worst aspects mindless urbanisation and disruption of old patterns of living. Also, the Saudi rulers buy huge stockpiles of Western arms which only increases their servility to the West. More arms they purchase from the West, more dependent they become on it.

HUMAN RIGHTS EQUAL MODERNITY

Earlier the Shah of Iran had also followed similar policies. He tried to impose forcibly the western modernism on a highly traditional society. The Shah also wanted to become regional satrap by stockpiling Western arms. There was no trace of democracy in Iran during his regime and no respect for human rights which are important parameters of modernism. Also, if women were allowed to wear mini skirts, could it be taken as sign of gender justice? In fact women were far from enjoying higher status in the Shah's Iran.

After the revolution Ayatollah Khomeini also tried to impose many restrictions on women. Chador was made compulsory. Also, the traditional laws as regards women were not changed. However, women in post-revolutionary Iran are becoming quite conscious of their rights. Iran is one of the few Islamic countries which allows women to contest elections and now a woman has also become Vice-President of Iran. In Kuwait it is still being debated whether women could be given right to vote. In appearance Kuwait is one of the most modern cities of the world but its society still continues to be medieval.

In all these countries except Iran there is total dependence on the West for arms as well as for economic development. They have no ability for developing modern science and technology or independent thinking in social or religious matters. Egypt produced many modern thinkers but it is also regressing now and fundamentalism has raised its head. In Egypt also there is a lack of democracy and human rights. In relation to women too, the 'Ulama of al-Azhar are resisting change. So the record of gender justice is not very bright in Egypt too. However, compared to other Islamic countries, Egypt is relatively more advanced.

Pakistan had much better record until Zia's time. Zia's political Islam pushed Pakistan, too, back to medieval thinking in religious matters. Democracy there is not more than a decade old. In post-Zia-ul-Haq period democracy is striking roots but the people of Pakistan are not very sure when military will intervene again. Zia's fundamentalist Islam also deprived women of their many rights which otherwise they had gained through their struggles.

Thus it will be seen that though Islamic society had much better record in terms of modernity during early period of Islam, the Islamic societies today have regressed to medieval ages though they claim to be superficially modern. Most of the Islamic societies have neither democracy, nor concept of human rights or gender justice nor capacity for independent development of science and technology.

BIBLIOGRAPHY

Akhtar, Wazir : *Economics in Islamic Law,* Kitab Bhavan, New Delhi, 1992.

Anwarullah : *The Islamic Law of Evidence,* Kitab Bhavan, New Delhi, 2000.

Arnold, Sir Thomas : *The Caliphate,* MacMillan, London, 1965.

Aurobindo, Sri : *The Foundations of Islamic Culture,* New York, 1973.

Baksh, S. K. : *Politics in Islam,* Kitab Bhavan, New Delhi, 2003.

Dawud, Rahbar : *God of Justice,* Mac & Jac Pub., Leiden, 1960.

Edward, Mortimer : *Faith and Power, the Politics of Islam,* Oxford, New York, 2002.

Fazal, Abul : *Akbar Namah,* Kitab Bhavan, New Delhi, 1977.

Guillaume, A. : *The Traditions of Islam,* Khayats, Beirut, 1966.

Hassan, M. : *Hadrat Abu Bakr Siddique (R.A.A.),* Kitab Bhavan, New Delhi, 2004.

Hughes, T.P. : *Dictionary of Islam,* Allen & Co., London, 1935,

Jafar, Sharif : *Islam in India,* Oxford, New Delhi, 1972.

Jansen, G.H. : *Militant Islam,* Pan Books, London, 1979.

Madhavan, A. : *What is Sufism ?,* Rupa & Co., New Delhi, 1981.

Qureshi, A. Iqbal : *Islam and the Theory of Interest,* Kitab Bhavan, New Delhi, 1994.

Sergeant : *Constitution of Madina,* Feroz Pub., Lahore, 1992.

Shemesh, A.B. : *Taxation in Islam,* MacMillan & Co., London, 1965.

Som, Tamarci : *A Brief History of Islam,* Blackwell, New York, 1992.

Walker, Benjamin : *Foundation of Islam : the Making of World Faith,* Rupa & Co., New Delhi, 2001.

Yusuf, S.M. : *Economic Justice in Islam,* Kitab Bhavan, New Delhi, 1988.

INDEX

P

Q

R

S

U

Z